DISAPPEARING DELMARVA

Portraits of the Peninsula People

Stories and photography by

Ed Okonowicz

Myst and Lace Publishers, Inc.

Disappearing Delmarva

Portraits of the Peninsula People

First Edition

ISBN   1-890690-00-7

Published by
Myst and Lace Publishers, Inc.
1386 Fair Hill Lane
Elkton, Maryland 21921

Printed in the U.S.A.
by Modern Press
(A family-owned Delmarva business in its third generation)

Photography
by Ed Okonowicz

Typography and Design
by Kathleen Okonowicz

Acknowledgments

This is where the writer tries to properly thank the people who helped during the planning and production of the book. As conscientious as one might try to be, unfortunately, someone is usually omitted. If this occurs, I am truly sorry.

My appreciation is extended to the men and women featured in these pages. They were kind enough to share their time, private thoughts and memories with a stranger who approached them with an idea. Over time and after several contacts, we became more than acquaintances. In some cases, I am honored to say some of these wonderful residents of Delmarva have become my friends.

From each of these everyday American heroes I learned a lot, and to each of them I am extremely thankful.

Special recognition and thanks are extended to photographer Bob Cohen, my co-worker in the Office of Public Relations at the University of Delaware.

At the start of this project, Bob took the time to share with me the principles of photography. In addition to his helpful instruction and frequent hints and suggestions, he processed the film and worked wonders with my photographs, printing them and making them presentable for these pages.

I appreciate his kindness, his professional assistance and his friendship.

In this type of project, word-of-mouth referrals are extremely important. Special appreciation for their introductions is extended to

Bob Bethke	Ben Pernol
Harry, Frank and Frankie Bartsch	Harry "Lefty" McBride
Gary Simpson	Bob Shultie
Rob Rector	Neafie Scarborough
Ronnie Byrd	Sean Mann
Shirley Justice	Rev. Edward Jones
Paul Anderson	Adolph Chappia
Lanny Parks	Ceily Butler
Lee Jennings	Joe Lofthouse

John Brennan and Sue Swyers Moncure, colleagues and friends at the University of Delaware, have proofread and edited my books in the past. I am grateful for their excellent suggestions and their willingness to share their considerable talents in the production of this book. Other proofreaders who were an important part of this project include Monica Witkowski, my sister, Ted Stegura, my friend, and Barbara Burgoon, my wife's mother. To all of them I am truly grateful.

Finally, this work could not have been accomplished without the patience, assistance and talents of Kathleen, my wonderful wife.

This project and others have taken her away from her painting, and I thank her for making this book a priority. She took all of these stories and photographs—hundreds of disjointed pieces of a story/photo/signature puzzle—and skillfully placed them into a finished work. The result of her graphic and artistic talents is a book that I hope you will find as enjoyable to read as it was for us to create.

Thanks so very much to all who helped and, again, my appreciation to the wonderfully delightful people featured in *Disappearing Delmarva*.

Also available from

Myst and Lace Publishers, Inc.

———◦———

Spirits Between the Bays Series

Volume I
Pulling Back the Curtain
(October, 1994)

Volume II
Opening the Door
(March, 1995)

Volume III
Welcome Inn
(September, 1995)

Volume IV
In the Vestibule
(August, 1996)

Volume V
Presence in the Parlor
(April, 1997)

———◦———

Stairway over the Brandywine
A Love Story
(February, 1995)

———◦———

Possessed Possessions
Haunted Antiques, Furniture and Collectibles
(March, 1996)

Table of Contents

Introduction   *1*

Family Farmers   *6*
Joe, Elaine and Dave Quigley, New Castle, Delaware

The Baker   *11*
Mitchell and Stella Radulski, Wilmington, Delaware

Seafood Shuckers   *15*
Sadie Sisco and John W. Tilghman, Rock Hall, Maryland

Drive-In Movie   *18*
Mildred Steele, Donald Brown and Leon Smullen, Felton, Delaware

Ferryboat Captain   *23*
Valerie Bittner, Oxford, Maryland

Decoy Carver   *26*
Delbert "Cigar" Daisey, Chincoteague, Virginia

Highway Gift Shop   *31*
Edith Davis Nichols, North East, Maryland

Scrapple Makers   *35*
Claude "Skip" and Jeff Burnham and Elaine Messick, Milton, Delaware

Fishnet Maker   *39*
Lydia Beideman, Milton, Delaware

Sportswriter   43
Matt Zabitka, Wilmington, Delaware

Boatman   48
Wickes Westcott, Galena, Maryland

Chair Caner   52
Marie Bradley, Lincoln, Delaware

Sawmill   56
Harry and Frank Bartsch, Townsend, Delaware

Veterans of D-Day   61
Joe Lofthouse, Elkton, Maryland, and Donnie Preston, North East, Maryland

Five & Dime   67
Julia Carucci deJuliis, Wilmington, Delaware

Waterfowl Hunting Guide   71
Andy Linton, Chincoteague, Virginia

Broom Man   75
William Hammond III, Felton, Delaware

Soda Fountain   80
Mary Sue Willis and Helen T. Durding, Rock Hall, Maryland

Trappers   85
Bud Holland, Blackbird, Delaware, and
Ed Hahn, Port Penn and Claymont, Delaware

Barber Shop   91
Frank Terranova, Elsmere, Delaware

Basket Makers   95
Bob McKnight and Pam Sargent, North East, Maryland

Band Leader   99
Joe "Smokey" Smolka, Wilmington, Delaware

Small Town Movie Theater   103
Ellen Combs Davis, Middletown, Delaware

Country Store   107
Erlyne Twining, Taylors Island, Maryland

Beer Garden   111
Theresa Okonowicz and Paul Okonowicz, Wilmington, Delaware

Printer   117
Randolph T. Faulkner, Smyrna, Delaware

Soap Maker   121
Mildred Wix Welch, Harrington, Delaware

Family Newsstand   125
Philip J. "Phil" Stanley and Debbie Stanley Storke, Elkton, Maryland

Disc Jockey   130
Bill Horleman, Wilmington, Delaware

Steam Show   135
Horace and Norma Davis Potter, Milford, Delaware

Fish Fry   140
F. Burgess Tucker, Bob Watson and Larry Compton, Rock Hall, Maryland

Clog Dancer   145
Frankie Bartsch, Townsend, Delaware

Country Musician   149
Harry "Lefty" McBride, Smyrna, Delaware

One-Room Post Office   154
Marlene W. Marshall, Sanford, Virginia

Neighborhood Restaurant   158
Josephine "Pina" Minuti and Robin Mabrey, Wilmington, Delaware

Record Collector   164
Joe Permar, Wilmington, Delaware

Roadside Barbecue   169
Tyson Cannon, Greenwood, Delaware

Accordion Player   172
Joe Ragan, Wilmington, Delaware

Mail Boat Captain   176
Otis, Darrell and Dale Tyler, Ewell, Smith Island, Maryland

Hardware Man   180
Otis Huff, Newark, Delaware

Butler   185
William Marshall Daniels, Greenville, Delaware

Railroad Man   188
William Bartosh, Greensboro, Maryland

Gravestone Cutter   192
James Tartaglia, Wilmington, Delaware

Bugler and Honor Guard   196
Dick Hires and John Murphy, Ocean View, Delaware

Afterword   200

Introduction

When I was a kid, growing up in an apartment above my grandfather's beer garden in Wilmington in the 1950s, I thought the block where I lived was typical of just about everywhere.

I didn't realize that there were places different than the city streets where I played among rowhouses and corner stores.

To me, everyone had a paperboy, and the newspaper would always cost 5 cents. The ice man would deliver blocks of frozen cold to small stores forever. Jake would come every week, tapping his blind stick down the street and yelling "BROOOOMSS! BROOOMM . . . MAAAN! BROOOMSS!" and Teddy the Huckster would appear each summer—with wooden crates of vegetables wired to the sides of his truck—calling out " 'MAAA-TAAAAASS 'MAAA-TAAAAAASS!"

Later, I found out that some of the things I experienced growing up existed elsewhere, but others didn't. Different places had their own characteristics, customs and unique characters, but progress was the one thing that affected us all.

Whether from the city, country or in between, no one was immune from the benefits and, in many cases, the unfortunate consequences of change.

As a result, my world, and everyone else's world, was changing. It was the kind of thing you didn't notice at first, since the differences were so slight.

Dominick's shoe repair shop closed down, and his corner storefront was turned into a house. Then, the Linden Grill shut its doors. Before we knew it, the man who brought his pony into town—and took pictures of us kids, sitting proudly in the saddle wearing cowboy hats and holsters—didn't come anymore.

My friends started moving to "the suburbs." They were going to live in "split-levels" that had "rec rooms." They'd keep in touch by phone, and promised to see us when they came back into town, to visit their grandparents and relatives who stayed behind.

The neighborhood fraternal clubs closed, too. Everybody was getting a new black and white TV. Why go out and talk to your neighbors when the fuzzy little screen would talk to you?

Eventually, there were only three neighborhood bakeries instead of five, but that wasn't a big concern. We could still get fresh bread from the surviving bakers, or from the corner groceries where they delivered.

Except . . . our regular market across the street wasn't open anymore. But the next one was only one block farther away. It wasn't too far to walk.

Local bars seemed a little less crowded on Friday and Saturday nights. More people were watching TV programs at home.

Ever so slowly, the exodus changed from a trickle to a stream. The vibrant soul of city life was silently disappearing.

The neighborhood theaters closed. Not all at once, but at an almost unnoticeably slow and steady pace. Parking lots, vacant buildings and storefront churches replaced the Ace, Park, King, Crest and Strand. The places where families spent their weekends and evenings, laughing and shedding tears, were gone.

No more double features. No more conversations with Pop the projectionist. No more opportunities to tease the teenager ushers or poke holes in the soda cups of the automatic dispensers. No more matinees with cliff hanger serials.

It didn't take long before the larger, fancier center city picture palaces, where the first-run movies had appeared, went dark. Shows at the Queen, Arcadia, Warner and Grand became fond memories.

Traffic grew as picturesque backroads became sterile, four-lane speedways. Interstates cut down everything in their way, leveling entire blocks, uprooting neighborhoods, separating families, ending friendships.

But the city was not alone. Similar steps toward modernization were happening in smaller towns as well.

In the hamlets and villages, general stores and family hardwares shut their doors, falling to competition from the new retail giants in "more convenient" shopping centers. Years later, "malls" would do the same thing to these suburban businesses.

Mom and Pop delis and candy stores—where the owners knew you by name—took down their shingles and sold off the counters and fixtures. Dark empty rooms, with silent memories and lonely ghosts, replaced soda fountains and drug stores. The places where people used to meet, talk and fall in love were gone, preserved only in faded photograph albums and fragile memories.

The next generation was going to be better off, and to accomplish that goal meant going to college. Nobody wanted to be a storekeeper, repair shoes or run a shot and beer joint. The kids were told to reach for the brass ring—jobs with big corporations, a government pension— become a doctor or maybe even a lawyer.

Gone by now were all the small town theaters and drive-ins. Multiplex cinemas were the latest places to go for entertainment—actually, the only places to go.

> *"These people never made the news; they made America."*

Residential developments gobbled up more of the landscape. Countrified names—like Green Meadows, Spring Hill and Babbling Brook—were the only reminders of what had been there before.

Farm supply businesses had fewer customers, so owners nailed up the shutters and hoped someone would buy their warehouse and turn it into an antique mall.

The remaining farmers had to travel farther for their machinery, supplies, seed and conversation with other keepers of the soil. The cycle didn't stop.

Fishermen still went out, but they returned with lighter catches. Pollution was killing the fish, crabs and oysters. Boats that once proudly cut through waves remained tied up at the dock, the water attacking their paint-chipped, stagnant hulls.

Hunters had less game to shoot. There seemed to be fewer geese and ducks with each passing season. The old timers talked of days when the game in flight would block out the sun, and listeners laughed and called the talk "tall tales."

Old time, familiar, one-room post offices were replaced with new facilities—sterile buildings with no character—to handle the influx of newer homes and more people.

Slowly, but simultaneously, neighborhoods died. The city decayed. The soul of small towns became silent, their streets empty.

Developers—who lived on private estates far from traffic and construction—devoured the open spaces as their suburban "planned communities" feasted on farmland. Empty silos and crumbling out buildings dotted the landscape.

Trips to the country took longer, because the country was forced to be farther away.

Pleasant drives to the beach were no longer relaxing, too many vehicles were heading for the same place at the same time—rushing to get there, rushing to get back.

More roads, larger highways and toll booths were built—gobbling up more farmland and forests—to try to handle increasing traffic. Wider toll lanes grew beside older roads, all going to the same crowded destination.

The downward spiral of progress hasn't slowed; it's only gotten worse.

And it can't be stopped.

The reason for this book

This book has been in progress somewhere in the back of my mind for many, many years, well before I realized it had to be compiled. Its origins probably began in the early '50s, when my father took me to places that other kids never saw—gin mills and junkyards, VFW clubs and railroad yards.

Those experiences and leftover memories had an influence on me. When I worked as freelancer for Wilmington's *News Journal* papers, the subjects of my features were a bit offbeat. Most were located in New Castle County, but I also traveled through downstate Delaware and on the Eastern Shore, looking for people with unusual stories to share. I noticed that things were quite different from the days when I was growing up. More importantly, I realized much of our culture was dying.

It doesn't take a rocket scientist to realize that life is changing very rapidly, at what I consider an ultrasonic pace, and many of the changes are not good.

Even discounting the advances of high technology, our everyday lifestyle—in the form of business and residential development and individual and family habits—is moving at mega-warp speed. The pace of progress is so quick, the changes so constant, that even the young can't absorb the latest advances before newer, better,

bolder and faster ones arrive—and they are imposed upon us all.

As this hideous, multi-armed monster known as progress moves in a large number of directions at the same time, it devours much of our culture and heritage.

Only afterwards, might we, and I stress the word "might," become aware of what has been lost. But if the monster pauses at all, it is only to refuel for the next assault on what little remains of our past and our too rapidly changing present.

Anyone who travels our highways, passes look-alike chain stores, malls and cookie cutter homes that stand where fields, forests and historic buildings once pleased the eye.

What's even more devastating is that in addition to the loss of historic sites and structures, our traditions, trades and family ties also are affected.

How many more years before the last shoemaker mends the last shoe, the lonely crabber collects his final catch, the tailor sews a last stitch, the sawmill's blade cuts its final log, the town movie theater plays the last picture show?

How many children ever play with their cousins, really talk to their grandparents and even know their aunts and uncles?

The growth of big business, retail chains, corporations, entertainment giants—plus changes in individual attitudes and cultural values—are affecting the way we live, work, learn and think, as well as what we stand for and respect.

While most of those who live in the waning years of the 20th century have seemed to accept our fate and ride on the crest of the murky wave disguised as progress, there is a small, disappearing handful of strong-minded, hardworking Americans who still embody the spirit of independence that established our land.

Many of these men and women work with their hands, performing tasks in the way they have been done for centuries. Their skills will not be taken over by a computer, robot or worker in a foreign factory. They carry on valued traditions that are slipping away, forsaken by the ultra-hip younger generations, who consider these practices corny, old-fashioned, embarrassing and not worth the effort and dedication.

Some of the survivors are self-taught. Others learned from elders. In many cases, their mentors have passed on, but still exist in spirit through the practices continued by their descendants and apprentices.

The peninsula

For centuries, the natural geographic inaccessibility of the Delmarva Peninsula—surrounded by the waters of the Delaware and Chesapeake Bays and Atlantic Ocean—made it a world unto itself.

Inaccessible except by water, these southernmost portions of the peninsula preserved a calmer way of life and were able to ignore progress longer than the more traveled areas of the growing East Coast megalopolis.

When U.S. Route 1 was constructed, the main road from Fort Kent, Maine, to Key West, Florida, traveled through every East Coast state except Delaware. Passing from Philadelphia to Baltimore, the well-traveled route was not connected to the northern tip of Delmarva.

Ferries were used to carry vehicles—west across the Delaware Bay from New Jersey, and east over the Chesapeake Bay from Maryland's Western Shore—onto Delmarva.

It was not until the 1950s that bridges made it easier to access Delaware, the nine counties on Maryland's Eastern Shore and the two counties of northern Virginia.

As roads become more numerous, as homes are built on farmland and waterfronts, there will be an impact. Just as there is absolutely no way

we can stop the natural movement from life to death, there is no way the individual—or even determined small towns and communities—can stop the sad, steady march toward modern, mediocre conformity.

What we can do is pause and try to capture what is left of our heritage and traditions. If we desire, we can reflect on a simpler era and make it a priority to remember those who worked with their hands and hearts, harvested the fields, operated storefronts, worked the water, lived simple lives and, actually, enjoyed their work.

They are the people who danced country style, played the fiddle and accordion, knew and watched out for their neighbors, patronized local stores, risked their lives in the service of their country, earned what they got and made America great.

> *"When an elderly person dies, it's like a library burning."*
> *—Alex Haley*

The purpose of this book is to capture the thoughts, beliefs and work of these people, to record their secrets and experiences in their own words. Each chapter profiles people who rarely made the news, but who made America.

To know who we are, it is essential to understand where we came from. These stories and statements represent the best of our shared cultural heritage, for we all are products of each other's lives.

In these pages, you will meet crabbers and cooks, shop owners and crafts people, bootleggers and bakers, mill workers and musicians. There are comments by historical perservationists who are active members of organizations and individuals who have appointed themselves independent guardians of our folklore.

They represent the three distinct populations of Delmarva: the water people, the agricultural families and the urban dwellers.

In no way is this a complete representation of everything that exists between the bays. It is only a sampling of the wide array of Delmarva's human and cultural treasures.

It contains the memories I could capture in 12 months' time. Several stories are from residents of Wilmington, Delmarva's largest city, but many others are from smaller towns, villages and hamlets, like Sanford, Taylors Island, Felton, North East and Lincoln.

Some of those who are featured in these pages reflect my background and contacts I made while growing up in the city. A few are people I'm proud to have known my entire life. Others I met more recently, but each has a significant story to share.

Someone raised in the country would have featured different subjects and, perhaps, taken a different perspective. But my interests could not be divorced from the heart of this project. To a degree, the preservation of the sources of some of my memories was one of my objectives and, probably, the essence of my motivation.

In these pages, you will meet those with whom I was privileged to share time. Many of them are the last of their kind. Some are silent heroes, men and women who are very willing to share their interesting stories of human sacrifice, high personal standards and even battlefield bravery, if only someone will ask.

Unfortunately, progress did not pause during the production of this book, and some of the featured people and sites are no longer with us. Since this project began, businesses have closed, storefronts have been boarded, meadows have disappeared and people have died.

Alex Haley, the author of *Roots*, said: "When an old person dies, it is like a library burning."

Each of us has a responsiblity to preserve the best elements of our history, to learn from those who have gone before. We must make the time to record carefully both the simple events and the significant sacrifices and accomplishments of the members of our individual families.

If not us, then who?

My hope is that, after reading this book, you will, so very soon, seek out those who have been featured and, more importantly, find others—including the elders in your own family— who should be noticed, respected and remembered, before they, too, are gone and it is too late for those of us who remain.

—Ed Okonowicz
in Fair Hill, Maryland,
at the northern edge
of the Delmarva Peninsula

Elaine Quigley and son, David, with Joe (left) on the William Penn Farm

Joe Quigley, 70

Farmer
From 1930 to Present
William Penn Farm
New Castle, Delaware

Family Farmers

At the end of the 20th century, operating farms are only memories in northern New Castle County. Shopping malls, auto dealerships, fast food restaurants and housing developments have devoured a tremendous amount of open space.

Rising costs make family farming an occupation that is unaffordable. High-priced offers are tempting established farmers to sell their acreage and give up the rural way of life.

Within walking distance of one of Delaware's most traveled intersections—at Routes 40 and 273 and within sight of the New Castle County Airport, mega stores and the New Castle County Farmer's Market—stands William Penn Farm. The property, that originally belonged to the Colonial founder of Pennsylvania, is still owned by the Trustees of the Commons of New Castle.

Joe Quigley, a man who has been in farming his entire life, his wife, Elaine, and his son, David, rent out the property, growing sweet corn on the 110-acre parcel, selling vegetables at a stand in the summer and supplementing their income with a well-established hayride business that began 25 years ago.

At one time, not too long ago, the entire area near Olde Historic New Castle was surrounded by thousands of acres of fields and farms. Now, William Penn Farm is about all that remains.

Joe Quigley said the trustees plan on keeping it the way it is. Hopefully, that will happen. Maybe, he added, the historic site will be turned into an agricultural museum one day, so people can stop and pause and try to remember how nice things used to be.

"*I was born in the house on Jackson Farm, my grandfather's place, right across the road. It's gone now. There's a big old post office there now. It's called the Airport Industrial Center. When you were big enough to do something, you were out there working. When I was 5 years old, I started milking cows at 4 o'clock in the morning.*

"*It was cold that time of morning, but it wasn't bad in the barn. We had a very modern barn at that time, one of the first loafing sheds, where the cattle could get in and out of the storm. The milking barn was warm, all sheathed with tongue-and-grove. With 30 head of cattle in there, you could go down to your shirt, and that's the way you worked all day long.*

"*I liked the cattle work when I was young. But about 20 years ago it got to be too much, so I had to get rid of the cows.*

"*But I love farming. It's all I've ever done. If I can get my 16 hours a day in, I'm happy as a lark. The thing I like best is to put in a full day without any troubles, when everything runs smoothly, but you don't find many like that. And then there's the changing of the seasons. It's a beautiful time of year now.*

"*Sometimes I go out and wonder what's out there. Last night, I went out and looked up at those stars, and I always say to myself: 'How far's out?' That may sound a little goofy, but I always wonder, 'How far's out? Where's the end of this?' You see a star and what's back of that star. What's back of the next star?*

"*We had a eagle land in our field earlier this year. It was quite a thing. My neighbor saw it first and called me and told me there was an eagle in the field. We sat there the biggest part of the day. Hundreds and hundreds of people stopped to see him. They were lining the road. Cars in, cars out. School buses slowing up so the children could get a look.*

"*A lot of people came to see it because they've never seen an eagle in their life. I don't think I could live in the city where I might never see a chicken, a cow or other animals. No way I could live like that. Neither could you if you was on a farm all your life— 70 straight years and never been off the farm.*

"*But the farm kept getting smaller. That's why we got into hayrides. It began about 25 years ago. I had three children in college at one time and I needed the extra money. We've done hundreds of hayrides over all these years.*

"*I've noticed one thing. When the people get to the bonfire, I don't know what it is, maybe it's because it's in an area where it's quiet and nobody bothers you, but the bonfire seems to mesmerize people. They seem to quiet down, enjoy themselves. They just don't want to leave the bonfire. Maybe it's an escape from the stress of the work that they're in. There's no traffic. It's like they're in a different world. I think a lot of these people go to work and it feels good to get away on the weekend, to sit beside the fire with family and friends and get close.*

"*One couple came in here and he got the wagon for just the two of them. He gave her an engagement ring at the bonfire. When the other campfires heard what was happening, they went over congratulating them. It was really a nice thing. But the most interesting part was the human side of it, that people who were all strangers would come over, and they were shaking hands and giving them a hug and congratulating them. That was really the warm side of the story.*

"But the hayrides help pull me through. Christmas trees help pull me through. Then you got a couple of months that's kind of lax, and you go right back into it in the spring. And you better believe that I do look forward to the spring and the summer when we have our sweet corn. In fact, I'm ready now and it's only October. In February, I got to get out of the house, got to do something. Go down to the shop, piddle around, work on machinery, or just bum as they used to say.

"What I really miss is the Aurora Borealis, the Northern Lights. I used to see them before all the glare came from the shopping centers over there. Boy, you could see them and they were beautiful.

"People don't go into farming any more. Land is so high, machinery cost is up the wall. I guess there's combines out there today that cost a quarter-million dollars. Unbelievable. Not a good enough return on your product. It won't encourage the young farmers to stay on the farm.

"It's hard work. Nothing like it used to be, but farmers don't mind hard work. They don't mind doing something that's theirs. A lot of conversation goes on here about farming. A lot of stuff you don't write down. It lasts with you forever. It's imprinted. You don't forget some things.

"I can even remember going to the old King Street Market. I guess I must of been 5 years old when I went in with my dad. It was super! Some days you couldn't hardly walk up and down the street. There was no room on the pavement for more people. Very, very good sales. It went from about Second and Third, up to about Eighth. Lined up with buggies and trucks, and people, with their grocery bags and baskets. That was Tuesday afternoon, all day Wednesday, Friday afternoon and all day Saturday. We'd go in when the crops would permit us. It was a wonderful, wonderful market.

"But then you got the supermarkets and things changed. When the supermarkets started, they didn't need the farmers anymore. They could get their medicines, vegetables, meats, whatever they needed at one place.

"It doesn't bother me none to be one of the last farmers left. You wish there was more open space. Everyone wishes that. So many of our customers say, 'Do not let the farm be sold,' or 'We want this open space.' I guess that's, basically, how most people think, that they want some open space rather than be bumper to bumper with houses.

"I guess within the last five or six years, Mr. Walker, one of my closest friends passed away. His son's still there farming. That's up the road about a mile. He's in grain. No cattle any more. I don't know where the next farm's at. I really don't, because all Hockessin is pretty well built up. Down Newark, I imagine, most of it's built up. What we call farmers in this area are all gone. I can't think of a one. When I moved here in '45, it was all farmland. Everything was farm.

"I don't get away much. Don't have time. I guess five years ago we went out to see our daughter in Colorado. You could see an awful lot of land there. If you go up in Pennsylvania to see the Dutch country, that's sort of what it used to look like around here.

"I'll keep farming as long as I'm physically able. It's what I do, what I love. It's just me."

Joe Quigley

October 13, 1996

9

"*I grew up in the city. I came to the farm when I married Joe, 44 years ago. When I moved out here it was different than what I was used to. We had people around us all the time. But we've had a lot of experiences, living in the country and in an old house, built in 1803. You can still hear all the things of the country and smell the skunks and all that, but there are a lot of lights from the shopping centers that weren't here before. It wasn't congested with all the things that are going on today around here.*

"*I've learned that farmers just like to farm. We talk farming all year long, different seasons different reasons. What you're planting, how you're going to take care of the corn. The whole nine yards of what we love to do.*

"*Once or twice we've gone on a hayride and it's fun. On a dark night, you can see the stars beautiful, because it's down in what southern people would call a 'hollow.' It's in a cove with a woods on one side and a grown up hedgerow on the other, so it's protection from the wind. People tell stories and some sing songs around the campfire.*

"*I enjoy farming. We get a lot of nice people who come here to our stand and go on the hayrides. We enjoy the simple things, like this morning, we saw the geese in the field and they flew off, and how pretty it is. I like farming as long as he does.*"

Elaine Quigley

October 13, 1996

"*I was born into this, I guess. I went to college for agriculture, studied plant science. When I came out, I stayed in farming. It has its good aspects. You work for yourself. You know what jobs need to be done and you do 'em. When they're done, you feel good about what you accomplished. There's a certain degree of history to it. My grandfather did it, my father did it and here I am.*

"*After a while, you get used to being at the mercy of the weather. I find a lot of personal satisfaction in fixing things that break down, machinery. I like the animals and I like to shoe horses. I do blacksmithing work, but that's sort of a widespread. I also make ornamental iron. That's a nice way to relax.*

"*I remember when this area wasn't so popular, and there weren't houses built everywhere. It was nice back then. Now, every little piece of ground is worth so much, and somebody wants to stick a building on it to make the most of it. You have to go pretty far to find a place that's as quiet as it used to be around here.*

"*I see what farming's turned into in the 40 years I've been around. I wonder what its going to be like after tacking 40 more onto it. By then, I have to believe the government will own most of the food production and everybody's going to be figured into how much of what is made.*"

Dave Quigley

November 3, 1996

The Baker

It was the smell that would grab your attention first--the aroma of fresh baked bread, rolls and pastries. Decades ago, every neighborhood and small town had their own bakeries, places where everything was freshly made each and every single day.

The aroma escaping from the hot ovens actually lured you into the shop. In many cases, a bell hanging on the back of the door alerted the owner when a customer arrived. Wooden display cases with curved, clear glass showcased a mouth-watering array of delicious, fattening sweets.

The bread was so soft, moist and warm that customers often nibbled a portion off the end of the loaf as they walked back home.

Stanley Radulski was the owner of one of these family bakeries. He left Poland and came to America in 1904, during the great wave with millions of other European immigrants who sought a new life as they landed on the Golden Shore. He eventually settled in Hedgeville, a Polish neighborhood in Wilmington, Delaware.

In 1911, he opened his small family bakery using basement ovens in a corner rowhouse at Beech and Harrison streets. Later, he built a larger bakery, along with garages and a home, a half-block away at 715 South Harrison Street.

In 1928, Stanley's 7-year-old son, Mitchell, began working with his father on the delivery route. Except for the years he served in the U.S. Navy during World War II, Mitchell—later helped by his wife, Stella, and a few oldtime bakers who also were good friends—worked in Radulski's Bakery for nearly 60 years.

Changing times and difficulty getting help caused the family bakery to lock its front door in 1980 and sell off its ovens and fixtures.

But, in the quiet rowhouse kitchen—two rooms away from the closed, dark storefront that used to be alive with customers and workers—the final family baker shared his experiences. He talked of early morning deliveries, never-ending holiday rushes, the trademark orders of regular customers, what it was like to make the bread by hand and why it will never be done that way again.

Stella Radulski with her husband, Mitchell

Mitchell Radulski, 74

Radulski's Bakery
From 1911 to 1980
Hedgeville
Wilmington, Delaware

"*I remember, when I was 7, we'd start deliveries at houses and stores at 3:30 in the morning. It was dark and we'd go door to door. My father would pull the truck up and I'd go up on the porch. I'd do the running back and forth. Then, when we got back about 8 o'clock, I'd go to school. It was like that six days a week. We went on the West Side, East Side, wherever the Polish people lived.*

"*The women worked in the house, cooking all the apples and fillings for the pies. When I was 15, I was driving the truck and delivering everything. Everything was made fresh every day. On Sundays, we'd clean out the truck and bakery, real good, and get ready for the next week and make the fillings.*

"*When I got done working and I could finally get out for a while, I was like a wild man just let loose. It was a lot of work, but we still had it better than a lot of other kids. I'd get a quarter a week, and they got nothing.*

"*I learned the baking business from working in it, and from the other bakers, mixing the dough and ingredients, how long the different breads and cakes had to set. We'd make cookies, pies, rolls, rye bread, pumpernickel, white and pound cake. We had our own recipes that we followed.*

"*On a regular day, we'd make about 200 loaves of rye, Vienna and white bread, plus 30 to 40 dozen donuts and 80 dozen buns. Then we'd have babki on Fridays. But when there was a holiday, like Easter and Christmas, we'd make 3,000 rye, 150 in a batch, and 1,000 pound cakes.*

"*You just worked without sleep, just worked the whole damn time 'til you could get ahead of it. The people were waiting in line, out the door and down the street. As soon as you brought the bread in, it was gone.*

"*It wasn't hard work, but you couldn't sleep. You put in long hours. Now, today, I can't sleep. It's because, except for the Navy time, I was getting up all those years at 3:30. But it was a good living. You worked like a dog. Stella, she worked like a dog. But we weren't starving.*

"*The customers, they knew what time the bread came out of the oven. They were there at 1:30 for rye. There was a guy from the railroad, he's dead now. He would take 25 or 30 loaves at a time. It wasn't anything for people, who took one or two loaves normally, to take 15 or 20 loaves during the holidays.*

"*All of the grocers, they were all your friends. When you delivered to them over the years, you got to know them. Almost all of them are gone now, too. Slowly, the big stores took over and the small corner stores closed out, then the city started rezoning. Once you closed, and you were out for a certain time, you couldn't reopen. They did it all to help the big chains.*

"*By the end of 1980, both the bakers who were helping me died. It was only me and Stella. It was too hard for me and her to do alone. There weren't any bakers around who knew how to make bread by hand. Who wants to work in a bakery? There was no pension. No benefits. Now, when you look back on it, you wonder how you worked the way you did. I was a baker in the Navy, but it was not as hard. You had help there.*

"*I had to close the bakery during the war, and when I got back we had to start it up again. It was hard at first. But we just kept at it and built it back slowly. You used to have salesmen stop by and sell flour, fruits and supplies and equipment. They'd take your orders and deliver to you. Now, you don't see them like you used to. The small bakeries can't order enough to make it worth it to them. Things have changed a lot.*

"It was a longer process back then, too. Now, everything is pre-mixed. You just throw it in right away. There's not as much time involved.

"Today, you go to the store and it's hard to find anything fresh. Before, when you delivered to stores, whatever was left over when you came back the next day, you took it out and gave them credit for it. So whatever bread they had was always fresh. Today, you just can't buy good, old-fashioned rye bread or pound cake. When we see some of our old customers, they always tell us how much they miss the bakery.

"I liked all of it, though. Everybody likes the money they get for their work. It's not that you make a lot of money to get rich, but that you make enough to make a living. Most people work to make things a little better, to make a future for your kids, so they don't have to go on welfare.

"But you miss it all. No matter how hard it was. In fact, if I wasn't so old, sometimes I think I'd like to start over again.

"I got a part-time job, with Louis Amalfitano. He's got an Italian bakery. Sometimes, I go in and use the ovens and make up a batch of Polish rye. I give him half and keep half for myself. I do deliveries for Louis. It keeps me active, lets me do something when I get up early in the morning.

"It's funny, though. When I sit here and think back, I didn't realize I did that much. It's a good feeling when somebody says, after all these years, that they remember what I did."

Mitchell Radulski   May 4, 1996

"It was hard to close. We had a lot of nice people who came in and I miss them. When you had time, and if it wasn't busy in the store, you'd talk to them and get to know them personally.

"During the holidays, we weren't able to answer the phone. We were so busy and had so many orders, we had to take it off the hook.

"But even today, 16 years after we've been closed, they're still talking about our bakery and our bread and pound cake. They used to come in and tell me that they were buying for their whole family. Some of them took our rye bread and pound cake to California and Texas."

Stella Radulski   May 4, 1996

Seafood Shuckers

At 5 in the morning the shucking crew arrives at Ford's Seafood at the edge of the wharf in Rock Hall, Maryland. For the next seven hours, as darkness turns into mid-day sunlight, the uneven banging of thick metal rods against muck-covered oyster shells echoes off the smooth, bright walls of the shucking house. The technique hasn't changed for the hundreds of years that the Chesapeake has given up its catch for hungry seafood eaters on the mainland and in cities up and down the East Coast.

Hit the shell, push in the knife, pry open the mouth, pull out the oyster . . . clean it, pack it and ship it.

According to 44-year-old Nevitte Ford, manager of the operation and a lifelong waterman, over the years the size of the catch and length of the shuckers' days have gotten shorter.

"Lord, yes," he said, "things have changed dramatically. Years ago, I could catch 50, 60 bushels a day, by myself. Now, today, the boats are coming in here with five and six bushels."

Ford said the influx of fresh water from the rain and hurricane in 1972 affected the oyster crop, and the lack of a state reseeding program has hurt the crop. The increase of recreational fishermen, clammers and crabbers has added to the problem and the end result is devastating to the livelihood of the full-time watermen.

Then there are the changes to Rock Hall. The small fishing village's charm and seclusion originally made it an attractive destination for vacationers, boaters and day tourists. Unfortunately, he said, newer, part-time residents try to change the area's character.

"I love this work, but Rock Hall's not Rock Hall anymore," Ford said. "When everybody comes here, they love it so much. They like the atmosphere and the flavor of the country. But they're here six months and they want to change everything, rezoning, changing this and that. So soon it will look like the city or where they came from. I really wonder why they decided to come here to begin with."

Ford's operation is the northernmost shucking house on the Chesapeake Bay. Where there used to be at least three such operations, his is Rock Hall's last.

"There used to be more houses on Kent Island, but there are less now, fewer shucking houses all throughout the bay. We send our clams up to New England," said Ford. "The oysters, they stay right here in Maryland. Some of the ones we work on come from right here, but not a lot. I keep a truck down Tilghman Island, and they haul them up here for shucking. There's a big market for oysters out west, but I haven't been involved in that yet."

With catch limits, harvesting by part-time chicken neckers, shortened seasons, lack of a state seed program and disappointing catches, Ford said, "It's just ridiculous. To tell you the truth, I used to make more money by accident than working all week long, hard as I can go now. I don't think there's any other work group that gets stepped on like a waterman does. It's definitely going to come to an end if something doesn't change."

While the shuckers still arrive, prying open clams 12 months of the year and oysters during the winter, their season keeps getting shorter.

If the catches continue to dwindle, who knows how long it will be before the last piece of rebar hits the final oyster shell? How many more seasons until the early morning sounds of conversation in the shucking house are just another memory of better days on the bay?

Sadie Sisco, 77

Oyster Shucker
From 1938 to Present
Rock Hall, Maryland

EATING LIGHT & HEALTHY

EATING OUT

Restaurants are more accommodating than you might think—a 1993 National Restaurant Association survey found that nearly 90 percent of all table service restaurants will alter food preparations on request. Here's how to design delicious, low-risk meals with a chef's help.

GAIN THE EDGE ON HUNGER by starting with a broth-based soup, fruit, raw vegetables, unbuttered bread, or a light seafood appetizer.

CHOOSE ENTRÉES that are steamed, poached, broiled, roasted, baked, or cooked in their own juices. Fish is almost always the best choice. Pass up anything fried or sautéed.

CUT THE FAT off red meats, and remove skin from chicken before eating it.

STAY AWAY FROM THICK, RICH SAUCES, and stick to ones that are thin and stock-based. Avoid hollandaise, béarnaise, beurre blanc, or anything that sounds like gravy. Choose red pasta sauces over white.

ASK FOR YOUR VEGETABLES STEAMED.

ORDER SALAD DRESSINGS ON THE SIDE, and then use them sparingly. Try lemon juice, plain vinegar, or buttermilk dressing as low-fat alternatives.

EAT SMALL PORTIONS, or order half-portions at a reduced rate—and never stuff yourself. As your stomach expands, so does your appetite.

THE RIGHT DIET

The best commercial diet programs focus on smart food choices. No plan is perfect, but the good ones all have the following features in common:

➤ Recommend food that is low in fat and sugar, high in complex carbohydrates, such as breads and vegetables.
➤ Teach you how to cook delicious low-fat meals that are quick and easy to prepare.
➤ Include an adequate supply of vitamins and minerals.
➤ Ask you to eat at least 1,100 calories a day.
➤ Allow you to eat a variety of foods and foods you like in moderation.
➤ Let you eat in restaurants occasionally.
➤ Encourage new eating habits and exercise.

CAUTION

AVOID CRASHING AND POPPING. Studies show that people who repeatedly go on and off crash diets actually gain weight over time. The sad fact is that the only thing crash dieters ever learn is how to starve. Try suppressing your appetite with most diet pills and you risk a number of nasty side effects, such as irritability, insomnia, high blood pressure, and chemical dependency. Plus, once you stop taking them, any weight you've lost will probably sneak right back on. Weight control is a learned behavior.

EATING LIGHT & HEALTHY

At one time or another, half the women and a quarter of the men in this country have tried to lose weight. The ones destined to try again and again are most likely those looking for shortcuts. There are none.

The only way to step off the diet treadmill is to find a weight-loss program that helps you lose weight slowly and steadily; one that trains you to adopt a healthy eating plan so simple it becomes a way of life. With that in mind, here is an introductory guide to the last diet you may ever need.

GOOD HABITS

START STRONG. People who eat a healthy breakfast generally feel less hungry throughout the day.

CURB YOUR APPETITE. Drink a glass of water or some tea just before a meal.

STOP COUNTING CALORIES. The best diet foods are complex carbohydrates. Low in fat, fast-burning, and rich in vitamins and minerals, they are also high in bulk, which means you can feel full on fewer calories. Eat whole-grain cereals, rice, breads, pasta, beans, nuts, and some types of fruits and vegetables.

EAT WHAT YOU LIKE. Nothing makes a diet more difficult than having to eat rice cakes when you can't stand them.

SIT DOWN. Train yourself to eat in one place, preferably at a table. It's too easy to overeat when meals are grabbed on the run or while standing in front of the refrigerator.

SLOW DOWN. Eat slowly enough to give your body time to release the enzymes that tell your brain when you've had all you need.

EXERCISE. It burns calories and suppresses the appetite, and it's awfully hard to lose weight without doing it. An easy way to get started is to strap on a pedometer and go for a walk, then work on increasing your mileage from one week to the next.

DON'T GIVE UP. Falling off your diet once or twice does not mean the effort is hopeless. Simply acknowledge that you overate, and get back on the plan.

REWARD YOURSELF. Treat yourself with a massage, or a piece of gourmet chocolate, or whatever, for each week that you maintain your new weight.

FIRST-RATE SNACK PACK

Air-popped popcorn seasoned with herbs
Bagels
Breadsticks
Broth-based soups
Cereals, low-sugar, low-fat
Cocoa, low-sugar, low-fat
English muffins
Fresh fruit
Frozen fruit-juice bars
Gingersnaps
Graham crackers
Low-fat or nonfat frozen yogurt
Matzoh
Milk shake of low-fat milk and frozen fruit
Pita chips with salsa
Plain nonfat yogurt with fruit and cinnamon
Pretzels
Rye crisps or rice cakes thinly spread with
     peanut butter or low-fat cheese
Sorbet
Tabbouleh
Vegetables marinated in vinegar or dipped in
     low-fat yogurt seasoned with herbs
Whole-wheat crackers

"*I been shuckin' 56 years. When I started off, I was shuckin' all day and I got a gallon and earned 50 cents. I was learnin' then. I've been doin' it ever since. We start like we always did, at 5 o'clock, and we go until around 12. Back then, we went until 2 o'clock. People ask if it's hard work. Not for me, but I been doin' it a while.*

"*In the beginning, your hands get sore. It gets you right in the palm of your hand, from the pressing. But you get use' to it. But you need the gloves. I never tried to shuck without gloves. I never thought about how many oysters or clams I shucked. It's a lot. I go through them pretty good now.*

"*You got to hit them and make them loose, then get the knife in the mouth. So you got to hit it where the mouth is. That makes it easier to open, when you hit them.*

"*It depends on the person, but the more you do it, the better you get. I was born and raised here in Rock Hall, and I like what I do. I just like to shuck oysters.*"

Sadie Sisco   November 25, 1996

"*I been at this work 50 years. Packin' oysters, shuckin' oysters. I'm 72 now. Done everything in here. In the old days, there were a lot more oysters. We'd start at 5 a.m. and go to 8 or 9 o'clock at night. Now, most of the time I'm done by about 3:30.*

"*There was a whole lot more comin' in than there is now. I'd say we'd shuck 500 bushels of oysters a day. Today, oh, the most we'd do is 200 bushels, and that's a good day. It's gettin' worse every year. I don't know whether it will be four, five years longer or what. But, yes indeed, I seen the good times.*

"*The packin' is real important. You got to keep it clean. Pick the stuff out of it. That's the main job, packin'. I'm the last thing they do. I like it. I been here 50 years. I know what I got to do to get it done, and I just like it.*

"*Shuckin' oysters is right hard. I didn't do that much of it. Cut your hands, stab your hands. It's hard on your heart, because of the pressure on your chest from pushin' the knife in. They're tough to open.*

"*I been gettin' up early my whole life. It don't bother me. But you don't see a lot of young people in here workin'. They won't do it. You know how young people are now days. They want somebody to give it to 'em. They don't want to work for it.*

"*When people ask me what I do, I tell them: 'I'm in seafood. We shuck it, wash it, pack it and sends it away!'*"

John W. Tilghman   November 25, 1996

Donald C. Brown Jr., 33, who operated a drive-in in Cape Cod, Mass., from 1983 to 1996, has managed the Diamond State Drive-In since 1995.

Mildred Steele, 80

Owner
Diamond State Drive-In
From 1949 to Present
Felton, Delaware

Drive-In Movie

It's believed that there were 5,800 drive-in movie theaters operating throughout the country in 1958. These open-air entertainment centers, with 60-foot by 100-foot megascreens, were popular local destinations for family outings. Many offered reasonable prices, snack bars and small playgrounds, where children could be entertained prior to the start of the feature film.

Drive-ins thrived in a post-war era, before televisions were standard features of every home. Later, these "passion pits" offered a secluded site where America's love of the automobile and adolescents' search for identity and independence met and meshed.

Eventually, changing tastes, suburban mall multiplex cinemas, multiple home televisions and the video rental industry killed attendance at the outdoor arenas under the giant screen. The open-air parking sites were empty, the box-like snack bars closed, the theater's tiny tot playground equipment rusted and, finally, the gigantic screens went dark.

By 1993, fewer than 900 drive-ins had survived. The same sad scenario was repeated throughout Delmarva—from the Naaman's' Drive-In near Claymont, Delaware, to Maryland's Bowl in Salisbury and the Dream in Chincoteague, Virginia.

But, somehow—through luck, coincidence and maybe because it was meant to be—one Delmarva drive-in has managed to survive in the closing days of the 20th century.

In 1949, central Delaware's first drive-in theater was built on U.S. 13, six miles south of Dover and two miles north of Felton. The builder was W. Courtney Evans, who also founded WDOV radio. One year later, in 1950, he moved from the area and sold the outdoor theater to Albert and Mildred Steele. They have owned the seven-acre drive-in site—which also includes the Diamond State Roller Rink—ever since.

That first year, three outdoor horn speakers mounted on top of the movie screen, provided the sound. But when the wind blew, they could hear the soundtrack in Felton. By the start of the next season, the Steeles laid wiring for 200 individual in-car speakers.

Mildred, Albert and their two sons operated the theater's movies and live country music shows until 1967. From the late 1960s through 1986, the Steele family maintained ownership, but leased the drive-in to operators from Baltimore.

In 1986—as a result of changing times, increased competition from other forms of recreation and lack of attendance—the Diamond State Drive-In's screen went dark, following the same road thousands of other outdoor theaters had been forced to take.

In 1995, Donald C. Brown Jr., from Cape Cod, Massachusetts, recognized an opportunity that others had overlooked. He arranged with the Steeles to open the Diamond State Drive-In from June through September. And now, once again, at least during the warm summer months, the antiquated, outdoor, big-screen relic, has become the only operating drive-in movie theater in the state of Delaware and on the entire Delmarva Peninsula.

"We bought the movie in 1950. We could fit about 200 cars. But, back then, we couldn't show movies on Sundays, because of the Blue Laws. So, we'd have shows. My husband, Albert, he used to play guitar in the Blue Hen Ramblers, a country music band. We'd play up and down the Eastern Shore for about 25 years. I told jokes, just like Minnie Pearl. I called myself Polly Peachtree. So we had country music shows on Sunday night. You could have a hillbilly show, but no movies.

"We built the stage up in front, just below the screen. We had some big names, like Tex Ritter, lots of local talent. We had regular customers come. A lot of friends would get together. They sat in the cars, and for applause they'd blow the horns. Sometimes, you couldn't get them to stop blowing the horns.

"We got us a good crowd. We sure did. Later, when we could have the movies on Sunday, we'd still have live shows before the movies, start before dark with the acts, and then the movie.

"The movie business was good, all during the '50s. They were lined up, those cars, down the side of the road to come in. We even had to move the box office back, so we'd have room to get more in. I liked it. It was like family. It was good times. You could put the kids in the car and go back to the snack bar and get soft drinks and candy bars.

"And the snack bar food was cheap! Popcorn was 10 or 15 cents a box. Sodas about 25 cents. We had hot dogs for 15 cents. I think it was 25 cents for a hamburger. In the beginning, it was $1 a carload for the first couple of years. All you could get in a car.

"We had movies every night, double features all the time. They didn't get done 'til about midnight. We changed the movies three times a week. We'd shut down about October.

"Everybody liked the movies, but I didn't have time to watch them. I was working in the snack bar. Most of the people didn't have TV in those days. It was something new back then. We didn't have a TV set. They were $800-$900 each. That was part of the reason they all came. Now, can you imagine days with no TV? But I can even remember when we didn't even have a radio.

"Then they got the Kent Drive-In, up the road. They got the first-run movies and we got the last run stuff. But we still ran it, did all right. But when my husband broke his leg, we decided to rent it out. People from Baltimore rented it and ran it until 1986. They were showing a lot of X-rated movies. Then we closed it up.

"A few years ago, Donald was going to Florida on this road. He noticed the marquee and stopped. I showed him around and he said he liked it and talked about renting it. He wrote me a few times. I didn't think he'd come back. I thought the drive-in's days were done.

"He came for a month, before the summer, to get it all together. Then, last summer he opened it up again and it was quite a fuss. This is the only drive-in that's operating in Delaware. They even came up from WBOC in Salisbury to take pictures and do a news story. I mean, I'd never think there was to be this much fuss over a drive-in.

"And the people came, they were lined up on the road to get it. And they brought their children and grandchildren, to show them what it was like in the old days. It was a good turnout last year. When we closed it up in 1991, I thought we might sell it off as a housing development one of these days, and instead it's a drive-in again. I never thought that would happen."

Mildred Steele

Mildred Steele

May 18, 1996

CHOLESTEROL

Shrimp is full of cholesterol. But the real cholesterol danger lurks in the slyly packaged "cholesterol-free" cookie. You see, shrimp contains very little of the saturated fat that makes that cookie taste so good. And it's the *saturated fat* in food—not the cholesterol—that has the greatest effect on your cholesterol level.

No wonder people are confused.

Here's your guide to understanding what it all means, because what *is* clear is the link between high cholesterol in your blood and heart disease. You'll find out whether you need a cholesterol test and what "good" cholesterol is, along with quick tips for creating a heart-healthy diet. What you won't find is a recipe for those cookies.

CHOLESTEROL AND YOUR HEART

Cholesterol, a white, waxy fat found naturally in your body, is used to build cell walls and make certain hormones. Too much of it, though, can clog your arteries and eventually choke off the supply of blood to the heart, which is the reason high cholesterol is a leading risk factor for heart disease. Other factors that put you at risk include:

➤ high blood pressure
➤ smoking
➤ a family history of heart disease
➤ being male
➤ diabetes
➤ obesity

PUTTING CHOLESTEROL TO THE TEST

WHO SHOULD BE TESTED: Everyone aged 20 and older, according to the National Cholesterol Education Program, although some researchers and medical economists believe this may be overcautious. Their advice: Men with no risk factors can wait until age 35 to be tested; similar women, until age 45.

WHEN: Once every five years.

BY WHOM: Preferably your doctor, who can measure LDL as well as total cholesterol. If you use an outside service:

➤ Check to see that the testers are doctors, nurses, or medical technicians.
➤ Get a written copy of your results to show to your doctor.

WHAT IT MEANS: The test measures the total amount of cholesterol in your blood: the HDL or "good" cholesterol, which cleanses arteries; plus the LDL or "bad" cholesterol, which builds up and clogs arteries. Here are guidelines for reading your test results.

Risk	Total Cholesterol	LDL	HDL
HIGH	above 239	above 159	less than 35
BORDERLINE	200-239	130-159	n/a
DESIRABLE	below 200	below 130	above 60

NOTE: If your cholesterol level places you in the borderline group and you have two or more of the risk factors listed at left, you're actually at *high* risk for heart disease.

CHOLESTEROL

EXERCISE

Thirty minutes of aerobic exercise three or four times a week may be all you need to raise the level of beneficial HDL in your bloodstream. Working out also helps control weight, lower blood pressure, and reduce stress. Suggestions: *Brisk walking, running, swimming, cycling, dancing, jumping rope, skating, aerobics.*

CHANGE THE FAT CONTENT OF YOUR MEALS

Following a low-fat, low-cholesterol diet can usually reduce your blood cholesterol by about 10 to 15 percent, thus lowering your risk of heart disease by 20 to 30 percent. Individual results will vary, depending on genetic makeup and former eating habits.

1. REDUCE SATURATED FAT, which raises the level of harmful LDL cholesterol in your blood (*butter, whole milk, cheese, ice cream, red meat, palm oil, palm kernel oil, coconut oil, hydrogenated soybean and cottonseed oils*).

➤ Cut out meat products high in fat (*hamburger, bacon, sausage*).

➤ Read labels carefully, and beware of foods that contain large amounts of hydrogenated vegetable oils, cocoa butter, coconut and palm oils, beef fat, or lard.

➤ Remove the skin from poultry, trim the fat around meat, and use lean beef, pork, or veal.

➤ Prepare at least one meatless meal a week.

➤ Snack on pretzels, air-popped popcorn, and fruit instead of candy, nuts, and chips.

➤ Drink skim or low-fat milk, and be aware that cream substitutes are made with tropical oils.

➤ Eat low-fat cheese, such as part-skim mozzarella.

2. REDUCE CHOLESTEROL (*eggs, meats, butter, whole milk*).

➤ Cook with egg whites instead of whole eggs.

➤ Avoid commercially prepared cookies, cakes, and pies.

➤ Limit portion sizes of lean meat, fish, and poultry to no more than six ounces a day, or about the size of two decks of cards.

➤ Eliminate organ meats (*liver, brain, kidney*) from your diet.

➤ Eat more water-soluble fiber, such as oat bran, legumes, and fruit, which may help lower cholesterol levels when made part of a low-fat, low-cholesterol diet.

3. EAT UNSATURATED FATS. Polyunsaturates lower your total blood cholesterol level—both LDL and HDL (*corn oil, sunflower seed oil, safflower oil*). Monounsaturates lower LDL levels but leave the beneficial HDL intact (*olive oil, canola oil*).

➤ Cook and bake with vegetable oils such as canola, sunflower, corn, soybean, and olive.

➤ Make your own salad dressing.

➤ Use soft margarine.

Kind of Fat	% Saturated	% Poly	% Mono
Canola oil	6	32	62
Safflower oil	10	77	13
Sunflower oil	11	69	20
Corn oil	13	62	25
Olive oil	14	9	77
Soybean oil	15	61	24
Margarine (tub)	17	34	24
Peanut oil	18	33	49
Cottonseed oil	27	54	19
Chicken fat	31	22	47
Lard	41	12	47
Beef fat	52	4	44
Palm kernel oil	81	2	11
Coconut oil	92	2	6

Source: *Compositions of Foods*, U.S. Department of Agriculture

WALKING

At a competitive extreme, walking is a track event. At the casual end of things, it's a surprisingly effective strategy for lifelong health. Walking has an unlikely virtue—its inefficiency. If you want to work major muscle groups, get your blood pumping, and take in oxygen, then efficiency is not your first priority. Studies show that walkers traveling faster than five miles an hour actually burn twice as many calories as runners going the same speed.

GETTING STARTED

To begin a walking program, keep in mind that you're in no big hurry. This is lifetime health, not overnight magic. For now, forget stopwatches, heart rates, and technique. Just go for a walk at a comfortable pace slightly above a stroll. Fifteen to 30 minutes would be nice. (If you are over 45 and this is your first step toward fitness, check with a physician first.)

BEYOND STROLLING

MEASURE YOUR TIME. Start by timing how long it takes you to walk a mile comfortably on flat ground. Chances are it'll take between 15 and 20 minutes. That's your starting capacity—build from there.

MEASURE SEVERAL COURSES. Use your car's odometer or the rule of ten city blocks to a mile to measure different routes. (Why walk the same path every time?) Two miles per course is enough for a start.

MEASURE YOUR INTENSITY. The recommendation for a "training heart rate" is 60 to 90 percent of the fastest your heart can beat in a minute. Figure your maximum heart rate by subtracting your age in years from 220. Multiply the result by 0.6 and 0.9 to get the bottom and top of your target zone for aerobic training.

SET YOUR FREQUENCY. The goal is three to five times a week, with a heart rate in your target zone for 15 to 60 minutes. Schedule your walks in advance, and keep the appointment.

GO. The proper technique is not as important as getting out there and doing something. Keep in mind that healthy people are well overall; their activities help fend off heart disease and circulatory problems. The key is to stay active.

KEEP IT UP. To make walking a habit takes willpower—and sometimes a strategy. Schedule regular walks with a friend if you need an extra push, or walk first thing in the morning before other commitments crop up, or vary your route to keep it interesting, or get a dog. Finally, don't think of it as exercise. It's time you've set aside for yourself. Enjoy it.

WHAT TO WEAR

All you really need is a good pair of walking shoes. Choose a pair with a firm heel cup for stability, a rocker sole to enhance a smooth heel-to-toe motion, and plenty of room for toes so they can spread out as they push off. Wear loose, comfortable clothes.

This information card compliments of HEALTH *magazine.*
HEALTH, P.O. Box 56863, Boulder, Colorado 80322-6863   HIC-19L

WALKING

FOR MAXIMUM GAIN

You don't have to walk any particular way, but there comes a point when refinements offer definite benefits. The correct posture, arm swing, and stride add up to higher-intensity exercise and lower risk of injury.

POSTURE. Lean slightly forward—from the ankles, not the waist. Leaning from the waist will only tire your back and make breathing harder. Keep your head level and your chin up.

ARM SWING. This makes walking a total body activity. Keep your elbows firmly bent at a 90-degree angle, and swing from the shoulder. Your hand should end its forward swing at breastbone height. On the backswing, if you're moving fast, the upper arm is almost parallel to the ground.

STRIDE. Make your stride long and smooth. It helps to borrow some moves from competitive race walkers: Keep your supporting leg straight as your body passes over it, and let the hip rise and relax. As that leg moves to the rear, keep its foot on the ground as long as possible before pushing off.

DON'T FORGET TO STRETCH

At whatever level you're walking, stretching is a good idea. Warm muscles respond better to stretches than cold ones, so walk for five or ten minutes until you're warm. Then stop to do at least three of the following static—no bouncing—stretches five times, 20 seconds each, for each leg. Repeat at the end of the walk.

ACHILLES TENDON AND CALF. With both hands against a wall or tree, place one foot well behind you. Keeping the rear leg straight and its heel on the ground, lean in toward the wall or tree.

QUADRICEPS. Put the left hand on a wall or tree for balance and with the right hand reach behind your back and grasp the ankle of the right leg. Pull it up toward your buttocks until you feel tension along the front of your thigh. Repeat on the opposite side.

HAMSTRING. Stand on one leg; prop the other leg parallel to the ground on a fence or table. Slide both hands toward the propped-up ankle as far as they'll go.

WHEN THE WEATHER IS BAD

Move your walk indoors. Shopping malls are a popular alternative—some 2,400 malls nation-wide let walkers in before shopping hours, usually between 6:30 and 10 A.M. In fact, many have walking clubs. To find the club nearest you, write the National Organization of Mall Walkers at P.O. Box 256, Hermann, MO 65041. If none is nearby, find a local health club that has an indoor track or treadmill.

RESOURCES

Rockport Guide to Lifelong Fitness. This is an easy-to-use test that helps you design your own walking program. Send a self-addressed, 45–cent stamped envelope to Walking Test, The Rockport Walking Institute, 220 Donald Lynch Blvd. P.O. Box 480, Marlboro, MA 01752.

The Manager

"After working at a drive-in theater during the summer of 1983, I became fascinated with the operations as well as with the mystique associated with the institution. At the time, I realized that the auto theater was not disappearing from lack of business, but rather from corporate apathy, as the major exhibitors shifted their focus away from single-screen theaters and seasonal drive-ins to the opportunities offered by multiplex cinemas.

"I came upon the long-shuttered Diamond State Drive-In site while traveling to Florida on Route 13 in 1993. After inquiring about the facilities with Mrs. Steele, she gave me a tour and I saw the theater's potential. Although the projection equipment was in dire need of restoration, the structures were sound enough.

"With new projection and sound equipment, a refurbished concession stand and an enthusiastic crew, the Diamond State Drive-In presented its first show in nearly a decade on May 19, 1995.

"To me, the atmosphere at a drive-in reflects much more than just an image on a giant screen. It's an event, as opposed to merely watching a movie. I like to say it's a venue where the stars glitter beyond the edge of the screen.

"The drive-in is an inexpensive alternative to today's multiplex cinemas. It also offers a much more relaxing and accommodating environment. Patrons certainly can't bring lawn chairs or pizzas to the local cinema, although that is standard fare at the drive-in.

"The Diamond State Drive-In's clientele consists primarily of patrons who grew up with the drive-in and who are returning today often with children of their own. It's a chance for some to relive the past and for others, younger people, to see what movies at the drive-in were like. It's also a family atmosphere, and that is the image that the theater wants to convey.

"The response to the reopening of the drive-in has been very positive and quite encouraging, especially from Mrs. Steele. Patrons are pleased to find a venue far removed from the confines of the modern multiplex. Many customers tell us they are very appreciative that we're back. On the first night we opened this season, I had a number of people drive up and say: 'Remember me? I was here last year.' I think they are very aware of what they have here.

"Personally, it is rewarding to know that a once-abandoned lot can generate interest and support that this theater has received.

"It all goes back to atmosphere. There is nothing quite like a drive-in theater. It's a reflection of an age gone by. I'm glad I can be a part of keeping this theater in operation."

Donald C. Brown Jr.   June 26, 1996

The Projectionist

"*I ran the projectors for the Bowl and the Delmar Drive-Ins for five years, back in the '70s. I never thought I'd get the chance to do it again, especially with so much automation, and the fact that there are so few drive-ins around. I came over here one night after they reopened and asked if I could see the booth. Now I run the show for Donald. It's great! Fantastic! That's why I came here. Theaters are just something you get hooked on. It just gets into your blood.*

"*Automation's become the big thing. In most theaters there are no projectionists anymore. The manager just arranges the show, puts the movies together on platters and pushes a button. But luckily, that's not the way it is here.*

"*We get 20-minute reels, so I have to thread the reels and change the carbons [lights]. I also have to watch the movies and know when to start up the other projector to change over the reels, so there's no break on the screen. That's a projectionist's nightmare, and it's all happened to us more than once.*

"*Most theater operators today couldn't run these old machines, absolutely not, unless they've been around a while. With movies now on platters, there's not much of a need for projectionists. Our days are pretty much over. There are very, very few places, that still want to use real equipment, but you can still find a few here and there.*

"*When there's a night with a good turnout, with lots of people and cars, it's great. I think it's rather exciting to see an older place like this come alive. I'm sure someday this will end and go by the wayside. But for now, I want to be out here and enjoy it while I can.*"

Leon Smullen   July 18, 1996

From 1974 to 1979, Leon Smullen, 40, of Camden, Delaware, was a projectionist at two drive-ins--the Bowl and the Delmar. In 1996, he worked as a projectionist at the Diamond State Drive-In.

Ferryboat Captain

Since 1683, a ferry has been transporting people, livestock and vehicles across the Tred Avon River, connecting Oxford, Maryland, on the south bank with Bellevue and Royal Oak on the north.

In 1974, Capt. Gilbert C. Clark, whose family had operated ferries between Shelter Island and North Haven on Long Island, New York, for five generations, came to the Eastern Shore to operate the Oxford-Bellevue Ferry. Today, his daughter, Valerie Bittner, her husband, David, and their children, Robb and Gretchen, all serve as licensed captains and have continued the family ferry-boating tradition into its seventh generation.

From March 1 through mid-December, the Bittner's ferryboat *The Talbot* —capable of holding nine cars and up to 80 passengers—provides pedestrians, bicyclists and vehicles with a seven-minute, 3/4-mile escape from the pressures of the day at a leisurely pace of 6 miles per hour.

The quiet, smooth journey progresses across the water. From the upper cabin, the pilot looks out over the river and glances at the deck, watching the passengers leaning against the rails. Some are operating cameras; others stand with their hands empty, their arms folded. Relaxed, they soak up the scenery.

As the boat docks, the travelers return to their vehicles. Doors slam. Engines restart. After they drive off, *The Talbot* picks up another load. In the wheel house, the pilot turns, faces the opposite direction, grabs a second, identical ship's wheel, and—as others have done for more than three centuries—silently guides the ferryboat across the Tred Avon River.

Valerie Bittner, 49

Ferryboat Captain
Oxford-Bellevue Ferry
From 1980 to Present
Royal Oak, Maryland

"*T*he summer is the busiest time—June, July and August. We have busy fall weekends. That's when we tend to see older people traveling when the weather is cooler and the children are back in school.

"A lot of our business is from word of mouth, but we are one of the prime attractions in the county. It's the only ferryboat system in Talbot County. It also provides an important link from St. Michaels to the Oxford area, rather than driving back up to Easton and down.

"I love being outdoors. It's just so unique to be able to enjoy nature, the waterfowl around us, to watch the weather change. There are four licensed captains in our family, including our children Gretchen and Robb. But, we say that they've abandoned ship, because they're currently living in South Carolina. They're not presently working on the ferry, but they're still licensed. They worked for a number of years, starting as deck hands, studying for their license and working their way up to captain.

"In the summer it will be full most of the day. During that time we work in short shifts. One captain cannot be down here for 10 hours at a time. My husband and I split it up. It slacks off in the fall.

"A lot of people are surprised and interested about what it's like to operate a ferry. Ferry boating takes you back in time. There really are not that many ferry boating systems left in the country at this point. This operation is unique because it is privately owned, and its the oldest continuous ferryboat operation in America. A lot of the systems are state-owned now.

"You see a lot of different reactions from people when they come here. When we have an all-female crew we get some reactions. Some people find it interesting, some people are a little nervous. But when we get to the other side, they tell us what a good time they've had and what a good job we've done.

"I find it very satisfying that we're carrying on a family tradition. How often can you find seven generations working the same business? That's unique in itself, although it's not in the same location, it's the same profession.

"It's absolutely beautiful out here when it's snowing. But it doesn't happen that often. The worst weather usually happens when we close during the winter. My husband, David, does most of the maintenance himself. We're always fighting the weather, trying to get things done and ready for the spring. Painting, sand blasting the decks, doing the engine work. There's a fair amount of maintenance that we have to do every year. We don't have all that time off.

"We have regulars, people who work in various boatyards. We have painters we ferry on a regular basis. We have cable companies, furniture companies, seafood people. We get to know them, and I enjoy that. They look forward to taking a relaxing cruise on the river, especially at day's end when the sun is setting. It's so beautiful. It's a nice way to end a busy day. People really look forward to it.

"Some people are so fascinated with the operation that they ask: 'How do I get your job?' or they say, 'I want your job!' And we say, 'You can fill out an application and we'll look it over.' People are envious. It's such a beautiful area and the job is unique.

"I love it. It's just wonderful to be working outdoors and meeting people from all over the world. I'll do this forever, as long as I'm able."

Valerie C. Bittner

Valerie Bittner

November 24, 1996

Delbert 'Cigar' Daisey, 68

Waterman, Decoy Carver
From 1941 to Present
Chincoteague, Virginia

Decoy Carver

For more than a century decoys have been associated with Delmarva. Along the entire coastline, watermen—and more recently professional carvers—have chopped blocks of wood, shaping them into everything from pintail and teal to canvasback and geese. In the beginning, the decoy was functional, made to lure passing game into killing range of shot and shell. Today, its purpose has changed.

While some rough, working decoys are still handmade, the newest generation of carvers—many of whom use power tools as opposed to hatchets and knives—concentrate on fine decorative pieces that will never see the wetlands, never float in the water of the marshes. Instead, these artworks are kept under glass or placed on high shelves as display pieces in offices and homes.

These days, Chincoteague waterman Cigar Daisey spends much of his time in the workshop, on the water's edge behind his home. In the midst of the frame building, with large doors that open at both ends, his figure forms a working silhouette against the calm background of the Assateague Channel. He had spent a lot of time on the refuge across the water, trapping birds, catching fish, shooting game. Now most of that's just a memory. The birds are gone, the water mostly empty, especially when compared to the past.

Listening to Cigar, you wouldn't know that some consider him one of the big names in the decoy world. Ask him if he's ever won any prizes and he answers "a few," then moves the conversation onto another subject. But mention his name at the Chincoteague Refuge Waterfowl Museum, where he's been the resident carver since it opened in 1978, and the staff speaks more enthusiastically. They point out some of his 800 pieces on display in its private collection, "but none are for sale." They take you to his work area, where he can come in and carve "when he pleases." Then there's the biographical display, featuring his photograph from an article in *National Geographic Magazine*.

Cigar explained that he got his name in 1945, while "relieving the game warden of some trapped ducks." In the process he lost some of his smokes. The next morning, his distinctive cigars were found, frozen in the ice that had formed in the empty trap.

"*I* was born and raised here. Worked on the water, mainly fishin', oysterin', clammin'. Did some fur trappin' in the winters, too. I was an instrument man on a survey crew for 13 years, and I worked as a blacksmith onshore.

"The first piece I ever made in my life was in the late 1930s. But then I made some decoys with my father in 1941. I got interested in it for huntin' purposes. They all were huntin' decoys back then. That's how this whole thing got started. It was huntin' decoys as far back as you want to go, back into the 1800s. There may have been a decorative decoy, but there weren't none around here. That started around the late 1960s, around this neck of the woods, I'll put it that way.

"I'm still not interested in decorative decoys. They're nice and take a lot of work, but it's just not the whole idea of it. Some people use my decoys for decorative purposes, but I still make some for people to hunt with. I make black duck, a lot of mallards, a lot of cork decoys, made from cork trees, pressed into forms. I paint 'em, too. Do it all.

"I don't know exactly how many pieces I done—17, 18 thousand, something like that. A lot of cheap stuff, real cheap stuff, you know what I mean? I made decoys for a dollar-and-a-half or three dollars in the early '60s. Now'days, I may get a hundred or so dollars for some pieces.

"But I don't like to do none of it any more. When you get older, the things that used to mean a hellava lot to you don't stay that way. They change. Nothin' lasts forever. Time has a way of changin' things.

"Same way with huntin'. Huntin's a lot of fun, especially when you're the right age. I don't like huntin' like I used to. I still hunt a little. But there's a little somethin' wrong with a duck hunter, anyway. Up at the top of their head there's a little somethin' there missin'. A man'll go out and freeze hisself to death, like I done thousands of times, to just get an old duck. One thing to it, if you didn't do your huntin' when you're younger, you won't do it from now on. Don't look like there's gonna be a whole lot to hunt.

"But you got people who never hunt a day in their life but like to collect decoys. I guess you gotta collect somethin', either money or decoys. I guess part of the attraction with decoys is people want to be part of the past, huntin' you know. Decoys were tools of the trade. Ownin' a good decoy was just like ownin' a good gun. Use 'em a lot and you got a lot of memories out of 'em.

"With decoys, you just have to worry about not bustin' 'em up too bad. These outboard motors is rough on stuff. They vibrate 'em so much. Jump around so much, ya know? Beat the paint off them when they rub together.

"I don't think too many people know what a good decoy is to tell ya the truth. A lot a people like a work of art. Somethin' real slick. Real smooth. They get their four fingers and their thumb around it and they seem to love it. But that don't make it a good decoy. A good decoy, it shouldn't be real slick, it should have a certain amount of roughness. It holds the paint better, breaks the light better. That's the reason cork is far superior to wood. It's got a texture to it. Most of mine are that way. I believe you can texture a piece of wood if you wanna take the time, ya got the same thing. But that requires a lotta time, ya know.

"I don't have to look at pictures too much anymore. If I don't know by now what they're supposed to look like, I never will, after all the years. But, a lotta times I'll go back and look. I save heads from huntin' season, ya know, to use as a model.

"I work by myself here. Don't keep nothin'. A decoy carver has a job just to keep himself enough decoys to hunt with. Most people'll try to talk you out of 'em.

"Some people come and ask for a certain kinda duck. But most time ya buy what a man's got. So I do this all year long. Ain't got nothin' else I can do now, at this age. Ain't no fish no more. Can't make a livin' on the water no more. Everything's dead on the water. Outboard motor's destroyed everything on the East Coast. Mixed up the oil and the gas with the water together is what I think.

"It's different here in the winter. No tourists. It's quiet. Feel like you got it back for a little while. Just as soon as you have a pretty weekend they're here again. They're somethin' like a necessary evil now. Used to be you had other industries around here. Had the seafood industry. Today, you ain't got nothin'. All your seafood comes from Louisiana and Texas, places like that. I'd say 90-some percent of it.

"We used to have plenty of oysters. I caught as much as 135 bushels a tide. In one day—four, five, six hours. Today, ain't 135 bushels from here to Smith Island. So the oysters is gone. The crabs goes and comes. They disappear and they come back. This spring ya couldn't catch a dozen around here. Now I see a lot of little ones comin' back.

"Don't seem nothin' wants to live around here. They got somethin' in this water, I don't know what it is. It's killin' everything.

"I liked carvin' all right. But now, if I wasn't doin' this, ain't much I could do at this age and this time. I ain't able to do an awful lot of hard work. There ain't a whole lot left for me when it comes to work. Matter of fact, I'm tired of work, anyway. I don't like work.

"I guess you could say some people know me from carvin'. I used to participate in the shows. Michigan, Iowa, New York, Maryland, Virginia Beach, different places. Traveled a little. Got some prizes sometimes, but they weren't really important.

"If people ask me for advice about carvin', I tell 'em to go buy a good book or tape. I believe anybody can learn it, anyone, with a little help and some books. A lotta people teach this. Most people, as soon as they learn a little somethin' about it, goes into teachin'. Ya gotta lotta people in this country loves to teach. They like to be an authority. That's probably what's hurt it more than anything. Teachers.

"What's happened is there's been an army of carvers since 1975. The woods is full of 'em. Some of 'em real good and some not so good. But that don't make no difference. It's there for sale. The average person that buys a decoy don't know a good one from a bad one, and it don't bother 'em none.

"I use a Fordham tool and a band saw. This is cedar, come from Maine—8 foot long, 4 inches thick, 7 or 8 inches wide. Saw off whatever you're gonna use. Just about all of it is knife work for me, but I'm from the old school. That's all I know is the knife. Some people don't use a knife. You can do the whole thing with a Fordham tool, do it just as well, maybe better. I don't know. You don't need a knife anymore.

"Most of the time I make 'em larger than real life. If you're gonna use them as a decoy, you can see it better the bigger it is. Don't want it a whole lot larger, but some.

"You leave the huntin' decoy and you start towards the decorative. Then you got betwixt and between. You got a lot more in it. You got too much time in it. I guess you'd call it semi-decorative. You can work forever on a decorative decoy. You can make 50 cents an hour on some of them, if you tell the truth. I worked on them myself forever, for nothin'. You gotta texture the wood. I've used a wood burnin' tool, used it many times. A lotta burnin', a lotta grindin' on grindin' wheels to make 'em look like feathers.

"People don't have any idea of the work goes into these. Don't know how time consumin' it is. They don't know what you put in it. They imagine you get somethin' out of it, but you don't.

"Most of the carvers are not full time. They gotta job makin' a livin' doin' somethin' else, and they carve part time, see, when they're not workin', which is the way to do it. Then you make what you want then, ya know?

"I wouldn't pay a whole lot for nothin' today. Matter of fact, I wouldn't collect fancy, high-priced carvin's. If you pay a lotta money for 'em, they got nowhere to go. They're already there. But if you buy an old huntin' decoy for a few dollars, and later on it begins to be worth a lot, why then you made a good investment.

"I used to have college students come out and see me carve, maybe 80 at a time. Used to have about 3,000 people a year come and look. Some passin' through would come by. Some from shows. I knew a lotta people in my life. Less now. See, most of my friends that's older than I am are dead. That's the way it works out. When you get to be 68-and-a-half, most the people that you know who were older are gone.

"There's some good young carvers. There's some real good young carvers. But I don't think the interest in collectin' decoys is there with the younger generation like it was with the older ones. Never will be, I don't think.

"To be a decoy collector today, and buyin' old antique decoys, and that's where the interest is, you gotta have a lotta money. You can buy a new decoy pretty cheap. Most of the people want somethin' you ain't got, somethin' ya can't get, ya know?

"Seems like nobody's decoys is worth a lotta money 'til he dies. Then they know damn well he ain't gonna make no more then. That's the way life is. People want what they can't have, what they can't get.

"If I'da been a decoy collector, I'da made some money. 'Cause I got in on the ground floor, years ago, ya know, in 1940. If I started collectin' decoys back then, today I could have millions of dollars. The money's in the antiques. It ain't in the new stuff.

"But it's nice workin' in here. I gotta lotta friends. They'll come in here with a few beers, and I'll sit here and make me a duck while we talk. First thing you know, I'll have 10 or 12 of 'em sittin' here, talkin'. It's like a beer hall. My wife says I do a lotta drinkin' and a little bit of carvin'. But, as far as I can tell, it don't affect my carvin'."

Delbert "Cigar" Daisey

Delbert "Cigar" Daisey   August 10, 1996

Highway Gift Shop

It was right after the Big War, in 1946, when the red, barn-like building was opened on Route 40. At that time, a half-century ago, the clientele was mainly enthusiastic travelers—sightseers who were heading along the then-busy, new six-year-old highway. Many made the Davis Gift Shop one of their landmark stops, to pick up souvenirs, including Indian moccasins, lawn ornaments, coonskin caps and chenille robes and bedspreads.

In the 1960s, newly built I-95 siphoned off most of the tourist and commuter traffic. The new generation of drivers seemed to prefer the sterile swiftness of the interstate over the more colorful roadside America of nearby Route 40.

But the Davis Gift Shop has survived, its racks filled with Maryland souvenirs, sweatshirts, painted plates, collectible spoons and painted ceramics for indoor and outdoor display.

It remains the last of the three stores that had been operated for decades by the same family. The others, in Bear, Delaware, and on Washington Boulevard, south of Baltimore, are closed.

Seven days a week, from April 1 through December 24, Paul and Edith Davis Nichols still offer personalized service to a steady family of regulars customers. But they also offer comfortable smiles to those newcomers who take a few moments to stop on the side of the road—perhaps attracted by the colorful glint of the outdoor display of "Gazing Globe" lawn decorations—and step into a fading, but still sparkling sliver of America's past.

Edith Davis Nichols, 77

Shop Owner
Davis Gift Shop
From 1946 to Present
North East, Maryland

"We used to have tourists, lots of tourists, stop in. The busses would pull up and they'd get off and come in and stay and talk and buy souvenirs. But that stopped with I-95.

"We would be open from 7 in the morning to 9 at night, and only close on Christmas Day. Now we go from 9 to 5, still seven days a week. But we close after Christmas for a few months, then open up in the spring.

"We have regulars who come back every year. I like repeat business. That means your people are satisfied. Today it's mostly locals, from Virginia, Pennsylvania, New Jersey, Delaware. I call that local.

"We had a man, one day, who bought a large hitching-post jockey, and shoved it in the back of a station wagon. Wrapped it real careful, with a blanket and all. My husband, Paul, asked him if he was going to travel far. The man said, 'Yes, to The Netherlands.' We thought that was one to remember.

"We keep our prices low, reasonable. We depend on word-of-mouth advertising. I heard some people knock on other people's doors and ask them where they bought the figure that's out on their lawn. They tell them, 'Go to that gift shop on Route 40.'

"I have my regular people who say, 'I don't know what I'm gonna do if you go outta business. Where am I gonna get my Indian moccasins?' Nobody else carries them.

"Some people come in and tell me that when they were little, their parents would bring them in, and if they didn't stop on a trip they'd look for us. We were like a landmark to them as they went by. They come in to remember and look around. One woman was taking a trip up I-95, and she took the exit off and drove over just to see if we were still open. I guess she expected we'd be gone. We fooled her.

"We used to have chenille bedspreads, from Georgia. They were made by hand in homes and little shops. When the carpet mills opened up, everybody went to work there and we couldn't get them anymore. I'd say about 95 percent of our items are American made, some from reservations in North Carolina and Minnesota. We try to avoid imports. Our people need the work instead of foreign people.

"I guess I must like it, or I wouldn't be here all these years . . . all except for the heavy work, with the lawn statues. But I do like being with people and talking to them. If I retired from here, I'd miss it and go to work. But my family's like that. My aunt died this year at 105. She retired when she was 92, but she was miserable. She told me she wished she was back in the shop. My mother died at 80, and she worked every day.

"My children say to me, 'You've been here 50 years. It's time to go out.' But what would I do? You have to do something. I can't just sit around and watch the TV.

"But the days of gift shops like this are over. Young people today are into different computers and other things . . . not the gift shop business. It's a dying part of America, especially shops that aren't in those new malls.

"This was good for us, though. We raised a family here, raised five kids who grew up with us in the business. They learned how to work with Mom and Dad. We were with them 24 hours a day. We had a good life.

"I wouldn't want my children to take over, though, not the way things have changed in the last 25 years. It's not like it was. Anymore, you don't know who's gonna come in. Places all around here have been robbed at one time or another. We've been lucky. Today, if they only get $10 they shoot you. Years ago that didn't enter your mind, and now you have to think about it.

Paul and Edith Davis Nichols in front of their gift shop on U.S. Route 40

"At the end of the season, you're tired. To tell the truth, each year, in December when I close up, I start to think maybe I won't open again. Then, April 1 comes and I'm ready to go again. Every year I think I won't, but I will, until my health goes bad and I can't do it anymore. Then you have to stop, 'cause you can't go on forever, and they'll be nobody else to take it on."

Edith Davis Nichols   May 2, 1996

Scrapple Makers

Philadelphia is noted for its soft pretzels; Louisiana has its spicy gumbo; and Texas has fresh beef, right off the hoof. In downstate Delaware, the trademark dish is homemade style scrapple. No visitor to Delmarva should miss the opportunity to sample the tasty pork product that is one of the region's delicacies, and the majority is made by a handful of long-established family businesses in Sussex County.

Many will agree that scrapple is especially pleasing to the eye and taste buds if you don't know, or ask, what's in it. The flat, rectangular fried slices are made mainly of corn meal and other grains, plus pig parts—including the snout, livers, heart, jowls and ears—that aren't used for anything else.

But spice it up, add some coating for flavor then put it beside a plate of eggs and you've got yourself the makings of a distinctively Delmarvalous breakfast platter.

Nobody knows for sure where the mixed meat originated. One legend says Philadelphia housewives collected meat scraps that they boiled and mixed with corn meal. They gave the mystery meat to Washington's troops at Valley Forge, during the winter of 1777.

German families cooked a similar concoction called "panhaus" for hundreds of years and brought the dish from Europe to their new settlements in the new world.

Despite its hazy origin, there are heavy concentrations of scrapple eaters on Delmarva, in Philadelphia and Southeast Pennsylvania, particularly the Dutch Country. But many consider Sussex County, in the center of Delmarva with four major producers, as the world's "Scrapple Capital."

In Milton, Delaware, on the banks of the Broadkill River, a white building houses Milton Sausage & Scrapple Company Inc., founded in 1930 by Robert and Morris Black.

The business has been in the Burnham family since 1940, when Dorsey V. Burnham Sr. bought the company. After his death in 1957, his two sons Claude L. and Dorsey Jr., continued operating the business. Today, the third and fourth generations of the family—Claude "Skip" Burnham Jr. and his son, Jeff—make the same "Old Home Made Brand" of meats that the family has proudly produced for more than a half century.

About 500 pounds of the Burnham family brand is made fresh every day. It's shipped north to retail stores near Smyrna and throughout the Eastern Shore and down to restaurants and hotels in Ocean City and the beach resorts.

Plant Manager
Jeff Burnham, 27,
with his father, Skip

Claude 'Skip' Burnham Jr., 52

President
Milton Sausage & Scrapple Company Inc.
From 1958 to Present
Milton, Delaware

"*I* started here full time when I was about 24, but I was working in the business in the summers since I was 14. When people ask about scrapple, they find out that it's a lot of the parts of the pig that are left over. After the hams are gone, the pork loins, the pork chops, you have all this other meat left. Years ago, they just put them all together, ground them up and made a meat we call scrapple.

"But the seasoning's the thing. The people I buy spices from is called A.C. Legg. Back in 1940, my grandfather talked to a man from A.C. Legg and they devised this seasoning, and we've used it ever since. It's never changed. The only people that know our seasoning are me, Jeff, Elaine, the USDA and our seasoning supplier.

"People come up to us and say, 'Don't change your recipe. I like it just like it is.' If they try another brand, they can tell the difference, especially with sausage, but scrapple, too. Our is a little bit hotter, a little bit spicier than the others.

"We start at 7 o'clock in the morning. We make up our orders and check our deliveries. Then we put the meat for the scrapple in the pot and start to cook it. The pots are big, cast iron, and hold about 450 pounds.

"We put it on at 7, then grind it at 9:30. Continue cooking. Put in our spices, flour and meal. About 11 o'clock it's ready to turn the pot off, then we pour the mixture out and we're ready to dip it in the pans. It's real mushy. We let it set overnight in the cooler. Then, the next day, we make our 1- and 2-pound packages, and others that are 5 and 10 pounds. When it's formed up, we wrap it and ship it out. We make about 2,500 pounds a week.

"We're good friends with our competitor Kirby and Holloway. There have been times when both of us have had problems. We had a flood here in 1962 and we did out processing over at Kirby and Holloway's. And one day their hamburg patty machine broke down and we had them come over and use ours. We're friendly competitors. They're nice people.

"My grandfather developed a good product. People come in and try to sell us new things, or tell us they can make our product better. But I'm an old-fashioned person who will not change. I think I got that from my Dad and my Uncle Jack.

"I believe carrying on the family business is satisfying, but it's hard work, too. Unfortunately, your work never leaves you. Even when you're home sitting down something will come up. Lucky for me I have a great secretary and a super manager.

"I tell you, when the pork is cooking, there's a good smell, real recognizable. I can tell when it's just about ready. Sometimes, I'll go back and get a cup of it, while it's cooling. I'll tell you right now, it's as good that way—right out of the pot—as when it's fried. You get some bread, slap it on there and make a sandwich, because it's already been cooked.

"It's not just for breakfast. This time of year, when it's getting cold, a lot of deer hunters are out and they'll have a scrapple sandwich. At our house, we eat it once a week for dinner.

"I like putting out a product I will eat for the rest of my life. I know what I put out of here is fresh, clean and has a good flavor. The only change in this business is when there are improvements in machinery. But, basically, our scrapple is done the same way it's always been, since 1940, and it will never change."

C. L. Burnham, Jr.

Skip Burnham   November 18, 1996

Plant Manager
From 1982 to Present

"Like my father, I worked here in the summer when school was out. One of my first experiences with the business was going to Philadelphia in the truck with my Dad to pick up products. We'd have a good time. Even when I went to college, majoring in journalism, I would come and help package products in the summer. One year, my uncle got sick and Dad needed help. Time went on and I just stayed.

"I like it, especially working with my Dad. It feels good when people say they like our products, and I think to myself, 'My family is responsible for it.'

"I'm pretty much my own boss. I manage the plant and drive trucks when necessary. Most of all, I like getting out on the road and meeting our customers."

Jeff Burnham

November 18, 1996

Office Manager

"I've been here since 1969. A lot of my friends went to work for large companies and they do repetitive jobs. Many have moved onto other jobs. I have been here since just before graduation from college, in 1969, over 27 years ago. I describe myself as Radar on 'M.A.S.H.' As office manager, I get to do a little of everything and I'm never bored.

"We have our regular customers who place orders through our salesmen or call our office. And then we have people who have lived in the area and moved away, or their children have moved away. We get lots of phone calls from people all over the United States—from as far away as San Jose, California, and Montana—who want 10-pound blocks of scrapple. We ship a lot to people who have retired and moved to Florida. We only ship in cold weather, mostly January and February. They treat our scrapple just like steak.

"We love scrapple. The first thing my daughter, Michelle, learned to cook was scrapple. She just sliced some off and started frying it."

Elaine Messick

November 18, 1996

Fishnet Maker

A Milton native, Lydia Beideman spent four years during World War II in Philadelphia, while her late husband, Alvin, worked in the shipyards. In 1945, when they came back to Sussex County, at Broadkill Beach, they worked with her father-in-law, Oliver "Dorry" Beideman, making and selling fishnets.

For 50 years, until recently when her doctor restricted Lydia from entering her basement workroom, Delaware's Net Woman has hung hundreds and hundreds of nets for commercial and pleasure fishermen.

She also has sold her product to customers who have never cast her nets into the sea.

"I've hung net for as far as Washington, D.C.," she said. "They wanted it to put in their yard to catch the leaves when they falled off of the trees. They took that net, laid it on the ground and folded it up and wouldn't have to rake. And I've sold it to keep birds outta the garage. I sold it to put over swimming pools. People from Florida, New York, Philadelphia."

But, today, times have changed. Fewer watermen working the river and bays have reduced the demand for her product, and even her long-time fishnet suppliers are gone. The Philadelphia and Connecticut companies where she knew the owners by name have closed. The few remaining net makers must now order from businesses located father away, in the South and the Midwest.

New laws restricting net fishing also have had a bad effect on the net making trade.

But still, on Delaware Route 1 between Milton and Lewes, the familiar red and tan sign stands, indicating the Beideman home, where for half a century, fishermen and regular customers would come to purchase the fine results of the Net Woman's work.

Lydia Beideman, 82
The 'Net Woman'
From 1947 to 1996
Milton, Delaware

"I started helping hang net when I had small kids. I'd go over there, to my father-in-law's and work with him and Alvin, my husband. Then, at that time, it was more commercial, I guess you'd call it, because you could use any size you wanted. Now, here in the past, I guess right close to 10 years, you gotta have a license now to use the net. Before, anybody could use the net.

"They were 100 to 200 yards, and anywhere's from 6 to 10 feet wide. Commercial fishermen can still use them, but I think the bigger the net, the more the license costs them.

"They'd ask for the net they want according to how deep the water they was gonna fish in. People ask me what kind of fish were they were gonna catch in these nets, and I'd tell them, 'Anything that would go in it.' They'd catch trout, rock, perch.

"When we first started with the nets, it was cotton. Then it went to linen and then nylon net took over. And now it's monofilament net. Don't ask me how to spell it. But it's been used a while. My husband's been gone 30 years. Before he died, somebody from Dover come down with a piece of net and said this is what's gonna come in now.

"It was heavy, and my husband said, 'That'll never catch fish.' But he was wrong. We use it now, but it's a lot finer than in the beginning. Of course, the finer your mesh or twine is, the more fish you catch. We used to hang anywhere's from 2-1/2-inch to 5-1/2-inch mesh. That's the spaces of the openings in the net. The smaller mesh caught the bait fish and such. The larger caught the rock.

"Early in my life, I could hang 100 yards a day. Now, in later years, I slowed up. Of course, now I ain't even allowed to do it. But a 200-yard net, if I stick at it, I could do it in two days. Five years ago, my sister, Dorothy Legates, come down from Millsboro to help me. Some days, we could hang 200 yards a day.

"This is all hand work. No machines. We get the net, the mesh, already made. Some people think I sew the whole net, but I don't. I buy the net, and I hang it for people. I attach two ropes, one has the donut floats on it, on the top, to hold it up. The other end has leads on the bottom, to hold it down. Today, we got braided rope, and we push the leads inside the rope. I think that's better than when we started.

"We repair nets, too. But I hate that job. The nets are all dirty and used. You gotta know how to cut the hole out, to match up the net and get it fixed and patched where there's the hole. My husband could do it, and all you could tell is where he done his knots, but I never got that good.

"Never were a lot of net hangers. Back then, they'd either hang their own or bring it to us to hang. I'm about the only one now, that's hanging net down here. A lot hung their own, but it took a lot of time.

"When I was in the hospital, I had quite a lot on hand to hang. So my two grandsons and my daughter, Patsy Brown, helped out and got me caught up with the orders. When customers found out I was going out, they didn't know what to do. They wanted to know if I knew anybody who could hang it. I said, 'I don't know.' I showed some of them how to do it, for themselves. They thanked me and said that's a lot of work.

"I got some strange things happened over the years, some good stories. They'd ask me, 'Are you guaranteed that this net'll catch fish?' and I said, 'If the fish is there it will.' Somebody from Dover come down and wanted a net, and he wanted it to sink, and I hung it to sink. But I never thought to *tell him, make sure he tied the rope to something, so he could find the net. So he takes the net and throws it overboard, and it went to the bottom and he couldn't find his net.*

"Another guy comes down and he wanted 400 yards of net to sink. And I said to him, 'You'll never get it outta the basement.' He says, 'Don't you worry about that. We'll get it out.' We had about 80 pounds of lead on 400 yards of net. So my daughter said to him, 'I'd like to see you when you put that net overboard.' I think they used it twice, then they brought it back for us to split half in two. We saw they had a time to get it outta the basement.

"I stopped hanging in March. From 1947 to now I hung a lot of net. But it's a business that you gotta have something to go with it, to make what you call a living out of it. My husband was a carpenter, and his mom and I would hang the net. Of course, he'd tell us what to hang. On weekends and at nights, maybe, if somebody was in a hurry, we'd both go down and hang net, down in the basement. I gotta television down there, now. Sometimes I listened to the soap operas and hang net. Before that you used the radio, or didn't use nothing.

"Nobody ever told me to my face, but I hear they'd say, 'Go up to see the Net Woman, over to Beideman's.' But everybody bragged about how good my net hanging was. I imagine I'd hang around 200 nets a season. It's all word of mouth. No advertising, except the Milton Lions Club calendar. My husband started that and I kept it up. Nothing else. Most people see the sign. They come up and say, 'I see you make fish nets. I'd like to have one.'

"Seems everybody thinks this work is hard on your hands. If you don't hold your needle right, you can get a blister. One time, somebody wrote me up and said, 'Do you care if I feel your hands?' I said, 'No.' They expect my hands to be all rough and everything.

"My business, I guess, is going out now. I got three kids and none of them is interested in the net business. And, right now, there's not that much money in it anyhow. But I really enjoyed hanging net. It was just something I liked, and I could stay home and do it, work home. If you don't like to do it, you just might as well forget it. See my kids don't like to do it.

"Some people say it's something like knitting. It's something like that, but I can't knit or crochet. But I've hung a lot of net, I mean a lot of net.

"I got congestion of the heart, and my lungs filled up with fluid. The doctor told me I couldn't hang net no more. He said, 'Stay outta the basement!' so that meant, 'Don't hang net!' I asked if I could go down and do the wash, and the doctor about hit the ceiling. So I got to relax I guess.

"It bothers me that I can't do nothing. I think it hurt me worse when he told me I had to give up hanging net than being sick."

Lydia Beideman

Lydia Beideman

July 12, 1996

Authors note: Mrs. Lydia Beideman died at home on Dec. 31, 1996, at the age of 83. Mrs. Beideman lived with her son-in-law, Raymond Brown, and her daughter, Patricia Ann Brown. According to Raymond, "There was a net had to be cut and she cut net on her last day. She was in good spirits and went to bed. She always said that, when she went, she wanted to be home and go in her sleep. She got her wish."

Sportswriter

There aren't too many of them left, the old-time, real-life sportswriters—those who came up through the ranks and learned the ropes about reporting on the street. They're the ones who can reminisce about time at the small town papers, where they wrote stories covering more than a half-dozen different sports at the same time.

Today's newsrooms are filled with the new breed of scholar-writers, most with journalism degrees and summer internship experience. Few newcomers, however, can serve as an athletic banquet toastmaster, host a radio program or entertain visitors for hours with stories about dining with such greats as Ted Williams, Joe DiMaggio, Jesse Owens, Joe Montana, Stan Musial, Bob Cousy, Wilt Chamberlain and Gene Autry.

At the Wilmington *News Journal*, Matt Zabitka remains one of the few old-time, pick-and-peck typist reporters who taught himself the trade. In 1962, after stints at such papers as the *Chester News, Kensington Guide, Marcus Hook Herald* and *Chester/Delaware County Times*, he landed a job at the Wilmington daily and has been there ever since.

Over the years, even while serving in the U.S. Navy during World War II, he's been a writer. His byline has appeared in such national publications as *Sporting News, Harness Racing, Golf Digest, U.S. Olympian* and *Tennis Magazine.*

While the procedures for getting the story are basically the same—ask the right questions, listen carefully and present the story accurately, and in a fashion that readers are able to understand and enjoy—there are few reporters like Matt, who have remained at a paper long enough to become an established part of the local sports scene.

Matt Zabitka, 75

Sportswriter
From 1934 to Present
Wilmington, Delaware

"*I* started writing when I was about 13. I was walking to Chester High School, and every Thursday they put out a paper. It was called the Progressive Weekly. It was a good paper, about 32 pages. I used to love to read it, because it was all local.

"I noticed that they didn't have any sports. Nobody asked me, but I sat down one day and wrote a column, 'Sports for All Sorts,' by hand. I didn't have a typewriter. I just printed it. I had good penmanship.

"I put in a lot of local stuff, a lot of names, information on who starred in the high school scene. I sent it into the paper. Unsolicited. I could hardly wait for the following week for it to come out.

"When I opened the paper, on page three, there were two full columns all the way down, it was all my stuff. Not only that, they had 'Sports of All Sorts' and my name, in half-inch letters, 'by Matt Zabitka.' I was shocked. To me it was like a million dollars, my name in print.

"So, I sent another column in the following week, and they printed that. Then they did the same a third week. Now, I didn't ask for any compensation. I was just thrilled to see my name there. A lot of people were calling me up, a lot of older guys, giving me information for new stories.

"The paper called and asked me to continue doing it for five dollars a week. Man, I was in Seventh Heaven. With that five dollars, I went and bought a used typewriter. I never owned one, didn't know anything about them. Later, I learned it was a left-handed. It didn't make any difference to me. I started typing the stories after that and taught myself to type. My pay increased to $10, $15 and then to $20 a week.

"I can't type with all 10 fingers to this day. But I can put out 60 to 70 words a minute, using three fingers. With all the copy I put out now, I have to move fast.

"I bought the typewriter for $35 and I was paying $5 a month until I paid it off. I kept that typewriter until 10 years ago, when we had a flood in our home. The water came over it, and I threw it out.

"With that typewriter, I sold stories to Sporting News. That was one of the top baseball papers in the country in those days. I sent a story in unsolicited, and they called me at my home and asked me if I had any more story ideas. I said, 'Yeah!' and I was writing for them for 13 weeks. That was big time. I remember interviewing Whitey Witt. His real name was Witkowski, and he played center field with Babe Ruth on the New York Yankees. I went over to his house in New Jersey to interview him. He showed me all his scrapbooks.

"He told me how happy Babe Ruth was that he was playing center field. He said that Babe Ruth liked to carouse all night. The next day—they played in the afternoon then—when the ball would come to the outfield to Babe Ruth, he was too lazy or too drunk to go after it. Whitey Witt would go over and catch the ball.

"After the story appeared, he sent me a note telling me to let him know if I had any other stories, 'cause he wanted to read them. I saved the note. Over the years, I saved letters from famous people. I have thousands of letters—Bear Bryant, Alabama coach. Jesse Owens, who was famous in the Olympics in Germany.

"I was president of the Delaware Sportswriters and Broadcasters Association, and I had to introduce him at the banquet. He was sitting next to me, and they have these huge name cards. Afterwards, I said, 'How about signing this, Jesse?' He gave me a little greeting on there.

"*Joe DiMaggio came to Wilmington to speak at St. Anthony's Sports Banquet. The morning of the night of the banquet, I'm at home sleeping and I get a call from Nick Grossi, who's in charge of the head table. He says, 'Would you like to have lunch this afternoon with Joe DiMaggio? It's at St. Anthony's Club, and it's closed. Just a few guys.' I said, 'Hell, yeah! I'll come down.'*

"*It was Joe DiMaggio, four other guys and myself. We got a gallon of port wine on the table. Joe's sitting next to me. We're talking about baseball and different things. He's telling me about his glove, when he played in the Pacific Coast League. It was like a winter mitten. He said he had that damn thing sewed and patched up so many times. It fit great so you used it. He said, 'When I went up to the majors I could have bought the best glove in the world. I had the money, but I didn't. You know, some bastard stole it last week.'*

"*The funny thing is, everybody was starting to leave, and the guy who brought Joe down says to me, 'You got enough for a story, don't you?' I had the tape recorder going, and Joe keeps patting me on the back and says, 'Let's keep talking. Let's keep talking.'*

"*I saved these tapes. Over three successive years, I interviewed three of the most famous outfielders in history who came to St. Anthony's: Joe DiMaggio, Ted Williams and Stan Musial. Eventually, this guy sent my tapes to the National Baseball Hall of Fame in Cooperstown. They sent me a lifetime membership in appreciation.*

"*I played all the main sports when I was a kid—baseball, basketball, football. But I write about everything, golf, swimming, horse racing, diving. When you're not knowledgeable, you find out the basics. You talk to people. That's how you learn a lot. You ask questions.*

"*I've been talking to people all my life, hosting a radio sports show for three years and doing newspaper work. When I think of the experiences I've had from newspaper work, I realize this job has taken me to places I never would have imagined.*

"*I was in Washington, covering the opening of the 1963 baseball season between the Washington Senators and Baltimore Orioles. President Kennedy was there. Here I am, in a tremendous seat, I took binoculars with me. I'm looking at Kennedy, on the opposite side. He's all dressed. After an inning he loosens his tie. After another inning, he takes his jacket off. I see him keeping score. Then, he put his sunglasses on top of his head. He's eating peanuts and throwing shells all over the place. Little did anybody know that in a few months there would be an assassination. If I wasn't a sports writer, I never would have experienced that. I covered the World Series in Yankee Stadium, in the Polo Grounds at Ebbetts Field.*

"*I have no college. But I've been in more colleges than most people because I was covering stories. Two of the most creative writers I ever worked for had no college—Al Cartright at the News Journal and Bob Finucane from Chester. They were a different breed, creative in their writing. Today, it's more specialized. This one's a business writer. That one focuses on something else.*

"*I learned from on-the-job training, where you had to do everything. I read a lot. I'd advise anybody going into the business to read the best writers they can find. You'll pick up stuff and develop a style of your own.*

"*I think today a lot of reporters like to move around. You don't get too many writers staying in one place like you used to.*

"Years ago, guys would ask me: 'When you gonna retire?' Some have left and some have died off, and I'm still going. I think your body tells you when you want to retire. It's like a baseball player, when his arms are gone or his legs are gone, he quits. But if you have enthusiasm, are in good health and you're still interested, hell, you keep going.

"When you're in prison, time doesn't fly. When you're sick in the hospital, time doesn't fly. But when you're enjoying what you're doing, everything goes rapidly.

"In May of 1995 I was nominated for Employee of the Month and they put my age in the newsletter. People were shocked. I was 74 at the time. All of the sudden people started looking at me differently. I didn't change. I guess they figured a lot of guys my age are in the old age home in a rocking chair.

"I remember when computers came in. Some people quit because they couldn't adjust. A lot were apprehensive about switching over. After a while you get used to it, then you never want to go back to the typewriter. Years ago, when they used paper, you'd come in and the wastebaskets and room would be full of paper, all over the place. News was coming in over the wire. You'd be going through all these reams of copy. You're always typing more paper and throwing it away. The only thing I use paper for now is to take down notes.

"What I like to do is write a column where you express opinions. What makes it all worthwhile is when you get a response. I wrote a story about this kid in Little League and something had happened to him. A teacher from Brandywine High School sent me a letter and said my story moved her to tears. She wrote that it was a beautiful, perfect story, and added, 'and I know because I'm an English teacher.' That made me feel good.

"To be successful, you have to ask the right questions. But the main thing is making a person feel comfortable. You can't come in there with an attitude like you're a New York Times reporter. If you make the them feel at ease, that's when you can get almost anything you want out of a person."

Matt Zabitka

October 4, 1996

Wickes Westcott, 73

Boatman
Gregg Neck Boat Yard
From 1959 to Present
Galena, Maryland

Boatman

Wickes Westcott enjoys walking the gray weathered planks of well worn piers, overseeing the hundreds of boats left in his care along the southern shore of the Sassafras River. His Gregg Neck Boat Yard is a workingman's hangout, a place where owners of wooden boats can still get the attention and hard-to-find expertise that they need.

In 1979, "Mr. Wickes"—as he's called by his workmen—along with his wife, Trudy, bought Gregg Neck Boat Yard. She would sew the sails and he was in charge of boat repairs. Today, he and his two sons, Dorsey and Scott, share the yard's responsibilities.

Standing close to the shoreline, wounded sailing relics patiently wait for busy craftsmen to provide the attention that will return the damaged craft to a second life on the sea. A short distance away, bobbing gently along the river's wake, are the brightly colored sailboats and larger pleasure craft that call Gregg Neck their home port.

The old yard's surroundings are very different from the modern-day marinas that are consuming more and more of the Chesapeake Bay shoreline. No in-ground swimming pool, manicured landscaping, antiseptic ship's store and smooth blacktop parking lot welcome visitors and customers. Instead, there is the hectic pace of a working boatyard—a place where craftsmen can handle all of the carpentry and machine work demanded by today's latest fiberglass beauties. But they seem a bit more eager to focus on the needs of 60-year-old, one-of-a-kind wooden classics.

It's the wooden vessels that put a sparkle in the owner's eyes. A slightly built, soft spoken man, Mr. Wickes points to each craft, sharing an anecdote about every boat's background, design and origin.

But the boatman can still recall growing up along the river in the 1930s, watching Chesapeake Bay workboats load their holds and decks with summer produce for the eight-hour trip downriver, across the bay and up to the Baltimore docks.

Those days are long gone, never to return. But, thanks to the workmen at Gregg Neck Boat Yard, a few of the wooden craft that made the trips still survive.

"*My family started coming to the Sassafras River for the summer in 1923. That was the year I was born. It was a beach cottage. Of course, back in the '30s, nobody had any money, so you had to do with what you had. Couldn't run off to Ocean City every week. I started workin' on boats when I was a kid. My father had little power boats and sailboats. We painted and maintained them, learned from the bottom up.*

"*It was all wood then. Some of them are still around. No glass came until the mid-'60s. Late '50s some people were foolin' with it. They didn't produce anything with fiberglass until in the '60s.*

"*Today, in the wintertime, we can store about 225 boats, on land and in the water. In the summertime, we can moor about 120 in the water. Usually have about 50 or 60 on land.*

"*We try to maintain them, and some of the people work on them themselves, and if they get into trouble we try to help out. We have about 40 percent wooden and more than half of them are glass. Wooden boats are still around, it's just that you don't have anybody that really wants to tackle the wood much. They all want the easy maintenance. Glass is easier, maybe, but you're still doin' the same type of work. I mean you're scrubbin' and polishin'. It's pretty similar as far as your action. But you don't have rot, which wooden boats are prone to. But they've lasted many years, and, if you look after them, they're gonna last some more years.*

"*You have those people who look for antique boats. They want to fix up the old ones and parade 'em around and show 'em off. If you maintain a wooden boat, I guess it can go straight on forever. We got some that are 50 or 60 years old. We got some older. That old bi-boat under the shed was built back in the '30s, I think.*

"*But they don't live by themselves. They gotta be maintained. If you let them leak, especially from the deck, they'll rot out fast. Boats are sort of like animals. You have a bunch of cows, ya gotta milk 'em every mornin' and every night. And the boats, ya have 'em in the water, you have to check 'em every mornin' and every night. Cows you're getting the milk out of, boats you're gettin' the water out of. You even have to check the glass boats that sit in the water. They can sit there, and nobody is using them. But you're watchin' them and, zip, something will happen. Water will come in. A sea cock will start leakin' or a hose will rot. You gotta keep an eye on 'em.*

"*They can sink on land, too. Scuppers will get stopped up with leaves or freeze up. Then the water goes over the bridge deck. Can sink her on land, too. It doesn't hurt the outside, but it ruins the inside the same as if it sinks in the river.*

"*A lot of marinas have ruled wooden boats out, because the ones that are left need more attention, and they don't want to fool with them. They don't have the people to work on them. A majority of their help is younger help, and they're glass workers and they don't have the knack to work on the wooden boats. But we have several wood carpenters, wood boatmen, that can do the job fine.*

"*Buster, he's been workin' on wood more than 40 years. Some of the older ones have retired. They're gettin' up in their 80s. They'll come over and give us a little consultation on a problem. But they just want to relax and enjoy life.*

"*Occasionally, we'll get a young one comin' up that has a knack for doin' wood, and can do glass, too. We'll utilize them. We got a young fella who went to a boat buildin' school in England. He's a real good fella. He can do a grand job.*

"*Usually, there's people who like those older trades. And if they're dying, they'll go back and pick up the old trades so they can be valuable to someone.*

50

"If you actually like workin' with wood, you couldn't find a better occupation. You get a lot of satisfaction in rebuilding a boat that has been around for years. A lot of other people have worked on it and you're keepin' it alive for future generations. Each of these boats has a story. If they could talk, you'd really sit up and take notice.

"It's just a pleasin' occupation, and those in it seem to be likin' it. They don't hesitate to work long hours when it's necessary. They're interested in it and they stay with it. When you're doin' work like that, competent in what you're doin' and enjoy it, it doesn't seem like a job. It's more like an avocation instead of a vocation.

"But we cater to the wooden ones, because the other yards are discarding them. We get them from all over the bay area. People will tell each other and we'll get a call from people who want to know if we can change something on their boats. We try to fit into each other's schedules.

"Most of the wooden boats in good shape should stay in the water in the winter, because it's better for them. They don't dry out and the seams open up and things like that. If there's a problem with a wooden boat, you should haul it out and fix it and put it back in the water. We got a bubble system around them, to keep the water moving and keep them from freezing around the hull. We keep a light on inside, to keep the pump warm enough to work. They all take care. Just like people, you don't just drop them and forget 'em. It's bad for them, too. Boats are the same way.

"We started in business with a little charter boat operation, mostly sailboats, in 1959, down Woodland Creek. Some of the people would come back in on Friday night and we'd get the boats ready, take the torn sails up to the house and Trudy, my wife, would sew the ripped sails on her sewing machine. The next people would come and pick the boats up on the weekend and go out for two or three days, or a week.

"We bought this place in 1979. I like what we do. I don't really think of it as a drudge 8-to-5 job. We're usually here 8 in the mornin', and it's about 8 or 9 before we leave at night. As long as it's daylight. We been farmin' quite a bit of our lives, and you go 'til you get the job done. You don't just stop 'cause the clock says stop.

"I like what I do, and sometimes I'll sit back and look at what I got done. My wife says I do that a little too much, and that I should keep moving and get more done.

"People like to go to amusement parks to have somebody amuse them. Down here you don't have to do that. You amuse yourself by looking at all the boats and thinking of where they've been and where they're gonna go, all the people they've made happy.

"Actually, it's a big release for people who live in urban areas. Their boss has been after them all week and then they come down here and they can yell at us and get rid of the steam, 'cause they're the boss down here. So we try to smile and keep 'em happy as much as we can.

"I like working with wooden boats. That's all I've ever owned. I guess it's what I was raised with. The glass, they're fine. But they just don't have the feel and the smell of the wooden boats. I'd rather smell sawdust than fiberglass dust. It's much more healthy."

S. Wickes Westcott

Wickes Westcott   June 13, 1996

Marie Bradley, 61
Chair Caner
From 1970 to Present
Lincoln, Delaware

Chair Caner

Unused chairs and antique benches are stored in attics and garages, tossed in dark lofts and shoved in the corners of damp basements. Their wicker cane seats and backs are damaged from moisture or, worse yet, by being used in place of a sturdy ladder or strong wooden stool.

Repairing cane furniture is not only time consuming, it's a very difficult task and one that's not entered into eagerly. Today, few people know the art of chair caning, and those who are able to perform the skill do so only out of necessity, concentrating on their personal furniture.

Most craftspeople readily admit that they would never perform the chore for someone else. No matter what they were offered, they would not spend a string of solitary hours weaving strips of wood through an endless number of intertwining strips to make a strong cane seat.

But Marie Bradley is different.

The Lincoln, Delaware, resident admits she enjoys caning chairs, and she is one of the few who will perform the task for others. She said she thinks it's probably because of her fascination with wood and a lifetime desire to bring old, damaged furniture back to life.

In the early 1950s, while she was attending Harrington High School, Bradley convinced the shop teacher to let her work with wood. Instead of baking cakes and pies in home economics, the class where young ladies traditionally spent their time, Bradley learned the skills that she's put to good use.

Today, she operates a small furniture refinishing business and also deals in antiques, but her real love and the primary source of her satisfaction comes from caning chairs.

"*I* learned how to cane in the early 1970s. My husband, Harold, he's deceased now, he was in the service, a military career man. He and I always messed with furniture for a hobby. He liked to buy and sell, and I liked to work with wood. We'd just refinish and kind of sell on the side.

"We had a set of four chairs and they needed caning. So I got a pamphlet, and that's how I learned. It wasn't hard, really. Just go step by step, and follow the instructions, just like crocheting. You just do one step and go back and see what you do next. It's actually weaving. If you can weave, you can do it. It's very time consuming and it's tedious. But I'm a slow steady person, so it doesn't bother me.

"With that first set, in the early '70s, he wanted them done by a certain time, and I was under pressure. When I got finished, I said I'll never do another chair. I think I got them done by when he wanted them, but I was never gonna cane another chair, ever. Other than a few, on and off, over the years, I don't think I did. I didn't do it steady until about four years ago.

"With caning, it's mostly chairs, some benches. There could be some dividers, screens, but it's mostly family pieces that I do for other people. People bring me their stuff. I'm backed up with about 20 chairs right now, and it's been that way since before Christmas. Not the same 20 chairs, you understand, but it's steady work, all year long.

"The old time farm days festivals and craft shows have been a very good source of advertisin'. The very first show was across the field here, at Wilkin's, for Plow Days. I've done Heritage Days in Harrington. I didn't even have business cards the first show I did there. So I wrote my name down on a piece of paper for a lady. Three years later, she called me up and said she found the paper with my name on it in a drawer and wanted something done. So three years later, I got business off that woman, when I didn't even have business cards made up. This year I've had 10 shows.

"These cane chairs won't take a lot of abuse, but I would say they'll last about 20 years or more, from what I can judge, if cared for. One day, I got one in and it looked like it hadn't been done that long ago. I said to the guy, 'Looks to me like a grandchild stood on this,' and he looks at me and says, 'Grandchild? My wife stood on it!'

"Some chairs go back to the early 1900s, or older. Some of the newer ones are made with pressed cane. It comes already made—in rolls and in different widths—in a flat sheet, all intertwined, and there's a groove in the chair. You just put it in around the edges, hammer it in and put some glue in there. It's caning, and I don't know how it's made, but it's not like with the individual strands.

"The size of the hole in the chair and how far they are apart lets you decide on the size of the cane you use for the weaving. It's rattan, some of it comes from the Philippines. I don't know where else. I get it in different widths, in hanks. You always keep learning things in this business.

"I refinish the wood if the customer wants it done. Take it down to the natural wood and refinish it to their desires, usually just a clear finish. Sometimes, I'll get a chair that comes in and I haven't done one like it before. That's when I tell myself that I better practice on one before I do that.

"With an average chair, I've got so I can do them in about eight hours. That's why nobody wants to do them. And, good gracious, one of those Lincoln rockers with the backs and the seat, they could run up to three days each. I know. I did four this winter. I'm workin' on one now. It's mine, I'm savin' it for shows.

"A lot of people have learned to do chair caning, like I did the first time. They've done one for the experience, and they don't want to do any more. They wouldn't do it for anybody else for any amount of money. They come up and say, 'I done that. I know how to do it,' or some will say, 'I only got halfway through and quit!'

"They don't want to spend the time on it, and they can't stand still. I don't know why I like it, it's just that I know that with those chairs that look like junk, I can make them look nice. That's the only thing that I can think of. But I can't do it sittin' down. I have to stand. It just kills my back to try to do it sittin'.

"In the beginning, I guess it was hard on my hands. But I don't notice, really, anymore. People don't really ask too many questions about how to do that. They just stand and watch me a while. I guess they know they wouldn't want to even try.

"I have to concentrate and look at what I'm doing, too. I can't watch TV, but I do listen to it or to the radio. I have to see what I'm doing. But I knew of at least three blind people that did this. How in the world they did it I don't know. They just have their fingers tuned and sensitive. I marvel at that. It's hard enough to do being able to see.

"I've done one chair from New Hampshire. She was visiting relatives and there was nobody up there who did it, so she brought it down with her. I've done a fair amount of work for people in Virginia, Pennsylvania, New Jersey, Maryland, and a lot of that came from the shows. I have had them go home from the shows to get their chairs and then bring them back to me.

"Everybody has a chair either in the attic or in the basement or the barn that was grandma's and that needs to be caned. When they come to pick up their chair, most of them say, 'That looks great!'

"I always said I wouldn't work under any pressure to get things done. Most everybody says, 'It's been up in the attic for 20 years. What's the rush now?' Now, around Thanksgiving and Christmas I got a little bit pushed. They want them for Thanksgiving dinner or a Christmas gift. I get them all done. I'm usually not under pressure.

"I'll be out and people will come up and talk to me and tell me they saw me at the shows, or I did a chair for them. Sometimes, it's hard to recall who they are, and that's embarrassing. I almost find, in my mind while they're talking, that I'm trying to match up the person with their chair.

"But, you know, I can't sew. Can't sew for beans. That just drives me crazy. But I just love to cane."

Marie Bradley

Marie Bradley

July 25, 1996

"We wood like to serve you."

At the family sawmill are, from left, Darrin, Frank Sr., Sharlene, Fannie, Harry and Frankie Jr.

Harry W. Bartsch, 82
Bartsch Sawmill
From 1951 to Present
Townsend, Delaware

Sawmill

Years ago, before everyone owned hand-held power tools and the big name, chain store, home improvement centers arrived, each community had its own lumber yard and sawmill. They were places where the locals would go to get what they needed to build a barn, outbuildings, a chicken coop or buy their fencing. If they needed to build a new home, make some interior renovations or put up a backyard shed, the local wood cutters served their needs.

Mill owners would cut wood to size and, oftentimes, help neighbors figure out how much of what it was that they needed. Timber from nearby forests was hauled in by loggers or delivered from farmers who were clearing more acreage for crops.

Plastic and metal materials were unheard of. Outdoor structures and interior work used only local wood—poplar, oak, ash, beech, gum and maple.

Today, finding a sawmill is like discovering a real silver quarter. Most of the small sawmills are gone, as are the independently owned, local lumber yards.

In New Castle County, Delaware, only one log-cutting enterprise remains. Bartsch's Sawmill, operated solely by family members, stands as a symbol of what things were like during the days when family members both lived and worked together.

Harry Bartsch, the elder statesman who started the present mill in 1951, provides decades of hard-to-find experience and knowledge. His son, Frank Bartsch Sr., who took over the operation in 1976, currently manages and runs the mill, which was newly built with modern equipment in 1995.

Frank's wife, Sharlene, works beside him with their two sons, Darrin and Frankie Junior.

They all split up the duties, running the board edger, head saw, loading, stacking, cutting, sorting and hauling the thousand-pound logs. The daily operation, that can go on seven days a week and well into the evening hours, occurs only a few hundred yards from the family home, which is located across the Delaware line, close to Golts, Maryland.

But the entire family agrees that Harry's wife, Fannie, who runs to town on errands, has the most important job . . . she does the cooking for the hungry crew.

"*I* lived up in north Wilmington. From 1930 to '40, I had a route, Bellefonte, McDaniel Heights, Carrcroft. It was like a store on wheels, with produce, canned goods, sugar and flour. In them days it used to be the butcher, the baker, the milkman and the ice man. I bought the farm down here in 1941.

"You know how I got started in the sawmill? When I was a little boy, the mill was off Wilson Road, right next to the school. I used to watch them saw at the mill when I was a little kid. We was 8, 10 years old, and at recess we used to stand at the school yard fence. I used to watch him saw and thought it was great, how you could take a tree and build anything you wanted out of it. It fascinated me. You could build a barn, build a house, a wagon or make whatever you like. After that I always wanted to have a saw mill. That was the first mill I bought. I've had three mills over the years.

"In 1951, I bought an old mill for $150 and rebuilt it on my farm that's nearby to here. There was three mills operating when I started, Charlie Roberts, Iron Hill and me, in New Castle County. We're the only mill left now. The nearest is Dover. I think the hard work drove a lot of them away.

"When I started, I sold lumber for about 5 cents a board foot; now it's about 60 cents a board foot. I had about 150 acres of timber, and, for the first few years, I got it out of my own woods. Cut it down with a chain saw, and the sawmill was right on the farm, so I just drug them logs in from the woods with a tractor.

"Back then, I just done custom work for someone who was buildin' a shed, barn or corn crib. I guess in the '60s I started cuttin' the pallet lumber for Iron Hill. They closed their mill, so I just cut the lumber and they took it and built the pallets.

"When I started, there wasn't no pallets. That business just got stronger in these last 15, 20 years. Everybody uses pallets to ship on today, not back then. Everything was done by hand then, too. We didn't have all this automatic equipment, forklifts. We rolled the logs by hand, with the cant hooks. It was hard work. Still is.

"Can be dangerous, too. One time, I hit a piece of iron in a log, and the 52-inch saw, at 500 rpms, was traveling about 120 mile per hour. As it came up, it went right by me, about a foot from my face, and went out through the shed and put a hole in the wall.

"It's hard work. It's hot in the summer and cold in the winter. The only good part is you have a roof over your head and you don't get the rain. You get used to it. Your hands would get hard since you had to use them to turn everything. But now, with the machines, it's not as bad on the hands as it was.

"After I retired, I went down to Florida in the winter, and I met a lot of people. When I told them I ran a sawmill, the first thing they'll do is look at your hands and tell ya, 'Well, you still got all your fingers!' I'm 82 now, but I still stay active around the mill.

"I'll give you a little sawmill joke. There was this boy, who come up one Saturday and said his daddy wants to order 400 2-x-4s. And I asked him how long he wants 'em? But the boy said he didn't know, his daddy didn't say. So I sent him back home to ask his daddy.

"So he come back in about an hour later and I asked if he found out how long he wanted them. And the boy said, 'Yeah! My daddy wants them for a long, long time. He's gonna build a house!' "

Harry W. Bartsch Sr.

Harry W. Bartsch

June 6, 1996

"*I* took things over in 1975. We make shoring lumber. It reinforces the ground, for jobs where they're working construction on subways and new buildings, up in New York City. When they build a 120-story building, they'll go in the ground 400 feet, and all that is reinforced with shoring. It's 12-inch x 12-inch in thickness, random widths. It's made from any kind of hardwood trees. That's the biggest thing we do. It runs from 10 to 20 foot in length. All that is shipped to New York.

"Another thing we do is pallets. A lot go to places in state. That and the shoring lumber are our main business. We also do lumber for barns and fences. Then we have a small dry kiln. We do cabinet and furniture lumber. A lot of that is sold to local cabinet makers. We sell mulch and a lot of firewood. We sell, I guess, over 300 cords of firewood a year.

"With the pallets, we do it both ways. We sell pallet materials and we make the pallets. Right now, we're averaging about 2,000 per month. It keeps us busy. Last month was a big month, we did 3,300. That was a lot of 80-hour weeks. That's not a normal working schedule, but we had orders to get done.

"Our lumber comes from within a 150-mile radius, sometimes we get it from as far away as Virginia, but normally within 50 miles.

"We get it from independent loggers. But, we have a lot of competition from other mills. Like, right now, it's pretty hard to get wood. The supply is not as good as it used to be. A lot of the better grades are sold overseas. They pay more. . . Japan, Germany. All the veneer logs are shipped overseas.

"My father bought a new sawblade in the late '60s and it was $700. Now, it's $2,350. That's a 56-inch blade from Richmond, Virginia. It has to be sharpened three times a day. As long as you don't hit a big chunk of metal, you're okay. See, people will hang a hassock in a tree with a metal hook, or put up a No Trespassing sign. Sometimes, people would lay a rock in the crutch of a tree and the tree would grow around the rock. It can be a four or five thousand dollar mistake.

"The hardest part is stacking the finished lumber. A lot of times, we have to move pieces that are two to three hundred pounds. We still do that by hand, put it in the bundles. Do that all day and it can be tiresome.

"This mill was put in new, last February, a year ago. It's totally automatic, it's a push-button mill. Eventually, we're thinking of putting in a computer that would scan a log. You could preset the sizes and get the most yield out of the log, track the lumber tally. Right now, we estimate by experience.

"We did a lot of thinking before building the new mill. Darrin was interested in the business, and the automation helped take the strain off my

Darrin Bartsch near the 56-inch saw blade

back. You have to be optimistic. I seemed to get into this business 'cause it was in the family. I grew up working in the mill. It seems like if you get sawdust in your blood, it just stays in your blood.

"I think it's an honest living. We do a lot of our welding, fabricate our own machinery. That keeps it from being boring. It's always something different. I think the best thing about it, we're not doing the same thing all the time.

"This work is taking a round object and making it square. It's like I was saying yesterday, we'd spend all day taking the tree apart and nail it all back together at night time.

"This work is very dangerous. Our workman's comp is 37-1/2 percent of payroll because of the nature of the business, the saws, machinery, conveyors. Especially the out-in-the-woods part, with trees falling you can get hurt. We're the highest rate of workman's comp that there is. This is why we keep it in the family. It's kind of hard to have employees with insurance rates like that. The workman's comp put a lot of people out of business.

"We've had some cuts and injuries. You've got to be careful. My father had a tree fall on him, and once, working in the woods, he had his cheekbone busted in three places.

"In the winter, it's very cold. We have frozen timber to deal with. Sometimes, we have to sharpen the saw every 15 to 20 minutes when conditions are really bad. Then it's actually cheaper not to work. But anytime when it's extremely hot or cold you have a problem with machinery. In the bad heat of the summer, we'll start 5:30 in the morning and break around 2:30, then go back out and start up again in the evening.

"I feel privileged to be one of the last of the small mills. Not everybody can do what we do. Each log is different. You're dealing with a tree that's 50 to 75 years old. You have to respect that and try to get that log to yield as much as you can get out of it.

"I worked in the big mills. All they know is production. They look at 25 to 30,000 board feet per eight-hour shift. I do what they do with less man hours. I try to utilize the log a little better. They have a lot more waste. It's to our advantage to get every board foot out of a log. But I didn't really like working for other people. I like walking out the front door and going to work. It's a challenge. It's always something different.

"When people find out I own a sawmill, they're a bit surprised. People also don't realize that Delaware has any timber at all. They don't think there's any left.

"In this work, you're always seeing an accomplishment, a finished product. And it's good to have the family working together and carrying on what my father started."

Frank J. Bartsch Sr.

Frank J. Bartsch Sr.   June 6, 1996

Veterans of D-Day

The men who landed behind enemy lines and on the French beaches on D-Day—June 6, 1944—represent the last generation of true American heroes.

Many of them had left home while still in their teens to fight the Japanese at one end of the world and the Germans on the other. They were from big cities and small towns, black and white, from families of American Indians and recently arrived immigrants. America sent its best and brightest sons to battle history's worst killers.

On June 5, the day before the joint Allied invasion of Europe, Corporal Joe Lofthouse of Elkton—a member of the 502nd Parachute Infantry—stood on an airfield in England with his comrades. He was just a few feet from visiting Gen. Dwight D. Eisenhower, and heard the Supreme Commander of the Allied Expeditionary Force personally tell them:

"Total victory—nothing else."

Later that night, Lofthouse and thousands of other members of the 101st Airborne Division boarded their planes. Sitting with their chutes, rifles and equipment strapped to their bodies, they knew their mission . . . to land and disrupt the Germans behind the front lines and, eventually, take out the shore batteries.

On June 6, D-Day, Staff Sergeant Donnie Preston of North East, Maryland, was aboard a landing craft with about 300 other members of the 115th Infantry Division, heading for Omaha Beach. They had been living on the ship a week, waiting to hit the shore, take out the German fortifications and move inland.

These two Cecil County, Maryland, soldiers, originally fellow members of Company E, 115th Infantry, the Elkton, Maryland, National Guard unit, landed at Normandy—one arrived from the air, the other entered from the sea. Here are some of their D-Day experiences.

Joe Lofthouse, 77

Corporal

101st Airborne Division

From 1939 to 1962

Elkton, Maryland

Donnie Preston, 77

Staff Sergeant

115th Infantry

From 1937 to 1947

North East, Maryland

Landing from the Air

"*I never really wanted to be a soldier. I joined the E Company, 115th Infantry, 29th Division of the Maryland National Guard in 1939, at the Armory in town. We drilled one night a week and got $1 a night. A lot of fellas my age were in there then. On the 3rd of February 1941, the Division was mobilized into federal service and stationed at Fort Meade, Maryland. We were to remain on active duty for one year. Of course, Pearl Harbor changed all that. We would be in for the duration plus six months. The tour lasted until September 1945. During that period, I participated in two parachute invasions and four infantry campaigns through Europe. Reenlisted in 1947 and served on active duty until November 1962.*

"*I volunteered for parachute training in the spring of 1942. The extra $50 a month jump pay looked promising. After qualifying, I was assigned to the 502nd Parachute Infantry, 101st Airborne Division, stationed at Fort Benning, Georgia. It was later moved to Fort Bragg, North Carolina. Late summer of 1943, my unit sailed to England and history.*

"*As the years passed, I thought most people had forgotten or just didn't care about what took place that day so many years ago. Some things are forgotten, but I try to remember the best of those times.*

"*In preparation for the D-Day invasion, we paratroops were taken to various airfields throughout England in late May. There, we would be briefed, issued 'chutes, ammunition and other equipment. Each man would be jumping with about 50 pounds of gear, including an M-1 rifle (disassembled into three parts), 195 rounds of ammo, six hand grenades, two C-4 grenades, two Hawkins mines, 40 feet of jump rope (for tree landings), toilet articles, a trench knife, trenching tool, six boxes of K-rations and two parachutes.*

"*Machine guns and motors were bundled and released from under the aircraft. Some men jumped with those items, making it an extra heavy load.*

"*D-Day was to be a great event for the Airborne. We were to spearhead the invasion with a night jump. During the hours from about 8:30 to 10:30 p.m., June 5, we entered our aircraft and in a short time were airborne on a one-way ticket to Normandy. That evening, time seemed to have stood still. Jump time would be approximately 1 a.m., June 6, H-hour minus six, meaning six hours before the beach landings.*

"*At first, there seemed to be complete silence. Some men started chain smoking, others trying to make jokes, but in reality they were lost in their own thoughts. I saw men kneeling, praying and saying the rosary. We all knew that it was to be a rough day coming, with no overtime pay. We also knew there was a good chance some of us would never see another sunrise. God, what a feeling.*

"*The door of the aircraft was opened, and the constant roar of the engines seemed to hum a melody. After a while, most of us fell asleep. The crew chief of the aircraft would awaken us 18 minutes before drop time. As we approached the coast, and flying at an altitude of approximately 1,500 feet, our aircraft began descending to about 700 feet for the jump. Low, but right for a combat jump. Soon we could hear the crack of flak from German guns coming up to meet us. We would be jumping about 8 to 10 miles behind the beach.*

"In a short time, the red light at the door went on and the command came to stand up, hook up, sound off for equipment check, stand to the door. It seemed a long time for that light to go green.

"It was a full moon and the opening shock of my 'chute seemed to rack every bone in my body. The sky was filled with tracer bullets, and I thought they were all aimed at me. Two passed nearby and tore into my chute. While descending and listening to all of the noise, I remember saying a little prayer.

"I landed in a small field, reassembled my M-1 as quickly as possible. We began to take some small-arms fire. The grass was like sage, a little high. We were crawling, keeping low, when suddenly I crawled over two dead paratroopers, still in their 'chutes. They were killed while descending.

"Welcome to Normandy.

"Some time later, a German soldier jumped from the hedgerow. I knew that he had the drop on me and, if he had wanted, he could have killed me. But he wanted to surrender. We were under orders to take no prisoners for the first several hours, until the beach head was secured. We had no way to watch them or control them. But I just couldn't kill him at that time. He was just a kid, younger than me, and just as scared. Eventually, I put a bullet between his feet and I pointed toward the beach. He took off, but I wonder if he made it that far.

"The paratroopers' main mission and objectives were to secure several towns, causeways and coastal guns and the personnel that manned them. Pressure had to be taken off the brave men that were coming ashore. Can you imagine what it must have been like, wading in water up to your neck, loaded down with heavy gear, taking everything the enemy had to give, and not being able to defend yourself? Those are your real heroes.

"Young men grew old that day. I have no idea why I lived and others died. There's no way to explain it, no logical reason why I should be here now. It was truly the longest day of my life.

"Sometimes, I've thought about what happened, especially when the 50th anniversary came about. Mostly, I remember the friends I lost. When you realize that 50 years have gone by, you also know you've gotten a lot older. But the guys that were killed that day will never grew old. Their young faces will remain with me forever.

"Looking back on it all, my memories linger. But I know I had the privilege of serving with the bravest young men of my time."

Joseph Lofthouse

Joe Lofthouse

December 14, 1996

Hitting the Beach

"Ijoined the Guard when I was in high school. We were inducted into active duty on Feb. 3, 1941. I was an operation sergeant, it covered all communications, transportation, supply, kitchen and all map work for my battalion, about 1,500 men.

"When we started out in 1941, we had 82 boys from Cecil County when we went to Fort Meade. On D-Day, we had 37 boys that hit the beach. People find that hard to believe. I think we had two men killed from Cecil County on D-Day. We had five more killed by the time we hit St. Lo. I'd say we had 15 more that were wounded. We didn't have anybody that wasn't wounded.

"While we were in England, we amphibious trained for eight months day and night, and went out on landings, on transports and LVCPs and hit the beach. Sometimes we'd do it three times a day. We knew something big was going to happen. But the Army headquarters, Bradley and Patton and all those big generals, didn't know what outfit was going to lead the assault. They trained these different divisions, and umpired and judged them and rated them to see which was what you would call a 'crack' outfit. When it all boiled down, the 1st, 29th and 4th divisions were the assaulting divisions.

"We hit Omaha, which was the hardest beach. We had no idea what we would hit. The 116th Infantry of the 29th were committed to hitting the beach first. The 115th was supporting them.

"The 116th was 80 percent casualties, and most of them were dead. They were taking such a beating, they called the 115th in early. We went in on ships called LCIs—Landing Craft Infantry. They throwed the ramps off the sides. Now the 116th, they went in on things called LVCPs. That was the landing craft that went in and throwed the front down. I'm happy I was in on an LCI, 'cause them boys were busted up. All the Germans had to do was put automatic fire right on the front of where that ramp came down.

"There was a tremendous amount of automatic fire from the German pillboxes. Even after all the Navy and aircraft bombing and ship and rocket fire, they were still there. It was heavy fire. Terrible.

"When we went in, we couldn't get in where the 116th went. There were obstacles, land mines, automatic fire, cannon fire, whatever the Germans could throw at us. That was right smack into Omaha. They landed right where they were supposed to land.

"We went down the shore about a half a mile and we was able to get in through the obstacles. The Navy took us in. The captain told us, 'I'll take you as far as I can take you.' And he done a wonderful job.

"We went in with what we call a light pack. Mess gear, raincoat, a change of underwear, and we had gas masks, your M-1. We grabbed all the ammunition we could off the Navy. They weren't going to use it. We had a tremendous amount of ammunition, and we were loaded with grenades, and they're not light. You got off that ship and if you was in over your head, you were at the bottom.

"The current in the English Channel is rough. You can't swim in it, only two times a year. And June wasn't one of them times. We went in at chest height. You had a hard time getting up on the shoreline because the current was so swift. A lot of boys drowned out there, I'll tell you that.

"A lot of things happened D-Day. A lot of things happened fast. You helped your buddy out. When you got past the beach, you were in what you call hedgerow fighting. You had to take it hedgerow by hedgerow. They didn't have fences, the French. They put their cattle in there. And there are more and more hedgerows behind them, miles of them.

"It was more like street fighting, a lot of it was man-to-man. It was rough, you had to be very careful. The fifth night in, we was laying on one side of the hedgerow and the Germans were on the other, only about two foot apart. You didn't dare stick your head up.

"I was wounded twice. I got hit in the ankle, but it was nothing more than a flesh wound. Then a German got me with a trench knife on the first day in. It caught me here, in the hand and the arm. It was a natural thing, to react by throwing your hand up. The lieutenant in back of me killed him. We was clearing buildings.

"When we were waiting to go in, the time went slow. Felt like we were sitting there for hours. People ask me when I was scared. I tell them, 'All the time.' Going in was the worst. I had six men killed coming down my ramp. After I reached the shoreline and got up on the ground, I felt more secure then.

"You couldn't get up and move around. You did a lot of crawling. D-Day the bullets were just snapping by. If you got through D-Day, you was lucky, very lucky. And, like I say, you try to do what you were supposed to do. I don't know how many lieutenants we lost. Couldn't keep track of them. More or less, you were worrying about yourself, trying to do the job you were supposed to be doing.

"We were trying to get a foothold. We got a lot of air support. I'll say this. They bombed the Germans day and night for months. And the United States and British had really knocked the German air force out of the air. If they hadn't of done that, we would never have been able to make that landing.

"I've never gone back. I never wanted to go back. Out of the 37 that hit the beach D-Day, there's only five of us left. In fact, we just buried two in the last two weeks. We always try to give them a military funeral. Here we are, our boys are 77, 80 years old and we do it. We may not be perfect or anything, but we still do it.

"I guess it's because we all fought so damn hard for this country, and gave up a lot. If we hadn't won that war, we wouldn't have these things today. We sacrificed so much, but it also was the homefront that made it possible. If we didn't have the homefront, we wouldn't have won that war.

"I've been asked to speak in different schools and classes. I tell it as it is. It was either kill or be killed. But kids today don't even know what D-Day was. They don't think about World War II and all the sacrifice. Our schools don't teach about it anymore. I can tell when I speak to them. When I talk, I can see it in their eyes. They don't even know where England and France are.

"Later, I got wounded bad, got hit with four shells. They took three out and left one of them in. I asked the Lord to help me and I guess he said, 'I'm not finished with you yet.' I was in a hospital for eight months as a bed patient. It took me two years to get back on my feet.

"War's a terrible thing, a bad thing. The Germans, they were professional soldiers, and we were there, a bunch of kids off the street just trying to do a job and get back home."

Donnie Preston   December 18, 1996

Five & Dime

On July 19, 1939, Peter J. Carucci and his wife, Elizabeth "Lizzie" Fidance Carucci, opened a 5 and 10 cent store in the heart of Little Italy, on the corner of Fifth and Lincoln streets in Wilmington, Delaware. After Mr. Carucci's death in 1979, his family continued to operate the small business. Mrs. Carucci, now in her 90s, is in a nursing home.

Her daughter, Julia Carucci deJuliis, who started working with her father when she was 8 years old, operates the store.

A fair number of five and dimes used to be found on city street corners. Large chains, like Woolworth's and W. T. Grant's were the big-time operations downtown, but family stores took care of the daily needs of local customers.

Today, even the large operations have fled the cities. But in Wilmington's Little Italy, beneath an old-fashioned, paint-faded tin roof and surrounded by shelves put in place by her father, Julia still sells many of the same type of wares that have been passed across the worn wooden counter for more than half a century.

The merchandise range is wide, from modern Bic razors to hard-to-find, old-fashioned, metal skeleton keys. Aisles offer such diverse items as spools of thread, sewing supplies, clear glass piggy banks, pasta machines, pizzelle irons, Italian language Christmas and Easter cards, rabbit's foot key chains and black-and-white, school composition notebooks.

Peter's is the last of its kind. Nearby, local restaurants and fruit markets have shuttered their windows. And time, which is so very patient and silent, and progress, which is so bold and heartless, have their eyes set upon Peter's.

Julia Carucci deJuliis, 63

Storekeeper

Peter's 5¢ and 10¢ Store

From 1939 to Present

Little Italy

Wilmington, Delaware

"When I come in here, it's like walking back in time. That's exactly what people say. When I'm in the store, I'm always remembering, always thinking back, to when my father was alive, when I was smaller. Now that he's been gone and my mother's in a nursing home, sometimes I get teary eyed. There's a lot of memories here.

"Everything's basically the same as it was years ago. The outside is painted red, because it was formerly an A & P. The shelves here are all wood. We have a metal ceiling. I wanted to get it painted, but everybody told me not to, that it's worth money the way it is.

"I spent my whole life here. When I was little, I played with the register. Later, I worked the register and my brothers worked as stockboys. While in school I worked for my father. I had it good then. Dad was a little easy on me, but I worked hard. He'd expect me to work a full eight hours. It was nice, working for family instead of strangers. I'm really contented when I'm here, I enjoy coming to work in the morning.

"People always tell me, 'I haven't seen one of these in 20 years,' or 'Where I come from they have these, but I haven't seen one around here in a long time.'

"We've got washboards, Mendits, to fix holes in pots, the rubber hose shower spray that attaches to the nozzle in the shower or bathtub . . . things that aren't sold everywhere anymore, like shelf paper with designs on the edging.

"But, today, we tend to call ourselves a variety store. The old name, 5- and 10-cent store doesn't mean anything anymore. Children come in and ask, 'What's a five and dime?' I say, 'That's just a name now. It doesn't apply to things for sale the way it used to.' Years ago, we had a lot of things for a nickel and dime. I can remember candy, cookies. Then you could get school supplies, books, pencils, dishes and glassware. Threads were a nickel then.

"A lot of people come back with their children. I hear them say, 'This is where Daddy or Mommy used to come to buy all the school supplies when we were little.' A few years ago, a man came in with a child. When they were done doing their purchases, he gave me $10. He said when he was small he used to come in and steal pencils. He told himself if he ever came back to Pete's 5 and 10 he would give them some money, and he did. He remembered my father as a very kind man, and I hope they think of me the same way.

"I still have things that my father marked with his own handwriting. I can't get rid of them. That shows how sentimental I am.

"I like being with the people all day. Every morning my neighbor down the street, Anne Barbieri, brings me my tea, and she stops in to check on me a few times a day. Josephine Brank, two doors down, she brings me a homemade lunch every single day. The people here are very, very nice. The whole neighborhood, they've been here for years and they're concerned for my welfare. It's like having your family here with you.

"My husband, Joe, he's a bricklayer. He helps out with the deliveries, the pick-ups and heavy construction work.

"My brothers help, too. My oldest brother, John, is a retired carpenter. He put in the floor. My brother Bob, a CPA, helps with the taxes and heavy duty book work. My youngest brother, Joe, a vice president of services for Dade International, helps with the electricity. But, basically, it's me here every day, running the store for my mother. Mondays through Saturdays, from 9 to 5.

Julia, in the store with a photograph of her grandchildren

"I know the store is in my blood. Most of the customers say, 'If you ever close I don't know what we'll do.' I feel good when they tell me they really need me, that they appreciate me. I know that they'll care when I have to give it up.

"I hate the thought of closing, I really do. I really know that time is coming within the next couple of years. And when I think of it, it's very upsetting, because what my father and mother started in 1939 will finally come to an end. It's very sad when something like this has to come to an end, be over.

"I've been doing this since I was 8. When I retire, then the business will be dropped. It's not lucrative for anyone to operate. This is the last of the old five and dimes. If my health keeps up, I'd like to stay until we're open 60 years. That will be 1999, if I can make it to that."

Julia V. de Juliis

Julia Carucci deJuliis   May 4, 1996

Waterfowl Hunting Guide

Each fall and winter, on the most wretched days when most people are planted inside, trying to avoid the wet snow, cold sleet and frigid air, waterfowl hunters are in the marshes and out on the bays.

Despite miserable weather conditions, they sit for hours in blinds—camouflaged boxes with no basic, modern conveniences like heat and toilet facilities. Their guns oiled, sighted and loaded, they pay for the opportunity to shoot down a passing mallard, brant, snow goose or merganser, and take the trophy home.

Andy Linton grew up near Assateague Island and he's hunted most of his life. During the last 30 years, he's worked as a waterfowl guide. His hunters often are amazed at Andy's ability to recognize the different fowl by name, but he tells them, "Son, that's not the first one I've seen. In fact, I used to raise them with my father."

But there's more to a successful day-long adventure than most first-time visitors realize. During the off season Andy builds and maintains his blinds, prepares his decoys and works on his boats. The night before each hunting party's arrival, the decoys must be set out, hunting stamps and licenses checked and meetings held with the hunters.

Andy also must be aware of the bag limits and keep track of each hunter's kills throughout the day. "Sometimes," he said, "I'll hear a shot, and call over to that blind over my radio. See, I've got radio contact with all of my people. And I'll ask, 'What did you shoot, men?' And they'll say, real excited, 'It had feathers on it!' But with every group, I always tell them Linton's Law: 'As long as they're comin' let them come. And shoot where they're goin', not where they been.' "

Andy Linton, 50

Waterfowl Hunting Guide

From 1965 to Present

Chincoteague, Virginia

"*O*ld Man Tom Read—he was a well-known fellow around here, a market hunter—he used to guide. There would be a few times when he would have more than he could take care of. So I helped him out, and sort of just fell into it. I sort of liked it. After that, in '65, I started, and my first year I had one man.

"Now, people call me up, mostly by word of mouth after hearin' from satisfied customers. I got federal judges that hunt with me, a lot of attorneys, doctors, psychiatrists. At the other end, you got the common, everyday worker who has to save up the money to be able to go that day.

"I take care of your motel reservations, find out if you need resident or out-of-state license. I tell you what kind of clothes to have, boots, all kind of stuff like that. I furnish you everything except whatever you eat and whatever you shoot.

"Mainly, it's from late November through the end of January. We leave from my dock at crack of day, between 5 and 6 in the mornin', dependin' on daylight. They got me until sunset, or until they want to come home. We go up this bay, where I got 13 blinds. I'll have decoys all set up, out in the bay or on the ponds. Every day is a little bit different, depending upon weather conditions and what they want to hunt.

"We're talkin' ducks and geese, and certain times is better for one than the other. After everything is set, we'll just sit there and wait. About the time when the sun starts rising off of Assateague, that's when the birds start coming off.

"I call for them, some with a duck call and some by mouth. They come over, and if the men are good enough shots, they get some. My pleasure is workin' the duck, gettin' him to me. Outsmartin' him. He'll go by and I call him, 'Whrea! Whrea!' Then here he comes, and I tell the men, 'Get ready. Not yet. Not yet. Not yet . . . . There he is!' Only 15 or 20 feet away from us, and sometimes they hit him and sometimes they don't.

"Sometimes, I'll go in the marsh, first thing, 'cause that's where I kill my snow geese. They don't pitch—that's land—in open water. They come onto the marshland. The ducks we used to kill on the Chesapeake side of the bay are different than what we kill on this side. We don't kill no canvasback and stuff like that. You see, that's closed now. As of last year, the Canada geese were closed. You can't kill none of them. They're talkin' about three to four more years of that.

"But the snow geese are here by the millions. Maybe 15 to 18 years ago, I've seen it here, in the first part of the season, when we could just start shootin' snow geese. They would get up and near about block the sunrise out. They would come over off the refuge by the tens of thousands. Now this was before you could shoot them. Some of them would be only about six feet off the water, like their wing tips would touch the water. Then, they would head over that marsh and just lift up enough to go over the duck blind. So close you could punch 'em with your gun barrel. Unreal.

"Today, the snow geese are out on the refuge. There's about two miles of marshland between here and the ocean. When they come up, it's just a beautiful sight, especially when they turn into the sun and they look all pink off the sunlight.

"When I first started shootin' snow geese, I was putting Clorox jugs in the marsh for decoys. Every day you'd kill your limit. Oh, did it work.

"Then, they started gettin' a little smarter, so I started usin' silhouettes, cut out of a piece of plywood. I'd have me about 50 to 75 silhouettes and maybe 100 jugs. Then, it got to where it was more silhouettes and less jugs. After years of shootin', you know the bird gets smarter, it got to where I was startin' to use the shell decoys, that's a full body on a stake, and some silhouettes. And now, it's all shell decoys and nothin' else, because they're just so smart. I'll put 200 to 300 of them to each blind, for when I start shooting major snow geese.

"There's pleasure in this kinda work, but when you're gettin' older, it's harder on you. There's a lot of preparation, when you have blinds you have to build and brush you have to cut, and then there's cedar for your camouflage on 'em. Then you have to keep your boat up and all your decoys. But the hunters don't notice that, usually.

"You come here, get outta your car, walk up on the dock and get into the boat. All you have to do is set there, everything else is done. Then you shoot a bird and I go out and get it.

"Meeting the people is the best part, some that have been huntin' with you for years and years and years. With a lot, it's on a first name basis. You know his voice on the phone when he calls.

"The worst part of the job are 'bluebird days,' when you don't kill nothin'. That's a day that's in the 60s and nothin' flyin'. And I tell the men, 'Listen, I'm a huntin' guide, not a huntin' god.' I can't do nothin' about the weather.

"But when we have good weather, and I'm talkin' real bad weather, it's different. The best huntin' day is blowin' nor'west about 15 to 18 miles an hour, down in the teens, snowin'. Freezin' everything that you can touch. The birds are up then. They got to move. They got to get out, 'cause it might freeze up that night. The worse the weather, the better it is. I left when there's been three inches of ice on this bay. You don't know what cold is. I've had my tears freeze on my cheeks before. Cold weather and spittin' snow is good.

"You got to be careful in this business. When I leave here and go up the bay and it's in the teens it's serious business. When it freezes salt water, it's cold, and I tell my men you got to be sure to have clothes on that are gonna keep you warm. It's a different kind of cold out there on this water.

"The one thing I miss is huntin' for myself. I don't get out anymore. This work took my pleasure in a hobby and made a job out of it. It used to be, when I was younger, when my hunters came safely home in the middle of the day, I got rid of them and I'd grab my gun and go back up for a few hours. Now, all I want to do is go on that sofa and lay down, and get ready for the next day.

"I like being on the water. I can't say I don't get no pleasure in workin' on my blinds. There's a lot of pullin' and haulin' and hard, heavy work that you don't even think about then. I guess my most pleasure is to see some people come down who have never killed no pintails before, or never killed no snow geese or no brant. Then that person is able to make that kill and be happy, and I hear them talk about takin' it home and mountin' it. I guess that's my pleasure.

"Some people come for just the pleasure of gettin' out. They enjoy feelin' the salt spray, watching me put my decoys out, just bein' here. On one hunt, when they didn't kill anything, I apologized to the men and one fella said, 'Andy. I've not heard that phone ring at all today.' To them, it was just good to be here. If they killed a bird, it's on the plus side.

"But you can imagine, in 30 years, I seen many a beautiful sunrise. That's the highlight of the whole thing."

Andy Linton

November 24, 1996

Broom Man

More than 30 years ago, while working for the state highway department, Bill Hammond's neighbor Charlie Hrupsa stopped by the Hammond's one night and suggested that the two of them get started into broom making. Charlie showed Bill a coffee can filled with strange looking, small seeds to grow broom corn. Eventually, they planted several acres of the special straw—that tapers down to a fine thinness—needed to make real, old-fashioned handmade brooms.

Today, Bill's garage holds the tools of the broom making trade: bales of drying broom corn straw, rolls of red and gold cotton broom twine, spools of silver galvanized wire, jars of tacking nails and three handmade, broom making machines.

Piles of whisk booms are scattered across a corner workbench, and racks of tall, standard-handled brooms stand upright, proudly waiting to be loaded and taken to new prospective owners at the several shows that Bill attends during the spring-summer season.

With a self-made, portable broom-making machine used for on-site demonstrations, Bill travels to shows throughout the Delmarva Peninsula. After years of visits to friendly, back-yard displays like Potter's Steam Show in Milford to more commercial three-day affairs in Salisbury, Maryland's, Civic Center, Bill Hammond has become known throughout Delmarva and beyond. In fact, he often receives mail addressed very simply . . . to the "Broom Man, Felton, Delaware."

William Hammond III, 75

The 'Broom Man'
From 1963 to Present
Felton, Delaware

"*It was pretty near to two years, of working with Charlie, and I was doin' the sewin' and he was goin' to the shows and all the rest. So, one day, I told him, 'Charlie, I got to get to myself to make a broom.' I didn't want nobody around. We were working together makin' 'em. And he said, 'Oh, Billy, you'll never learn how to make a broom. You'll drop out.'*

"*But after a few days, he told me to get my 2 x 4s and he helped me make my own broom machine. We made it over in his shop. I went over on nights and weekends. After we got it all together, he made a broom on it. And he says, 'It's gonna work!'*

"*So I put it in my pickup, and I told him to fix me up a bundle of straw and took it all home with me. When I come home from work the next day, I puts myself in here to work on it. And I still got the first broom I every made. Here it is. It was about two years after I started with him.*

"*I never showed it to nobody, but I did show it to Charlie. I took it up and said, 'Well, Charlie, I messed up,' But he said, 'You know, you ain't messed up, 'cause that's the old-time way they made 'em. His Daddy, he come from the old country, way off. He wasn't our nationality. You got to take an aeroplane to get out there, or a boat or something. He said that's the way his daddy made them, but it wasn't with wire. He put string around them. But, anyway, he said, 'It ain't too bad. It ain't too bad.' So I kept on, and kept on, and after a while I got to goin'.*

"*I was a bit backward and shy in the beginning. But, after a while, when I got to doin' it, I got so I didn't care. But I didn't want anybody to watch me while I was doin' it. But that was back in the beginnin'. So, he said, 'I gonna have to give it to you. You're startin' to get to make a broom.'*

"*Now, today, with the shows I go to, I make somewheres around 300, 400 a year. I just love to do it. I just enjoy it. I'm gettin' away from home, go to these shows. That's the only place I go to anyway.*

"*I meet a lot of people, from way off. They watch me make a broom and talk and go on. I enjoy it. There's a lot of work to it, a lot of hard work. Whatta you gonna do? Anything you do is work, ya know.? But I was used to work anyway. My Daddy was a farmer and he tried to till all the land there was in the country, and he milked a mess of cattle and stuff like that. So I was used to it, anyway, so work didn't bother me.*

"*You gotta grow the corn, dry it out, take off the seed, cut the stalks, work it into the machine, then ya tie it up with wire and gotta sew it together. Broom makin's a lot of work. Most people I think know all the work that goes into it, but there's some that don't . . . don't appreciate it.*

"*People, they tell me, 'There ain't but one thing wrong with your brooms. They last too long!' There was two or three women come to me on Saturday, and she said she's got the first broom, and it's been five or six years ago. She said she's been buying a broom every year, every year. Been stocking up on 'em, and said she's still usin' the first broom she bought from me, and it's five years old. And I've had several tell me that.*

"*I made seven brooms, for seven people, and had to autograph them. They all said they were goin' to put 'em in their shops with their antique motors and hang them up and never use 'em.*

"*They said, if somethin' happened to me, or somethin' happened . . but they don't want somethin' to happen to me. But they know they won't be able to get no good brooms. They liked that it had written the day and date on it. Some say they're buyin' 'em and keepin' 'em for Christmas.*

"It makes you feel pretty good. It seems like everybody that's bought these brooms, they come back and say they love 'em, and they say they sweep good. They say they're stockin' up every year, 'cause they don't want one of them store-bought brooms, 'cause it ain't worth takin' home.

"I never had one come to pieces. I never had one to come and say, 'Your broom ain't no good,' or this, that and the other. They all got a pleasant word and they enjoy the broom and they like it.

"You have to give me a pretty good half hour, that's to make it and sew it. And then I got to go right on. You know what I mean? I can't stand around and talk too much. I can make the broom quicker than I can sew it, that takes the longest. When you get inside them stalks, that's pretty tough sewin'. That's all by hand.

"See, all these brooms you buy in the stores, they're sewed with electric machines. That's the reason they're half sewed, 'cause they miss and hit. They ain't sewed right. I get in there, and I never had a string to come out.

"I make smaller whisk brooms. . . fireplace brooms. I got some with fancy handles. This here handle is a little tree. It's sassafras. Crooked. A lot of people likes it. It's short. You can sweep the trailer out with it. I also do those crooked brooms, some people bring me handles that they want the new straw put back on it.

"Some like those crooked handles, twisted from where the vine grows around it. I used to make a mess of them, but you can't find it anymore, where that old honeysuckle and old vine twists and grows around the wood. Man, I made a mess of that, and they go. People go for that kinda stuff.

"A lot of people'll come up and say, 'What kinda broom you gonna make?' And I say, 'Well, I'm gonna make the kinda broom that you're gonna sweep the house with.'

"I tell ya, there's a lotta people come up, and they don't even know what a broom is, the way they ask. They wanna know what I'm a makin'. They just go on like that. I don't know. Must be city people, I guess. I don't know. You run up on some queer stuff, I tell ya.

"But they come from Pennsylvania, New York, North Carolina, from all over. They wanna take the broom back with them, but you can't take no broom on an aeroplane. So they don't get one. They ask me to ship it out, but I can't do that. You gotta have a special box and whatever.

"I made a mess of brooms. I couldn't tell you how many I made, but never kept count of it or nothing. I got enough to do, just thinkin' about makin' one. Last year, I think I done a little bit better than 400.

"Sometimes, I can't make 'em fast enough. They don't want brooms that's in that rack, they want the broom you're making, that they're standin' there lookin' at ya.

"I make an awful lotta brooms in my sleep. When I wake up, I ain't got none. Well . . . I enjoy it. People comin' to the shows, they ask, 'Is the Broom Man gonna be here? I gotta have brooms.' They send me letters: The Broom Man, and I get it. The mailman, he knows me and that I make brooms. I get the letters. They want me to come to their shows.

"The world is the same, but it's the people in it makin' the world what it is. There ain't nothin' wrong with the world. They just come out with this and that and the other. They don't wanna work. All they wanna do is ride, do things easy.

"There's a lotta women who come up and say, 'I wouldn't carry a broom home with me. I use a vacuum cleaner!' I say, 'You go use a vacuum cleaner!' That's what I tell 'em. You see, that's too *much like work. That's these city people. You know what I mean? Yeah . . . Well . . . there's some queer people in this world.*

"I like to talk with people and meet 'em. See a lot of friends and they seem to like to come to the shows and see me. A lotta people come and don't even buy brooms. They say they just had to come to see me.

"I started doin' the shows with Charlie, for about four years we went out together. Then Charlie went into the hospital. The day before the operation, he told his wife he wanted to talk to me. So I went up there. He says, 'Billy, I give your telephone number and address to a lot of these shows. They're gonna operate on me tomorrow. If I don't pull through it, will you try to keep it on for me? Carry it on as long as you can?' He says, 'You're doing good.'

"The last year, he didn't make no brooms. All he did was just sit around. He was getting bad.

"I said, 'Charlie, I'll do the best I can. What I tell ya, I'll try to do.' So he said, 'Okay.' They operated on him the next day. When they opened him up, they sewed him right back. He had the lung cancer. They couldn't do nothin' for him. The next day, he went unconscious. He didn't know nobody.

"So I told him I'd try the best I can and go as long as I can, and I have.

"But I like it, the whole works of it, all the way through. There ain't no certain parts that I like any more than the others. It's all together. I'm doin' somethin' that nobody else is doin'.

"Broom makin' is pretty much a lost art. You take this generation, now. There's been a lot that says they wants to learn, but when they come in for 15 minutes or a half hour, you don't see 'em anymore."

William E. Hammond III

William Hammond III   June 20, 1996

Mary Sue Willis, 48

Proprietress, Durding's Store

From 1988 to Present

Rock Hall, Maryland

Soda Fountain

If you've ever wondered how you'd react if you were transported back in time, take a trip to Rock Hall, Maryland, and walk into Durding's.

The building on the corner of Main and Sharp streets has been there for more than 100 years. Today, following extensive renovations that occurred in the late 1980s, the small town soda fountain and drug store is an exact replica of its former self in the 1920s and '30s.

Places like Durding's used to be commonplace. At least one such site was a fixture in every town, small and large. But the days of the soda fountain—with its marble topped counter, whirling stools, comfortable booths, hand-dipped ice cream and bubbling seltzers and spritzes—are long gone. Such businesses with history and character have been replaced by fast food chains offering institutional menus of premade soft sweetness that plops out of a sterile machine.

The modern day service is impersonal, served by counter help who ask, in a programmed tone:

"Can I help you?" then punch your order into a computer and shout out "Next?"

At Durding's there's friendly conversation as the staff creates your order, from traditional double-dips and vanilla Cokes, to sundaes, exotic banana splits and special orders. They use the original syrups and ingredients from companies like Evan's and Fox that have supplied soda fountains for generations.

Everyone agrees it doesn't take long for Durding's to make an impression on first-time visitors. It happens immediately. Those who are old enough to remember the glory days say: "When I was younger, this is how it used to be."

Those who have never experienced the old-time charm usually stare in amazement, inspecting everything from the worn wooden floor to the ornate pressed tin ceiling and hanging brass lamps. Then, very comfortably, as if they've been there before, they sit down at the counter and place their order—eagerly becoming part of the long line of satisfied Durding's customers.

"We bought the store in 1988 from Helen Durding, the last generation of the Durding family to operate the soda fountain. My husband, Art, and I spent several years restoring Durding's to its 1920s charm and grandeur. We were very fortunate to have Helen's help with the restoration. Her family had the floor plans from the last time her father refurbished the store in the 1920s. She also had pictures of the store from earlier years. Between the floor plan and pictures, we were able to get a very accurate representation of what the store was like in the mid '20s.

"In addition, Helen and her mother had stored the cabinetry, shelving and furniture when they changed the store around years ago. So all of the original pieces were here. We just put them all back into the old floor plan. We were very, very lucky.

"A nice surprise was the telephone booth. It was in Wayne Baker's barn, and when he heard we were restoring Durding's, he asked us if we wanted it. Of course, we were delighted. The ship's carpenter from our marina was able to restore it. I think Wayne was delighted that we were restoring Durding's, and he was pleased that the booth would be used again.

"Most of the comments I hear when people walk in is that Durding's immediately takes them to a time and place that reminds them of their childhood, when they had very happy and pleasant memories. They're reminded of a time when the pace was a little bit slower.

"For example, I think people are just so amazed at our milkshake maker. Today, they're accustomed to buying a milkshake at a place where they pull down a lever and it drops into a paper cup and that's it. Here, they actually watch our staff put the milk and the syrup and the ice cream into our milkshake machine, and it whirls around and around. Then it's poured into a glass from a stainless steel cup that's set in front of you, and it's filled with, actually, another milkshake to drink.

"We get so many people who come in here who are eager to relate their own stories about coming in here as a child, or else they've had experiences at a similar soda fountain in their past.

"Both Art and I grew up in Chestertown. When you're raised in that type of setting, you become aware of the historical presence and the importance of the need to preserve it. When we came to Rock Hall there was a lot of development going on, and in many instances there was an attitude that it's better to tear down and start again rather than take what you have and preserve it.

"We told Helen to contact us if she ever decided to sell. We didn't want Durding's to be torn down. It was a site that served generations of residents. You can imagine how many great-grandparents and grandparents and children have passed through this store.

"As we were involved in restoration, we knew the store had a soda fountain, candies, cards and gifts. In trying to bring the very best in here, I thought we should approach Hallmark. Initially, they declined our request because our square footage was too small. But we asked them to come and see the store and they decided that, in spite of its size, Durding's was appealing enough to become one of their stores. We had to have shelves and card racks, but we didn't want to use modern fixtures. Hallmark was wonderful. They went into their archives and sent us pictures of card racks dating to our period. We then took their pictures and designed our racks to make it look like they were part of the store. We're proud of the significant amount of thought, care and effort that's gone into the restoration.

"Our most hectic time of year is during the Rock Hall Fourth of July celebration. There are just so many people in town at that time and this store is just filled. We have our windows all decorated and we have flags. This is a fun place to decorate, all through the year.

"To present the store's happy appearance takes a lot of attention to detail. It's almost like planning a party. Because we're a Hallmark store, we follow the seasons, from party to party. We go from Halloween to Christmas to Valentine's Day, St. Patrick's Day, then Easter, Mother's Day, Father's Day, Fourth of July and then we go to autumn, back to school, and we're at Halloween again.

"The very best part I like is interacting with the people who come in. You listen to them reminiscing about their past, speaking about their childhood, about when they went to a soda fountain. People will relate how they courted their future wife in the store. They'll talk about the telephone booth, about calling their friends after school. We play the big band music and you can watch people tapping their feet to the music. I feel the store has always been a source of happiness for people, and it gives me a lot of pleasure to be a part of it and, hopefully, help further it.

"You can see the faces of people who remember coming here as a child light up when they talk about the various things that went on in the store. It's just amazing to see 50- and 60-year-old women sit here giggling like school girls. Some people will come in and sit at the same soda fountain stool and order their same ice cream that they did as a child.

"Most of these places are gone. Honestly, in my travels, I haven't found another Durding's. Even in magazines, you rarely see soda fountains like this that date back to the 1920s. I'm sure this place would have been gone if we hadn't bought it.

"But the continuance of the past is still going on because Helen Durding, a member of the original family has been so helpful to us during the restoration and even afterwards. She's given us information on where to get ingredients and even instructed the staff on how to operate some of the equipment. We couldn't have done it without her.

"In fact, we still get people who come in the store and ask about her. Since she lives upstairs, when that happens, she comes down and talks with them and they have a private reunion in the booths."

Mary Sue Willis

Mary Sue Willis   November 9, 1996

Family Manager

"*I was here all my life, because my family had the store ever since I was born. I started working part time on weekends about 1938, when I came home from school. I guess you can say I got a college education to make sodas. Then I was allowed to be the janitor, the bookkeeper, the soda jerk. I was everything.*

"*In 1962, after my mother died, my brother, Ben, worked with me. Then, later on, I was totally in charge. The best part of working here was meeting the public. I had some of the best friends here. We should have kept a book. I have a lot of wonderful memories.*

"*I was glad to retire, but I knew the store would open up again, because Art and Mary Sue were after me to buy when I was ready. They've done a beautiful job here.*

"*They make good sodas and sundaes, almost as good as I used to make. I always said that you get what you put into it, and if you use the best, you'll get your customers back.*

"*At least once a week I come down here to keep checking, to see what's going on. I have a lot of old friends that come and I talk to them, plus people who want to learn about the history of the store.*

"*Christmas was a favorite time. The windows were all decorated and we enjoyed it. I liked all the holidays. It was really wonderful.*

"*This store is part of my life and part of the community. I have seen little kids, when my mother was alive—her name was Daisey. They would lay right down flat out there, on the cement, when their mothers were dragging them along, wanting to come into this store. They wanted to go into Daisey's.*

"*It's been in the family for over 100 years, and it was a happy place. The only sad part was that my father died when he was 48, and left my mother with two children. She was English, and she had never worked before. And she came down in this store and built the business all up again, and it was wonderful.*

"*I wish she was here, I know she would be proud of this now. I'm crazy about what they've done. It's very satisfying that it's still going on.*"

Helen T. Durding

Helen T. Durding   November 9, 1996

Helen Durding, 76, who worked in the store from 1938 to 1988, and Emil Myers, at their favorite booth in Durding's.

Trappers

You don't just find trappers in country wetlands and woods. Marshes on the edge of the city also attract their share of hunters, seeking game for food and sport.

Bud Holland is a more traditional trapper. He started in the late 1950s, when he was 9 years old in his home state of Pennsylvania. The terrain, animals and weather conditions were quite different from the wetlands and farmland along the Delaware Coast where he traps today.

A full-time postman, Bud has been president of the Delaware State Trappers Association for the last 10 years. But not all of his time is spent outdoors. The organization is involved in a number of educational programs, training courses, environmental clean-ups and informational sessions. Oftentimes, Bud finds himself in the hallways and offices of Legislative Hall in Dover, trying to explain to city-raised politicians how certain laws will adversely affect the state's trapping industry.

On other occasions, he has been asked to explain how the ancient trapping skills can be used to solve some of the area's problems, many associated with the effects of rampant residential development.

But in the wide-open basement lair where Bud keeps his supplies, his conversation continually comes back to the outdoors, where he enjoys himself the most. His conversation includes words that you'd expect to be associated with a trapper, terms like independence, solitude and self-reliance.

Ed Hahn, 76, grew up in the city of Wilmington in the '20s and '30s, during the Depression. He started catching snapper turtles when he was 10 years old, in the marshes and ponds off South Heald Street, with brother Amos and their father. They would put a pan of water out on a winter night, to see how thick it would freeze. "If it was a good, thick layer," Hahn said, "we would go out catching on the water. Out on the water, if we could see the air bubbles forming under the ice, that's where there was snapper."

After chopping a hole, he learned how to stick his arm into the icy water and grab hold of the snapper's neck and pull it up to the surface. A normal catch of a dozen snappers was tossed in a box in the basement and the turtles sat, until they were to be used for snapper soup. Through the winter, the family would kill two turtles at a time and make up a 20-quart-pot batch of snapper soup, mixing in onions and barley along with the turtle meat.

After returning from the service in World War II, Hahn caught snapper near Port Penn, Delaware. In 1963, he suffered a stroke and couldn't catch any longer, so he began walking the marshes each spring, collecting unhatched snapper eggs before they were destroyed by raccoons. In a child-size plastic pool at his home in Claymont, Hahn kept the eggs until they hatched. For nearly 20 years, each spring he took hundreds of baby snappers to the Port Penn marshes and released them on the banks of the Delaware.

In an age where government seems to be intruding more in our lives, where people in offices and high-tech laboratories are forced to work together, where age-old skills that survived into the middle of this century have disappeared, the trapper observes nature, works according to the motion of the tides, listens to the temperament of the wind and silently survives.

Bud Holland, 46

Trapper

From 1959 to Present

Blackbird, Delaware

"I'*ve been down here since 1972. There's still a lot of trapping in this area. To those of us in the business it's no big thing, but I guess a lot of people are surprised to find that we're still out there. I basically do muskrat trapping, but I also do 'coons, otters, beavers. You need to set out different types of traps for the different animals. Basically, with trapping what you're into is following the cycle of life. In the spring, when the young stuff's born, the season's out. Then, in the fall, whenever they become fully furred, is when the trapping season starts. So it's pretty much December 1 until the middle of March.*

"I'd say about 90 to 95 percent of the trapping's done on the tidal marsh. Most of our people are working their traps on the east side of Route 9, from Wilmington to Rehoboth. You get mainly muskrats in the city of Wilmington. The raccoons, otters and beavers start up the farther south you go. In this area around here you're allowed to trap raccoons year round, there are that many of them, and they devastate the sweet corn crop. They wear it out.

"With increased residential and commercial development, that's basically the destruction of their habitat, the animals are moving to the protection of the wetlands. So you're getting an abundance of animals in one area, and fewer farms. But there's only so much room, and as traffic goes up and down the roads, you start whacking them. Then there are developments on the edge of the open land where raccoons go in and start to cause problems. That's when you get a different kind of trapper going in. He's called a damage controller and nuisance trapper—or exterminator—and he charges you to take the raccoon out of the chimney.

"What people don't realize is that after we trap a muskrat, for example, the entire animal is utilized. The meat is consumed, the hide is processed and sold for coats. Even the musk gland is used for perfume and as a lure to attract other animals. With beaver the same thing happens, and beaver meat is a delicacy. It's the first thing to go at a sportsman dinner. It's hard to explain what it tastes like. But beaver is a vegetarian, so it's a wholesome meat.

"Super Bowl Sunday is usually the big one, when everybody's going to a sportsman's banquet. The guy who goes elk hunting brings some elk, and the guy who goes bear hunting brings some bear, and alligator or whatever. It's at a house or at different clubs around. Some of 'em might have a hundred people there, and a lot of it's invitation only. It don't matter if you're the governor of the state, if you're not in that particular group, you're not getting invited.

"Raccoons used to be a big seller, but since the rabies scare people backed off. What they don't understand is the rabies virus was killed two ways. When you froze the meat, it was dead, and then when you cooked the meat it was double dead. There was nobody in the state who could have gotten rabies from eating raccoon, but it's one of those things that people got in their mind and it lives with people. In a case like raccoon, when the meat's not consumed it's used for bait.

"Now probably the hardest animal to catch in the state is otter. They're here, but very few trappers have caught an otter. It's been one of the most expensive furs in the last two or three years.

"I buy a trapping license, but I also have a fur dealer's license. There are some dealers who come down here to the house from Jersey or Pennsylvania to look at a good size lot of furs. They offer you a price, and you go with the dealer who's gonna treat you the best.

"Most trappers mark out their boundaries and check with the other guy so there's no dispute. I also mark my traps with high poles, so it's easy to find them.

"Like most trappers, I use conibears traps for muskrat and foot traps for the others. For tidal trapping, you're setting your trap at low tide and a majority of animals are traveling at night. But the tides around here are erratic, you got to keep an eye on them. Then you've got the storms to contend with. An east wind won't let the tide go out and a west wind 'll keep it out all night. One time, I didn't see a low tide for four days. You got to watch the weather, that's a big factor.

"A lot of people look at the trapper as a mercenary whose only interest is money. But I look at trapping a bit differently than most people. For instance, if you set a trap for a mouse and you catch a mouse, you've trapped it. If you set a trap for ants and you catch ants, you've trapped ants. If you put out a bag for beetles, it's called a beetle trap. You've trapped beetles. That's where I have a problem with these groups that say they don't believe in killing anything.

"I saw a situation the other day where people were catching wild cats and using a trap. These are the same people who condemn what trappers do. At that moment, when she had that cat in a trap, she was a trapper.

"There's a lot more to trapping than catching an animal and selling the hide. We provide a lot of services and we're important in managing a natural resource. If there's an over population, it's going to be reduced by disease or cause problems. A marsh with too many muskrats is called an eat-out, where they decimate everything that's edible and they starve. The trapper is important in solving that problem and helping make sure it doesn't happen. Most of the time trappers don't have to look for places to trap. A lot of the time farmers find us. That's what happens with me. They want someone on their property who is safe and knows what he's doing.

"During trapping season you're busy, from sunup to past sundown, carrying traps and your catch back and forth on your back. Sometimes you'll go twice a day. I wash the animal's fur right there where I catch it, so it starts drying right away. Then I come home and skin 'em. Hang the pelts on the line downstairs. Put the meats away and start the process of fleshin' and stretchin'. There's an awful lot to it. It's a cycle and you don't take a day off.

"It's pretty much the same type of mechanisms with the traps that's been around for years. There's been some modifications by the manufacturer and by the trapper himself that have made it a little bit better. Using an outboard motor instead of paddling, you get around a lot faster than before. There's still a lot of walking, and you still have to move your traps.

"If you set out a hundred traps, you have to move 75 percent of them the next day to continue to be successful. That takes a lot of time. You've got to get out there early to empty the catch in your trap. The raccoons and Norway rats, they're the predators, who will follow you and eat the muskrats caught in your trap and damage them. So you got to worry about the animals in front of you that you're trying to catch, the ones behind you, then you got the two-legged kind that like to take everything. People. Poachers.

"They're not so much a problem down here, but when you get up into Wilmington it can be bad. But it's simple deduction. The more populated the area, the more thieves are around, and the more chance you have of losing something.

"In the off season, I catch turtles, snappers. Get my equipment ready. Go over traps I've put in preservatives. Check out the mechanics, make sure I've got a well-operating trap before I put it over the side. 'Cause if you go out there with trash, you're just cheating yourself. You're not gonna catch anything. In fact you make animals smarter, because once stung they're gonna be a little more leery of that area.

"We have trappers who are kids and retirees. A lot of it's handed down. Trapper education comes in when a young person's interested in it but the father's not around, or when a father might not know what to do. In those cases, we fill a void and teach how to do it properly. We have classroom and practical training programs.

"Trapping is pretty much a one man operation. No dogs, because they scare the game. There are a few guys who may trap together, but it's mostly you out there alone. Over the years, you develop a sense of the sound and smell of the marsh, the sense of the touch of the animals, and of course the site.

"I love it. There's a certain solace and solitude. You don't have anybody bothering you. You've got the owner's permission to do a service on his land. I'm out there doing something I love, I'm not bothering anybody and I foot my own bill.

"I guess there's a sense of satisfaction in all of this that has something to do with you doing the same thing people have done for hundreds of years. You wonder how you compare with somebody who did it a hundred years ago. I think the sunrises and sunsets are special. It's just, really, being there. Everybody has their priorities. To some people it's ballroom dancing. To me, the solitude of the marsh is it. It don't get any better than that."

Bud Holland

Bud Holland   August 4, 1996

Snapper Catcher

"**M**y hobby was to find a she one laying. I'd put a red marker flag there and come back a few hours later to take the eggs out, because they don't hatch out in the wild. Raccoons eat every one of them eggs. Very few ever hatch in the wild that I know of. I could take you down there and show you a hundred nests with the eggs all broken up.

"I kept them here all winter and let them go in the spring. I really enjoyed myself. I marked down where I found them, how many eggs they laid. I watched one lay 61 eggs at one time. That was back in '72, in Port Penn. When she got done, she was so tired I had to pick her up and take her down to the water. She couldn't get down there herself.

"See, the she turtle lays them and leaves them. I'd walk up and down the banks, about 2-1/2 miles a day. One day, there were so many nests I ran out of markers and had to use beer cans. If you don't mark them, you don't find them. You have to be careful digging them out. The biggest she snapper I ever caught was 14 pounds. She had 55 eggs in her. But a big snapper can be 40 pounds or more. The eggs, they look just like ping pong balls, but harder.

"People ask if they bite. I say sure. I had them bite my pants while I'm carrying them. But they let go. As long as they don't latch onto any meat, they're okay. I'd carry them in a bag on my back, and I've had them bite me through the bag. You just have to lay down until they stop biting you. I know it sounds crazy, but I enjoyed it.

"I went down there every single day. I figure I hatched 2,700 snappers all those years. I'd get the eggs on Memorial Day, right when they laid them. Keep them through Labor Day, when they started hatching. Had hundreds of them in a kid's, plastic swimming pool down the basement. I'd keep them over the winter and take them out in the water in April, when the water starts getting warmer. I hatched between three and four hundred every year. They were about as big as a quarter when I took them back down to the river. Put them in a bucket and just stuck them in the water at Port Penn and they'd swim off.

"I had some great experiences. It was hard work but I enjoyed it. There was this one guy, a good turtle catcher, but he was always drunk. He went into a beer garden one day, showing off that he was going to kiss a snapper. He held it up and it got hold of his lip. They had to take him to the hospital, it took his lip off.

Ed Hahn, 76, currently of Claymont, Delaware, caught snappers from 1930 to 1980. In the latter years, he hatched the eggs in his basement and released the baby snappers into the marshes around Port Penn.

"They bite pretty hard. They can't break a broom handle, like they say, but they'll put a dent in it. When you carry them, do it by the tail. They're faster than you, but they can't bend back up and get to you from that angle.

"I was a city boy, but I hunted and fished my whole life. We ate bullfrogs, muskrats, rabbits, squirrels, robins. There was 11 of us in the family—eight of us kids and my grandfather and mother and father. He made $8 a week working in a leather factory, so we had to eat all this wild game and stuff. I enjoyed it. I experienced it when I was young, I got a lot of water in my boots.

"I really do miss it, though, being outside, finding them turtles. But I can't go out anymore. I fell and broke my back, that slowed me down. So I guess it's best that I quit. But everybody in Port Penn knew me. They thought I was doing a good thing."

Ed Hahn   July 27, 1996

Barber Shop

There's nothing like a real barber shop, a place with that trademark red-white-and-blue rotating barber pole out front. Inside, there are stacks of old, beat-up fishing magazines, lots of hair clippings on the floor and a heavy razor strap dangling from the worn metal and leather chair.

It's a place where both the regulars and newcomers feel right at home, complete with good natured joking and enjoyable conversation, and you get a real haircut from an experienced barber at a reasonable price.

More importantly, your barber is a friend, someone who knows your name as the result of a relationship established over the course of years. In fact, there are older customers who proudly admit that they have only been to three or less barbers in their lifetimes, and they will only switch if their barber dies.

Unfortunately, many of today's kids grow up having their hair cut in "trendy," delicately decorated, hair styling "salons," complete with ferns, pastel colored walls, plush carpeting and an ever-changing staff of "stylists," who aren't there long enough to establish a relationship with the customers.

Frank Terranova started barbering in 1949, when he was 13 years old. He talks fondly of how he used to stand on a small wooden box to reach the hair of his first customers.

Today, in his small, old-fashioned shop, he shares stories of 50-cent haircuts and how he practiced his craft by giving free shaves to grime-faced hobos he would pull in from off the street. It was during those early years that he learned to use leeches to suck blood out of his customers' swollen faces on Saturday mornings, after the local gin mill Friday night fights.

In the last decade of this century, genuine barbers, like Terranova, are disappearing from the American scene, victims of high overhead, and the marketing glitz of stylists and studios, that are pushing these real artisans out of the market.

Frank Terranova, 60

Elsmere Barber Shop

From 1949 to Present

Elsmere, Delaware

"*M*y mother wanted me to become a barber. My father had a sub shop on Fourth and Poplar, Joe and Tony's, it opened in 1938. I started working in there when I was 8 years old, part time after school. When I got to be 15 or 16, my father said I would have to work in the store day and night, and I couldn't go out, or I could be a barber and go out at nights. So, I decided to be a barber. That was in 1949, when I started out working for Tony Monaco. I was just in my early teens.

"I was working at shops in Wilmington and then in Claymont. I ran into Joe Casalvera one day, and he asked me to come with him to Elsmere. Since my girlfriend, now my wife, lived on Lincoln Street, I figured it would be easier to see her if I worked with Joe. Besides, I was born in Brack Ex, so it was like I was coming back home. I came here in 1955, and I bought the shop in 1957, when I was 20 years old.

"When I got here, we had a radio and air conditioning. Not too many barber shops had air conditioning in 1955. Today, we've got color TV, a VCR. Everything's modernized. The kids today would be lost if they came in here the way is was back then.

"Across from me, where Wawa is now, was the old Hearn's supermarket. It was the only big market in the area. Behind it was a big water tower. I remember they used to have an auction at Prices Corner. There weren't too many cars. You could drive down the Kirkwood Highway, and there was no traffic at all. No red lights all the way to Limestone Road. We moved to Newark in 1961. Nothing but cornfields and farms all the way back and forth. It used to take me 15 minutes to get to work. Now, it's a half hour.

"But none of the other shops that were here when I started are around. Only me. On the corner, there was a drug store with a soda fountain. The Three Little Bakers were in one of the stores years ago. There was a cleaners. A shoemaker shop, Joe Nardo's, was next to me. I guess when you stop and think about it, I'm one of the oldest businesses left in Elsmere. I've seen them come and go.

"I've had some customers for 38, 40 years. A lot of them come from out of the area, from Maryland, Middletown, Smyrna, Penns Grove. I even have a guy who comes from Ocean City, Maryland. I think he comes once a month. But I had a chance, when I was 21, to go to Hollywood to cut movie stars' hair. They wanted me because I use shears, scissors. A lot of guys only know how to do clippers, and that's the way it is today, too. But, my wife, she didn't want to go. It didn't work out, so I stayed right here.

"But, oh, yeah, I'm happy. I like Elsmere. It's a nice town. It's convenient. Vilone Village reminds me of the neighborhood you would see on the Dennis the Menace TV show. Everybody's friendly and they're nice to you. I also like being here because my granddaughters, Maria and Michele, who live in Hockessin, go to Corpus Christi. They can come by after school and see me.

"Getting along with people is the most important part of the job, but that's just like any job. A lot of the customers have problems. I help them out. Talk to them. It's more like a family in here.

"They come here because I got a positive personality. You've got to be nice to people. You get to know them when you cut their hair for a long time. A lot of the guys who come in here, I did when they were kids. Lawyers, doctors, senior vps come to my shop. And I cut their kids, too.

"I got a lot of friends, local guys, who come in during the day. Talk sports, numbers, drop in to say a quick hello. So many of them   . . . Ed, Cas, Fitz, Rags, Leroy, Ed O'Neill. Fitz, he says we're all going to hit the lottery and I'll retire, close the shop. Then we'll all go out to Vegas or California. We have a good time with each other.

"But, this won't go on forever. There used to be more barber shops than beauty shops. Now, its the other way around. At one time, in the city of Wilmington, there were between 50 and 60 barber shops. Now, there are about 15 to 20 barbers, at the most. Barbers are fading out. The rent today and the overhead is too high. Health care insurance and the rent kills them. Then, today, with AIDS, you got to be careful. Barbers will start using throw away blades if they do any shaving. And they'll have to start wearing gloves. There's a lot of good barbers out there, but they aren't cutting because they can't make out. It's too expensive.

"But, I'll keep going, maybe about four to 10 more years. I'm going to see if I can hit 50 years total in Elsmere. Then I'm through.

"I guess when all the barbers are gone, you'll have to get your hair cut in beauty shops. There won't be any barbers left, unless they charge $20 to $25 for a haircut. It's hard to be a barber. It's like an art, and it's hard on your feet. But, someday you have to go. Someday it's going to happen."

Frank S. Terranova SR

Frank Terranova   July 19, 1996

Basket Makers

In 1876, shortly after the Civil War, brothers Edward and Samuel Day of Massachusetts came to North East, Maryland, and established the Day Basket Factory. Using strips of wood from fresh logs of white oak trees that were plentiful along the nearby Susquehanna River, the factory manufactured hand-made baskets that were shipped to cotton pickers in the South and workers in industrial factories in the North.

Today, if you try to buy authentic, American-made baskets, you will find yourself involved in a frustrating and time consuming search.

Highway gift shops and big-name department stores display shelves and racks filled with attractive, pretty-to-look-at, ready-to-buy baskets of all shapes and sizes. But, when you look at the tiny tag on the bottom, in very small lettering, you will find the words: "Made in China" or some other distant, third-world locale where cheaply paid help cranks out cheaply made goods to be sold at cheap to moderate prices.

Unfortunately, these inferior imports won't last through too many Easter egg hunts, nor will they carry the heavy loads or last as long as "Made in the U.S.A." products. But to find genuine American products, the trick is in knowing where to go.

At the south edge of North East, Maryland, the Day Basket Factory's 20th-century weavers, strip cutters, bottom makers and finishers still use the identical by-hand basket-making methods that the American Indians taught to the white man during the days of the early settlements in North America.

The owners and artisans are proud of their work and encourage bus travelers and visitors to browse the building's gift shop and, more importantly, step back in time in their factory and see how things are done, and made to last, American style.

Bob McKnight, 46

Manager and Basket Maker

Day Basket Factory

From 1989 to Present

North East, Maryland

"The basket business had been for sale and others who were interested were looking to buy it and take it out of town. Myself and three partners felt it was important that the Day Basket Factory stay in North East. We also wanted to make a living and conduct business in a Christian environment, a place where we could set a positive example in the workplace. There is never off-color language, no loud music. We promote positive attitudes that, I think, help foster a positive employee/employer relationship.

"We make everything here, just the way it was done when the basket factory started in 1876. We go from a flitch cut—which is a thin, white oak board with bark on both sides—and process it to a complete basket. It all happens right here. The process is able to be watched by the public, and a lot of visitors seem to enjoy watching the baskets take shape.

"We make about 40 different styles and sizes. There are market baskets, that people take shopping, plus picnic baskets, bread, gathering, firewood and fruit baskets. We have four different bushel baskets, from half-bushel to three-bushel size. The larger baskets are used for toys and laundry and decorative purposes. Also, twice a year, at Easter and Christmas, we make collector editions. We produce 150, which are a different new style and decorated especially for that particular holiday.

"Our customers are from about every state in the Union. We mail throughout the country. We ship to Texas, California, Florida, Canada. We have shipped to England and France, but honestly the shipping cost is prohibitive. We have orders from the U.S. Park Service, the National Arboretum in Washington and the Mt. Vernon Memorial Park in Virginia.

"We warrant our baskets forever, with a full, lifetime guarantee. If it's used for its intended purpose and it doesn't last, we repair or replace it for you. We've honored it for baskets that have been 20 or more years old. The normal shelf life of our baskets is 20 to 40 years.

"Imported baskets are not competition for us because it is a totally different animal. Our baskets are a lifetime investment, family heirlooms in the making, and our customers know this. They realize the difference. They tell me 'I remember using my grandmother's basket when I was a child, and now I want one of my own to give to my child.'

"There are other American basket makers, but they use a different process and different materials. For one thing, many of them will use maple—which is easier to work with, but not as good a wood—instead of oak, which we use. I think we're unique, because of our material and our totally handmade process, in the East Coast and probably in the entire country.

"There's a sense of satisfaction in offering a product that is American made, that has a lifetime value and that is done in a way that's continued in this country for 120 years. There's a sense of satisfaction in being associated with all of this. We're 100 percent American made, and that is very important to us. It's one of the things we made a priority."

Bob McKnight   June 1, 1996

97

Basket Maker and Finisher

"I was just out looking for work and Ross Gibson owned the factory then. I went in and his father, the older Mr. Gibson, he saw me and said, 'As little as you are, what possibly could you do?' I said, 'Give me 30 days and I can show you what I can do.' And that was the deal. I had 30 days to make a basket to go through their grade of inspection and, well, I'm still here.

"When people find out I make baskets, they always ask me what it's like and they want to come down and try it one time. They don't realize how hard it is. You tell someone you're a basket maker and they think it's a gravy job.

"I've seen people come and go. When they first start here, they don't realize the soreness in their hands will eventually go away. In the beginning, it's a raw feeling, because you lose a lot of skin, a whole layer, off your fingers. There's a lot of pulling and tugging. Your fingers are so sore and raw, but you get used to it. My hands right now are so hardened, I can go away for a week and come back and it don't bother me. It was terrible in the beginning. Sometimes, I didn't want to return. But I would remember what Mr. Gibson said to me. It sort of gave me the extra will to keep on going.

"I have a job not many people have. I've thought about how special and interesting it is, how you can turn a tree into a basket. Robert, who does the stripping, will show us an oak board and say, 'This will be a basket.' We have a gentleman who weaves the baskets, but I'm the only one right now who knows how to finish them. That's putting the handles and yokes, or reinforcement strips, on. I also decide if it's ready to sell and qualified to pass. Some of them I don't pass, if there's a split or the weaving may be rough or uneven.

"You have to like your work to make a good basket. It has to be something you like doing. There's a lot that goes into each of these baskets, and they last a long time. We guarantee them for life. That's how much we stand behind them.

"I just like doing something all by hand, that can be used and last. I can look at it when it's done and say 'I did that,' and no part of it was produced by a machine. I really believe I'll do this the rest of my life. I know it. I like my job, and I like the people I work with."

Pam Sargent, 36, has been creating baskets since 1984.

Pam Sargent

June 1, 1996

Band Leader

There was a time when local musicians were as popular as sports heroes. Before the days of portable electronics and amplification, guys who could play a horn and female vocalists who could carry a tune were minor celebrities. They provided entertainment for weddings, private parties, church socials and fraternal society weekend dances.

To create music was a skill that had to be perfected over time. Most old-time musicians were self taught, and they could play several different instruments. Many also gave private lessons in their homes, hoping to pass on their skills to the next generation.

In the summertime, the scales and simple songs of young students floated through screen windows. At the start, the melodies were peppered with mistakes and repeated often.

Later, combos, trios and small bands formed. Neighbors were treated to free entertainment whenever the musicians got together to practice.

No one thought of hiring a disc jockey to play recordings at a home wedding party or dance at the hall. Live music, played by real musicians who talked and laughed with members of the audience, was the only way to go.

In 1953, when he was 8 years old, Joe Smolka began playing saxophone in the Pulaski Legion Band at the club hall across the street from his brick row house. His three sisters also were members, two were majorettes and another played the saxophone.

Today, Smokey is the sax player and leader of the Seventh Avenue Band, the last of Delaware's authentic polka bands. All three of the musicians are named Joe, and all can remember days when such standards as "E-I-E-I-O," "Beautiful Brown Eyes," "Mamo Moja Mamo," the "Polish Lullaby" and "Beer Barrel Polka" were played for hundreds of smiling, enthusiastic dancers in crowded halls and clubs every weekend.

Joe 'Smokey' Smolka, 50

Polka Band Leader and Musician

From 1953 to Present

Wilmington, Delaware

"*The whole neighborhood belonged to the Pulaski Legion Band. That's where you learned your instrument. All the older guys who had their own polka bands started out there. I remember thinking that I wanted to have a polka band, but only better than theirs.*

"*A nun in the eighth grade knew a bunch of us guys needed a way to earn money. She suggested that we have a band. We had three or four accordions, two or three saxes, a drummer. We didn't stay together too long, but it was our start. We didn't have a name, and we got a job and were supposed to play, so somebody suggested the Polka Dots. That was my first band. Since, I've played in the Gladiators, Golden Bells, Now and Then and now Seventh Avenue.*

"*All you needed to get started was an accordion, a clarinet, drums and a stand up bass. In the old days they had a violin. No amplifiers, because most of the parties were in the homes. And when you had a party, the neighbors came over. The old musicians would play two or three instruments. They just picked them up on their own. They say the best musicians were the old ones. They didn't take any lessons. They learned and handed the music down from generation to generation and would improvise.*

"*Back then, it was fun playing, because we were having a good time. People supported you and gave you a nice hand. The families all came out, to the picnics and parties, weddings and church hall. People appreciated the kind of music then. It wasn't just rock and roll, like today. The older people danced with the younger kids. It was a family thing.*

"*The best feeling was to be up there, on the bandstand, and look out and see people having a good time and knowing it was because of what you were doing. You see, to be a musician in those days was a big thing. Musicians were respected. People would say, 'Hey! You play in a band!' That was great. It made you feel good if people saw you performing.*

"*The music wasn't that difficult. It was music from the heart. It was for people who worked hard and went out to have a good time. Some wanted to dance. Some wanted to sing along with the folk tunes that kept them all close together. You'd start playing an old tune, and they would recall the melody and sing along. It was a chance to release their frustration.*

"*Up to about 20 years ago, nobody was ashamed about polka music. They would sing and play and be proud of it. People respected the band. Families would get together, bring as many as 30 members with them to a dance, and they'd meet other families there. Everybody knew everybody. If the church had a dance, every club showed up with its gang and they each had tables.*

"*Now, everybody is trying to fight for the handful of people who go out. But there aren't that many anymore. People are working two jobs. On the weekends they need to rest. They can watch TV and movies at home. The kids don't listen to polka music. Only a handful of people bring their kids to dances. Nobody teaches polka dancing anymore. Families don't do it together.*

"*In our neighborhood, there were at least eight clubs and a half a dozen church organizations, and they all had their own dances, and they were all packed. On one weekend, you could go out polka dancing, between Wilmington and Chester, to at least a half-dozen different dances. Today, there are maybe three clubs left. We used to play for 250 to 400 people at a weekend dance. Now, you'd be lucky to get 100. We have to travel out of town to find jobs. But the dancers are traveling, too, to find somewhere to dance. There are a lot less polka bands, less jobs to share and fewer dancers to come.*

"*Now, you have DJs. People don't even get bands. I never thought I'd see the day when people would use DJs instead of live music for their weddings. That would have been something people* would have been embarrassed to do. Now, it's normal, the thing to do. They even have specialty polka DJs, but it's not the same thing. Not at all.

"Why, years ago, I can remember, just here in Wilmington, there were the Regents, Grenda 4, Merrymen, Joker and the 2 Jacks, PenDels, Royalists, Golden Bells, then Golden Bells II. All gone now. We're all that's left.

"Then, everything turned too commercial. Dances started to move to bigger halls. They needed amplification and the bands needed extra equipment. The tickets got more expensive. Then people didn't like kids being in the halls. It wasn't like the old church family picnics anymore.

"Sometimes, I wonder why we still do it. But I know the answer. Because we enjoy it. We take pride in trying to carry on traditional music. We enjoy the reaction when we travel out of town, and people appreciate the music we give them. Every now and then, though, when you play at some of these old, big name polka places, you get little glimpses of the old days. Like when people came up and asked you to play a song for them, it made you feel good. They'd even give you a $5 or $10 tip. Guys would impress their girlfriends by giving the guys in the band a tip.

"To keep going today, you have to make deals, run bus trips, play in festivals. We have equipment today that we would never ever dreamed of having. But we still have the main thing. The accordion, the core of the polka band, is the most important instrument in the polka band.

"We want to keep it alive as long as we can. I guess we'll be at it until we're physically unable to do it anymore, even if it means playing only two or three jobs a year. We'll do it because we enjoy it, and we think we're good at it . . . and there's nobody else doing it.

"We'll keep it alive for even one more year, one more time, so people will remember, so that people will know that there was once another kind of music that made people happy and dance and sing. Someday, all that will be left will be the recordings—the old 33s and cassettes and CDs. They'll be saved somewhere. And people will turn them on and hear the fun music that, at one time, was the cornerstone of the hard working people who did their jobs and wanted to have a good time after-wards, which meant singing and dancing and drinking.

"You see, this is where I came from. This is what I am. This is part of my basic make-up and values. To me, polka music is an expression of simple family life. It means remembering the gatherings we had with friends and relatives, all together, and music was an important part of it. But I'll admit that the slow dying, the gradual disappearance, bothers me.

"It's all going to be gone after a while. I can see the day when we're the last band and there's no place to play. So we'll play for ourselves. But there will be some arts council out there somewhere that will want to remember the good old days. And they'll call us and we'll get together one more time and pull out our instruments. We might be sitting in our rocking chairs.

"I do have hundreds of memories, all good ones, from the many jobs and the songs and the dances, from local dances and faraway trips. The only sad feeling is that one day we'll be gone, and this will all come to an end."

Joseph Smolka (signature)

Joe Smolka   May 16, 1996

Small Town Movie Theater

Soon after the Civil War, in 1868, Middletown opened the Town Hall and Opera House that offered live performances until it was destroyed by fire in 1918. A second theater built at the site burned to the ground in 1921. The current and third building on the same spot was built of concrete and plaster and opened on Dec. 7, 1922, Delaware Day.

For more than five decades the Everett Theater offered live vaudevillian performances and moving picture shows as generations of families grew up at The Everett.

Eventually, drive-ins, shopping malls, multiplex cinemas, television and changing lifestyles pulled away the audience, causing the distinguished, small town, Main Street movie house to follow the path of thousands of others through the country. The Everett darkened its screen and shuttered its doors in 1979.

Ellen Combs Davis, a local insurance broker and Middletown native, was instrumental in organizing a group that was interested in preserving the theater. In 1981, several concerned citizens formed Associated Community Talents Inc., a non-profit organization that purchased the theater and transformed it into one of the few remaining active downtown movie houses on the Delmarva Peninsula.

Broadway musicals, recent movies, community programs, talent shows, film and drama festivals, organ concerts, workshops and neighborhood school events all play a part in the life and purpose of the restored Everett Theatre.

Touchstone Pictures selected The Everett for scenes in its film *The Dead Poets Society*, starring Robin Williams. As a result, Middletown's restored Everett was featured on movie house screens throughout the country.

On a spring Friday evening in 1996, a mixture of young and old, children and parents, bought tickets under the lights of the outdoor marquee, lined up for fresh popcorn in the lobby and took seats in Middletown's dimly lit "real movie theater."

In front of the big screen, beneath the grand proscenium arch and surrounded by ornate decor created by workmen generations ago, the audience relived the grand old days when films were king, when theaters had character and when going to the movies was a very special event.

Ellen Combs Davis, 73

The Everett Theatre

From 1922 to Present

Middletown, Delaware

"*A very good friend came in and he told me the theater was on the market and he thought it would make a great indoor tennis court, and that sort of got my dander up. So I called a group together, people from the community, some ex-school teachers. About nine or 10 of us met together to see if saving The Everett would be a viable project. I really wanted to save the facade for Main Street. I never had a clue that it was going to grow and touch so many lives as it has. It's like a pebble in the water, it just makes circles and circles.*

"*We met once a week to plan our first show, which was in February. We sold ads in the program. We hoped it would be a success, and the theater was packed. The three acts on the program were a local country band, a classic trio from the University of Delaware and the men's choir. The building was very run down. When we had our first variety show, the roof leaked badly. A man sat in the balcony and caught rain in a bucket.*

"*But the first show was so successful, that we decided we would try to show movies. We drove to Dover to get the lenses for the projectors from Mrs. Schwartz, who owned most of the movie houses on the peninsula. When she closed down the theaters, she took the lenses to the projectors to Dover.*

"*We started to show Disney films, and then a local talent show. I tell people it's the only stage on the East Coast that anyone can get up and make a fool of themselves if they want to.*

"*We do three plays a year, like Nunsense, which we did last year. We've done South Pacific, The Student Prince, Jesus Christ Superstar. Next year we'll do Into the Woods. It's a showcase for local talent. Nobody gets paid for anything, not the projectionist or anybody. We have about 50 to 60 volunteers involved in the operation. When there's a performance, that number goes up to about 100. It's from ages 6 on up to retirees, and mostly just local people.*

"*We used to have over 400 seats, but we received a donation and we took the old ones out and put in 310 downstairs, with more leg room, and about 50 in the balcony.*

"*We're in an enviable position where the children can walk to the theater from the elementary school in town. The shows that people do in cafeterias that last 40 to 45 minutes for children, we bring here to the Everett stage, during the school day. And the teachers and students love it. We had a show not too long ago and three busses came down from the Commodore McDonough School in St. Georges and three came up from Townsend. We had 300 children in the theater for one show on stage.*

"*Last year, the middle school students were studying the Holocaust and they didn't have time to plan a bus trip to the museum in Washington, so we arranged to show Schindler's List over two days. One of the projectionists took off from work to show the movie, and there were about 175 children who walked down here to see it.*

"*When they needed to raise money to restore the town's World War I monument, we did a local variety talent show and raised $1,000 for the monument. We had a show for the senior center, and a lot of the seniors did their line dancing and appeared on stage, so the community is very much involved in our performances, and we're very much involved in being an active part of the community.*

"*Some youngsters broke in and stole some candy and there was a story in the newspaper. I mentioned that a security system was on our wish list and I received a call from a man who told me his boss was donating a system and sending someone over to install it.*

"When someone found out we needed to have termite work done, a woman called the theater and said they couldn't afford to give us a donation, but if we paid for the materials they would do the work, for free. It's some way that these people feel they can help, can do something for the community. A man from Levittown used to visit his daughter in Kent Narrows and occasionally drive through the town. He came to see the theater and later arranged to get us a large Rogers Trio organ.

"We did get some publicity associated with the filming of The Dead Poet's Society. When we had our showing of the movie, we decided to only charge a dollar, so that anyone in the area could afford to come. It was amazing. A lot of people came from Wilmington. They had already seen the movie once, but they wanted to see it in the venue where it was made. And to look at that proscenium arch and see the film, within the proscenium arch, was really quite exciting. We had over 2,100 people come to see the film.

"But being in the movie hasn't made that much of a difference in The Everett. It was five minutes of fame. Today, it's the local people who still come to our theater; we don't get too many from out of the area.

"I went to see The Merry Widow in Philadelphia and was talking to a gentleman up there. When I told him the dimensions of our stage, he said we could do anything we want on a stage this size. The size of the stage is excellent and the acoustics are as near perfect as you can get. We have two of the original backdrops from 1922. They're hand painted on canvas. One is a street scene and the other is a garden scene. We were told it would cost $25,000 to restore each one.

"There are very few community movie theaters left. I was asked to speak to interested persons in Pocomoke City, who are interested in preserving their theater. I told them, you can't do it with a community performing group as your focus. There are more people who care about preserving historical buildings. That's really the way we approached it, from that angle and that's what's made the difference.

"But we're unique. There are parents who drive up and let their children out of the car and pick them up when the movie or show is over. Where else can you do that today? Once, we were showing a Disney film and a pipe burst during the matinee. There was water up to the first four rows. We shut down the theater and took the children next door, to the annex. There was a school teacher in the audience and she and I called every parent to come and get their child. Some of the children even call me Mrs. Everett.

"When I was growing up, you'd go to the movies every Saturday. It was 10 cents up in the balcony and 15 downstairs. Then the price went up, and you had to pay a quarter. We had Western serials every week. There are some young boys, now in the 50 age range, and they remember coming every Saturday to see the serials. There were double features, too. Then, it just went downhill, but that was a natural way of life at the time for small town theaters.

"I wanted to save the facade for Main Street. But the project has touched so many lives. It's satisfying that it's such a success and that it has made such a positive impact on the community. When the theater is filled, it's exciting. I stand in the back and look at everybody, and I think: Isn't it great!"

Ellen Combs Davis   June 7, 1996

Country Store

"If people come here, they're either coming to see you or they're lost. There isn't any other reason, because there's nothing here. We're at the end of the line."

That's how Erlyne Twining describes her "Taylors Island General Store," located on the right side of a quiet road about a mile across the Slaughter Creek bridge. The trip to Taylors Island is a scenic, 20-minute drive southwest of Cambridge on Route 16.

Save yourself the time if you want a gift shop with scented candles and local trinket souvenirs. Take another road if you're looking for junk food, newspapers, film and cappuccino.

But those searching for the unusual will find their effort rewarded. Older visitors will be thrilled as they step back in time; and younger travelers will be amazed to witness an authentic, working remnant of the past.

There's no exterior sign. A single gas pump sits in front of the old frame building that at one time was a working cannery.

The overhang of the front porch protects the weathered entrance. Inside, the main section of the store is dark. A long, two-sided bench is the meeting place for regulars sharing morning coffee and conversation. The worn wooden floor supports shelves that rise toward the ceiling, holding a conglomeration of antiques plus modern household goods and automotive supplies. The latter are for sale, the antiques are Erlyne's private collection, on permanent display.

In the rear, a back door leads to the docks. Watermen, who work the Slaughter Creek inlets leading to the Little Choptank River, tie up their boats, then come in to eat, swap stories and catch up on the latest news over a cold beer, homemade soup and crab cake sandwiches.

Beer signs, rusted license plates and pictures of the regulars cover the walls of the store's Slaughter Creek Pub. But, a hand-printed notice, tacked up in a frame beside an old Baltimore fire alarm box, tells it all:

There ain't no place just like this place,
anywhere near this place.
So this must be the place.

Erlyne Twining, 65
Owner, Taylors Island General Store
From 1984 to Present
Taylors Island, Maryland

"We opened it back up in '84. It had been closed for less than a year. When we started, there was so much room, it had so many shelves that if you put a can of peas up there they'd get lost. So I started putting up baskets, odds and ends, dolls, antiques and interesting things. Pretty soon, people were coming in looking for the junk more than they were the peas.

"We had a deli and served sandwiches, but the people asked for soups. They said: 'It's awfully cold out here. We have to work and we don't have anyplace to get anything, and it's 20 miles to town.'

"So we started doing soups, several different kinds a day. Then that evolved into dinner specials every night—chicken or ham and cabbage. Of course, we always have crab cakes and oysters in season.

"At first our customers were just local people when we first started. I remember some guy from Annapolis came in one day and said, 'Oh my goodness! Aren't you afraid somebody will find you're here?' And I looked at him sort of funny and said, 'We wish.' 'Cause we were just starting out.

"Then, more and more people kept finding us. It was like a secret that people enjoyed telling. They'd say, 'I know where you got to go.' We get them from California, New York, had people from Alaska in here one day. Now they didn't come all the way from there to here, but somebody told them. It's fun to see their reaction. A lot of them look like they can't believe it. They walk around and look at everything. Then they eat, and the food is good, and they're even more surprised at that.

"When the store was built, there was no road, no bridge to get on the island. This building was a combination tomato canning house and a general store. Then there was a fish packing place just down the road. They had a pot bellied stove in the front. That double, back-to-back bench out front used to be straight down the center aisle, across from the counter. When you came in, it was like walking the gauntlet, because all these people would be sitting there, having their sodas, staring at you and had a few nice things to say as you went by.

"They still meet there every morning at opening time. Have their coffee, discuss the weather and whether or not they're catching crabs or oysters, or whether the wind is blowing too hard to go out. This is their morning ritual, still today. A lot of these people are original Taylors Islanders.

"Out front we have books and videos. We call it the Taylors Island Library. You just bring a book if you're finished with it. Leave it there, and pick up one that somebody else's left. Bring it back whenever you want. We don't keep any record.

"It's a community center, here. When someone has a problem, or there's a fire, we collect for them here. People drop things off. We have community potluck dinners. Everybody brings a covered dish.

"For our Halloween parties people really get dressed up. You wouldn't believe the costumes. You can see the pictures on the wall. We have our Easter Egg Hunts. New Year's Eve is a big event in here. Of course, our Taylors Island Christmas Eve Caroling is the most beautiful thing you ever saw. At 7 o'clock people start gathering in. We bring in a piano or organ. It's packed. You can't get them all in. Some are standing outside singing carols in the night.

"It used to be just the people from around here, but now we get them from everywhere, even congressmen from Washington. I notice people with Airstream trailers pulling up. I hear they've been doing the caroling for about 33 years. We continued after opening back up.

"We give everyone a full buffet dinner, with turkey and ham and desserts for everyone. Even cracked corn and bakefish that night as a special treat. It's our Christmas gift to them. Everybody, black, white, and members of all the churches are here. People bring things, too, special treats they make that they want to share.

"We're open every day of the year, except we close on Christmas Day and for a half day on Thanksgiving. I think people depend on us to be here. It's a long drive to anywhere else. When they run out of something they come here. We've got the milk and bread and gas. There's no other gasoline nearby.

"We run accounts for our regulars. There are a lot of watermen that don't have the money. In the wintertime they'll run their bill until they get their money in, and they'll pay it off. We don't ever lose any.

"There's no sign out front. It wasn't there when I came and we never needed it. Everybody brings you things, that's what's so strange and nice. They'll see something that they think would go on the walls in here, or on the shelf, and they bring it in. A lot I've collected, but an awful lot people will bring in.

"I like people and I guess I have the need to please people, so this is a good place to do that. And I'm not Pollyanna, but I honestly think the community needs something to sort of hold it together. If they need something, this is where they come. If they want to find out where to buy firewood, whatever, it's an information center.

"It's a family place. It definitely is. We know about 95 percent of the people by their first name. Of course, you know when it's a tourist, 'cause it looks like a tourist. But you do get to know the people. You know their problems. You know which ones can't drink. You make sure there's somebody to take him home when he has too much. The big thing I've always said is: 'Here, you are your brother's keeper indeed.'"

Erlyne Twining

November 25, 1996

Beer Garden

From the earliest times, public drinking establishments have been meeting places for travelers, neighbors, strangers and members of fraternal and secret societies. The Founding Fathers of the American Revolution often met in Philadelphia pubs to discuss the young country's future, and their decisions, some made while sharing the juice of the barley, have affected history and continue to impact our lives today.

Great ideas and petty crimes have been discussed and planned over a cup of brew. These sites have been called by many names—Wild West saloons, city gin mills and cafes, highway taverns and inns, country stores and ethnic beer gardens. But whatever the name, they provided a site to relax, rest and socialize.

Adolph Okonowicz left Poland, came through Ellis Island and arrived in the promised land of America in the early 1900s. After working in the Pennsylvania coal mines, he moved to Wilmington, Delaware, and worked as a riveter in Harlan's shipyard and in shipyards in Baltimore. He opened a corner, city saloon in 1926, taking advantage of the opportunity provided by the U.S. government during the wild and daring days of Prohibition.

His Maryland Avenue speakeasy and the high quality of his whiskey attracted some of the city's more colorful characters, including politicians and judges, as well as a steady clientele of cops and working class regulars.

In 1933, when liquor again became legal, the neighborhood beer garden expanded and became known for its hard shell crabs and Adolph's famous hot spicy crab sauce.

The names of 10 U.S. Presidents—from Calvin Coolidge to Jimmy Carter—were taken in vain across the bar at the Maryland Avenue shot and beer joint. Over the years, the customers ranged from railroad winos and local factory workers to racetrack handicappers and union tradesmen. Neighborhood patrons and an assorted cast of regulars mixed well with passing travelers who were in need of a quick one for the road.

Family members continued to operate the business until 1977, when Theresa Radulska Okonowicz, the last owner and widow of Ed Okonowicz, finally shut off the lights of the gold, black and white Schaefer beer sign that hung above the entrance for the last time.

Paul P. Okonowicz, who was born in 1920 and grew up and worked in the establishment during its heyday, is the last living son of Adolph and Helen Okonowicz, the beer garden's original owners.

Theresa R. Okonowicz, 71

Owner

Adolph's Cafe

From 1971 to 1977

Wilmington, Delaware

"We owned a soda fountain in Wilmington, not far away on Harrison Street. My husband's mother needed help when her older son moved away. I thought if my mother needed help we wouldn't hesitate, so we sold our place and went over to help her as best as we could.

"I was brought up in a bakery where you sold your donuts and your bread. Family people would come there. I had never been in a bar before I met my husband. It was an entirely different world, a whole different life. People were buying drinks, and I didn't drink.

"But the people were very nice. We had people from DuPont shops, next door, who would come in for lunch, after work. A lot of them were young engineers in the Engineering Development Lab. They were my regulars, they were all budding geniuses, very smart, the cream of the crop. They were from the best schools. Then we had people from the neighborhood that would come in. Some worked on the highway, a lot of construction workers from I-95 when it was being built.

"You got to know the people quite well. You're like a lawyer, they tell you everything, about their family, where they go for amusement, what they do on Friday and Saturday nights. Our place was a stopover. They would come in and then go somewhere else for the rest of the night. Other people liked to come in and talk to the regulars. It was like 'Cheers' in a way, a lot of talking, a lot of socializing.

"Some talked about work, fishing, hunting, some about how to build a highway. You learned a lot listening to them. The philosopher, J.B., could talk about anything. He especially loved art and history. Most of them had nicknames—Jersey Jack, Tequila Kid, Motorcycle Harry, the other Harry was Storm Window Harry, Wynnie, J.B., Tricky Dick, Reds, Sambo.

"The names were based on what they drank or what they did. You knew what they drank. They didn't have to ask. When I was busy, they'd just wait on themselves. They were my watchdogs, my protectors. I think they'd appoint someone every night to stay until I closed so nothing would happen to me. They were great.

"We also had the winos come from the railroad tracks, nearby. They drank that cheap, sweet wine. It was sad to see them. They only lived for the drink, and they'd bum cigarettes. I'd give them whatever I had until I was told not to do it anymore. Only one ever stole from me, because I was in the back room. He took whiskey off the shelf. My husband went out with a baseball bat and was going to break every finger on his hand. Thank God he didn't find him. You see, he'd rather give it to you than have you steal from him.

"He was something. He'd invite the regulars over for Thanksgiving dinner with the family. Anyone who didn't have a place to go would be with us. It was fun. The kids would look like it was a little strange, but I think they enjoyed it. It made them better, socially. They learned how to talk to people.

"We were closed on two holidays a year, only Good Friday and Christmas, and on Sundays. It was hard work. You might as well say you worked 16 hours a day. You opened up, you had the cleaning to do, cases to fill up, then you'd order the liquor, beer and food, plus keep the inventory and raise a family.

"There were so many crazy things. One night, during a full moon, a man ran in like a bat. He said he had dynamite in his cellar and he could blow the place up. They say during the full moon all the nuts come out, and I think I had one that night.

"It was a working man's place. A lot of them thought they owned a special seat. If somebody sat in their seat they would glare. But the stranger didn't know what was the matter. The regular customer didn't get there in time and it would bother him that somebody else was in his place. It was like it was upsetting his routine.

"The people who came to Adolph's were like family. Some lived in rooms, in boarding houses, and they would get up and come and sit in the bar. They would nurse a drink all day long, until somebody else came in, so they could sit and talk. Some of the younger guys would take them in town if they needed a ride to go shopping, or even take them out to eat. When one of the regulars died, all the pallbearers came from the bar. They all attended the funeral and the family was grateful.

"They were social drinkers and the bar was a place they used, a way of communicating with other people. They just liked to sit and talk. In Revolutionary days, the colonists always went to a pub or tavern to make plans and discuss matters. It's the same way in today's world. People go to gather with other people. They're like soulmates that have something in common. If it was just tea being served, people would still gather, but we had beer and whiskey.

"I really learned to like it, the people especially. I came to realize that most people are good, and even the lowliest have good in them. I think my children benefited from growing up there. They were in the bar all the time, meeting the customers. Today, they don't look down on people. They know it doesn't matter where you come from or what you do, it matters how you are and how you act.

"In a way it was hard to close, but the city changed and you were afraid to walk down the street. The crooks took over, the robbers. I had a few close calls. If my customers didn't stay with me it could have been bad. I still keep in touch with some of the regulars. We closed in 1977, right after my middle daughter got married. That was the biggest bash we had in there, Connie's wedding.

"The people were super, they gave me a party when I was leaving. I hated to leave, but life goes on. You have to think about your family. I couldn't have the whole world as my family, although sometimes I thought I did.

"I really thought of them as part of the family. I was interested in them. They would stop to visit me. When my husband died I never saw such an outpouring of love. They brought food. They just were there. I remember how much their friendship meant, how caring they were. You can tell in an emergency how people are. They were great all the time, but they were just outstanding when something happened.

"They were always looking out for me and my children. Storm Window Harry used to bring us vegetables, to make sure we had enough to eat. You can't forget that. He's gone. So many people are gone. But you always remember them, a certain thing touches off a memory. Some are good, some are bad. But you let those go by, because it eats you up inside. You have to think of the good things. You don't realize when you're sitting and talking and laughing with someone—that's a good memory.

"Some of their lives didn't pan out the way they wanted. You cry with them when they lose somebody, you sympathize with them when they're hurting, and you laugh with them when they're happy."

Theresa R. Okonowicz

June 23, 1996

114

Bootlegger's Son

"*I was born in 1920, but I guess I started working when I was about 7, as soon as you could do anything. I'd carry booze from one station to another, those were other houses in the neighborhood that handled Pop's booze. I'd be a delivery boy.*

"*When they would raid the house, sometimes Pop would know and sometimes he didn't. It depends on who got paid off. He had a special bar built, with a chute that opened down to the cellar, where there was a giant, granite rock. When the policemen came, Pop would drop the whiskey bottles down the chute and they would smash. No evidence.*

"*There was a little room in the back, with a big radio. People would come in with girlfriends or wives and listen to the music, drink whiskey and have a public discussion. Our doors and windows had bars, and we had a great big German police dog. It would go after any strangers. Sometimes, the police would knock the door down. When they got into the house they would knock over furniture, break it and tear the place up. Me and my brother, Eddie, we were sleeping on a mattress upstairs, and two or three of the cops lifted us up in the air, looking for booze. After they threw us back on the floor, they went to another room.*

"*One time they raided us and we got caught with the liquor. And they had a trial. When the judge called for them to bring in the evidence, it was gone. Somebody drank the booze! Case dismissed!*

"*We had people from all over. They came because they heard we made a good brand of whiskey. Widows used to come to Pop and ask him how to make booze, so they could get clothes and food for their children. One woman still prays for him every night. After her husband got killed, and they had no money coming in, Pop went over to her place and showed her how to make a living with the booze.*

Paul P. Okonowicz, 75, grew up in Adolph's Cafe.

"*Pop knew all the politicians. They drank booze, too. It's just that they would send somebody else over to pick it up. He knew the other bootleggers. They would give each other tips. Who was an easy cop, and who was a hard cop. Also, there were two or three or four cars to a bootleg family. Some were for local use. Some were high speed cars for delivering booze.*

"*When they ran him out of town, we lived on a farm in Townsend, Delaware, not far from Golts, Maryland, for a few years, way out in the country. Pop rented the beer garden out until it was safe to come back to town. But he still made the whiskey and delivered it up to the city. The cops used to put roadblocks out, so Pop would travel at night, with the lights off, from Golts up to the city. He'd drive a load of booze in the truck across the farm fields to get around the roadblocks. They never caught him.*

"*We knew all the people. They'd knock on the door and we'd let them in. Everybody had nicknames. Double Gin, he worked for the carnival across the river. He'd come in during the daytime and ask for a double gin. We never knew his real name. He never said, and we never asked.*

"*When they didn't have any money and couldn't pay their tab at a particular time, people left watches and rings. Pop had a box full of watches. Eventually, we took them for ourselves.*

"There was always something to do. On Sundays, you got up early, by six o'clock, and cleaned the beer garden, or we'd cut up the crab barrels, so we could burn them for heat in the winter. But there was always food on the table, always clothes and shoes. We didn't have to worry about that.

"I remember helping make crab cakes on Fridays. We were noted for our crab cakes, 250 we'd sell over the weekend. If you weren't in school, you'd sit in the back kitchen and cook them to order when the people came in. In 1934, we sold a crab cake, crackers and a pickle for 25 cents.

"But life was different then. Not like today. When anybody in business patronized you, you patronized them back, whatever they were selling. We bought bread and cakes from Radulski's and he bought whiskey off of us. There was more of a feeling of comradeship in those days.

"We were noted for our snapper soup. We had a sand bin in the cellar that had 30 or 40 snappers in there. Every Friday morning, we'd go down and drive a nail through the snapper's tail and hang it on the wall. Then Pop would cut the turtle up and let it drain the blood for a day. We'd make about 40 gallons of snapper soup.

"When he sold crabs, in the '30s, we were getting 20 to 30 bushels delivered every day in the summer, six days a week. People would come from Philly, Chester, Reading. . . all over. I remember being about 17 and cracking, cutting and cleaning them. You did it so long your gloves wore out and your fingers were all cut up.

"Whenever you needed something done in those days, you did it yourself, or you got the guys in the bar who knew what to do. Fireworks was a good bricklayer. Dog Shit Charlie was an electrician. Eckerd was a carpenter. You didn't get a permit. They just got a crew together. In those days you had a good meal, good booze and friendship and got the job done and that was it.

"Children in those days had to take care of themselves. I remember asking a guy in the bar to help me with my homework, and he asked me, 'How can I do that for you? I don't know how to do it for myself.' What you learned you did on your own. You taught yourself.

"There was no such thing as a vacation. Once in the while we'd go to White Crystal, and we'd swim while Pop went to visit a man who owned a beer garden there. To do that twice a year was a lot. We never had bicycles or trucks or little cars. Whatever you made is what you played with. Roller skates was a great gift. It was like the people in Poland. You got fruit and nuts, and that was a special gift, especially when the fruit was out of season, like in the winter.

"But it was a good life, because it learned you how to take care of yourself. But it was bad because you didn't have time to play or to do sports of any kind.

"What I remember the most is meeting people. Talking to them and getting along with them and finding out their needs. I met hundreds and hundreds of people in the beer garden. Even now, when they find out I'm from Adolph's, quite a few will say, 'I used to go to your place to eat crabs.' And they say how good they were and how the place was always full.

"That makes you feel good. Especially since the building burned down about a year ago, and there's nothing left except the vacant lot . . . and a lot of good memories."

Paul Okonowicz

May 5, 1996

Printer

Some consider the invention of printing the "greatest event in the history of the world." Johann Gutenberg of Mainz, Germany, is believed to have introduced modern printing in 1455 with his version of *The Bible* and the invention of movable type. No longer were educated monks needed to transcribe history. Education became more accessible and was shared with all through the art of printing.

For centuries, through the days of America's most colorful printer Benjamin Franklin and into the latter half of the 20th century, the actual contact of inked paper with metal type produced finished documents.

Whether they were powered by human muscle, animals, steam or electricity, metal presses—built to last centuries—created documents through mechanical movement. In each town, printers skilled in the ancient craft worked at small local papers. Their noisy, ink-stained surroundings also produced advertisements, fliers, wedding invitations, entertainment billboards and political posters.

The printer was a skilled artisan and recognized as a central figure of the community.

Today, high technology has delivered laser, ink jet and bubble jet printing equipment that works silently and efficiently, producing everything from pamphlets to complete books. Noiseless, odorless and without character, the antiseptic soul of modern printing equipment resides within a complex computer housed in light-weight plastic. The process is so simple that school children can produce camera-ready copy with the ease of typing a letter.

While new technology accomplishes the job, some of those brought up in the old ways of the black arts believe there is still a place for the iron presses of the past.

Throughout America, hundreds of small presses survive. In attics, cellars, small rooms and garages, older printers have saved some of the trustworthy relics of a long-gone age. One such site is in Smyrna, Delaware, where Randolph T. Faulkner is the sole owner and operator of Three Owls Press.

Randolph T. Faulkner, 74

Printer, Compositor

Three Owls Press

From 1941 to Present

Smyrna, Delaware

"I worked for a number of letterpress shops and newspapers. I was at Hambleton Printing and Publishing Company in Wilmington in 1941. Then I went into the service during World War II for 44 months. When I got back, I worked for the Dover Index, doing work in the job shop, which was everything but the newspaper work. Later, I established Enterprise Printing in Clayton, a commercial job press.

"I learned my apprenticeship on the letter press, where the paper was printed direct from the type. Basically, for about 550 years, up until the 1960s, the principle was exactly the same as Gutenberg—type to paper, directly on the page. The mechanics changed over the years. You had new and bigger machinery, automated equipment, you even had the different ways it was powered. But the principle was the same, type to paper.

"When the computers came in with the electronic stuff it was, basically, to make things happen faster and more economically.

"But here, I have machines from back into the late 1800s. My objective is to have the old equipment in good condition and to preserve this method and explain it to people who are interested in it. A lot of colleges, in their graphics art departments, are trying to preserve the same thing.

"Some of the equipment I have is pretty old. There's an 1890s Rosbeck large perforator. Over here is a rare piece, an 1878 Mustang Mailer. They would set up the type by hand and roll the ink roller, a brayer, over it. It was really an old time label printer. I have a cutter that works just like a guillotine. It weighs over 1,500 pounds. It can cut a whole ream, that's 500 sheets, of paper.

"Most of the different equipment has come from 12 states and I've had it shipped here from Virginia, Cincinnati, Ohio, Nebraska, Massachusetts, New York and Pennsylvania. This garage is filled with machinery, but then I also have the type in all sizes and compositions, wood, metal, brass, copper. I have a set of rare Victorian wood type that came from the Seaford Leader. Altogether, I've got about 18 cases of wood type. It's very hard to get now. Most of the type is made of metal, it's called foundry type. They used the wood type rarely, for special sale bills and special fliers as accent designs. I've got about 150 cases of the metal type.

"I've also got six small Kelsey hand presses. They operate on what I call renewable power. There's little noise and no mechanical energy needed, because you operate them by hand. I can print if the power goes off, just like in the days before electricity. There are different size hand presses for different sizes of paper.

"My largest press is a Chandler and Price, C. & P. That's a 10 by 15, it will handle a poster. It weighs 1,600 pounds and was made in 1885. It was converted to run on electric. Would you believe, years ago they used to operate these by hand?

"I was involved in all phases of printing. I worked in the composing room at the News Journal from 1956 until I retired in 1984. One of the most interesting jobs I had was working on the make-up of the front page of the Morning News when Sam Caufman was the editor and sometimes with Emerson Wilson. I worked the night side for the morning paper. There was a lot of deadline pressure, but it was very exacting work, especially when you had to change a page close to deadline because of a breaking story. You didn't want to be under that pressure all the time.

"There's a lot of nostalgia in the printing business. If you've been involved in printing, once you move away from it, there's something missing. We had 34 linotypes on the floor in the News Journal at that time. There was a certain type of sound that goes with them. It wasn't a bothersome sound.

You'd get used to it, but it was hard to explain. You just liked the whole thing, the sound, the excitement, the atmosphere.

"I went from the old days of letterpress operation all the way up to the computers. I still had some of my equipment from Enterprise Printing when I stopped that business in 1962. In 1985, about a year after I retired, my wife saw an ad in the paper that somebody had some printing equipment to sell up in Pennsylvania. I went up with the idea that I would get a small hand press and a little type. I found out that he had all the equipment from an old Philadelphia job press. It was about 4,000 pounds of equipment and type, and I bought it all.

"I've got a little over 400 square feet here. To be comfortable, I really need about 2,000 square feet of space. I decided to concentrate on artifacts that were in good condition and which would help preserve our methods, based on what space I have. I found out that there were a lot of others around the country—during the '60s and '70s when changes were being made—who had the same idea, to preserve the traditional methods of the 'black art,' that's what they call printing. A person in California put out an International Directory of Private Presses. These are people who, basically, write their own works and print it. Some do work for churches and charities. Some even do small jobs and others will put out private editions of books. I think there are two private presses in Delaware. The other one is up in Newark.

"This was a rural area, and I was brought up on a farm in Kent County. I have a great interest in acquiring metal cuts—zinc and copper engravings—that have anything to do with farms and animals. I try to find those pieces. I found some from a person in Ohio that go back to 1905.

"We lost a lot of this equipment to Third World countries and China. The owner of Turnbaugh in Pennsylvania, one of the biggest dealers in printing equipment through the years, told me he took large truckloads of printing machinery to the Baltimore pier and sold it over to India. I hear Mexico is buying it, too. A lot of those countries are not as technically advanced as we are, and many have trouble with electricity. Some only can use it about two hours a day.

"Another idea I have is that China bought a lot of our molds, and I see a lot of stuff in the stores, marked made in China, using what appears to be foundry type. That's my observation.

"Most people don't realize it, but a number of famous writers and people were printers, including Horace Greeley, Walt Whitman, Thomas Edison, the Wright Brothers, Carl Sandburg, Robert Louis Stevenson, Mark Twain, Edgar Allan Poe and Rudyard Kipling, who bought a Kelsey hand press.

"There seems to be something in our civilization where there's an attraction if a person can compose something and put it down on paper. It provides a lot of satisfaction. It's a statement, a record for others to see and reflect upon.

"The French philosopher Rousseau said, 'Life is not breath, but action. The best way to lengthen life is to enjoy it.' Sure, I don't have to do this, but I guess I'm living proof that once you get ink in your blood it's there forever."

Randolph T. Faulkner   July 31, 1996

Soap Maker

Mildred Wix Welch was born February 6, 1903, one of 13 children in a farm family in Whites Church, near Whiteleysburg, Maryland.

A long-time resident of Harrington, Delaware, she is known throughout the community for her talents as a seamstress and as a baker. Her homemade cakes and pies are popular items and fetch high prices at community fundraising auctions.

In 1976, during the Bicentennial Celebration, she began marketing her special lye soap. Today, she is recognized throughout the region as an expert in the field of soap making. All of the proceeds of her soap sales are given to such charitable causes as the Fuel for the Needy Fund, Senior Center, Harrington Fire Company, Jaycees and Harrington Historical Society.

In the days when families were more independent and barely had money to spend on the essentials, much less luxuries, home soap making was a common practice. Mildred started making soap when she was a teenager. Today, she follows the same formula that was used by her mother, and her mother's mother, well over a century ago.

Some still believe that a bar of old-fashioned lye soap can serve very well as a combination shampoo, beauty bar, house cleaner, spot remover and laundry detergent. According to Harrington's Soap Woman, it had so many uses that, if it was marketed today, lye soap would replace an entire shelf full of popular cleaning products.

According to Mildred's daughter, Lillian, "It's good for just about everything but your eyes and your mouth."

Recently, because of her health, Mildred has stopped making her soap, but the family tradition is being carried on by her niece, Norma Jean Bradley of Denton, Maryland.

Mildred Wix Welch, 93

The 'Soap Woman'

From 1920 to 1996

Harrington, Delaware

"*I was 17 when I started helping my mother, Nettie, start making soap. We didn't buy store bought soap, we just made what the family used. Back then, we only used lye and grease, or meat skins and scraps from the hog killin'.*

"*My mom made her own 'cause there was 13 of us, and you had a lot of pants and shirts and overalls to wash. At first, when I helped my mom make it, it was a necessity, 'cause we were poor and lived on a farm. Killed our own hogs. Had our own scraps.*

"*Now, I have a man that has a sawmill, right at the edge of town. They kill around six hogs between Thanksgiving and Christmas. They had been throwing the nice lard meat out in the woods for the animals, but now they know I can use it. I bet I have 30 gallon of lard in my cellar now that's been donated to me to make soap.*

"*You do so much yesterday. You start preparing the night before. I have certain utensils that you dissolve the lye in the night before. It has to be agate, or the lye would eat it up. That lye is powerful stuff. My pans, pots, kettle are all agate, even the stirring spoon.*

"*Mine is a beautiful serving dish, agate lined over iron. It's white, like porcelain.*

"*Everything has to be room temperature. It's a production, it's nothing that takes just a few minutes and you're done. You have to let it cure for two weeks before it's completely ready. I would never give anybody my soap until it's had time to cure and it's perfectly ready.*

"*I use one can of lye and six pounds of grease. It could be pure lard, or it could be kitchen grease. If it was kitchen grease, you had to wash it and cleanse it. It makes nine pounds, and that makes 24 cakes.*

"*My friends bring me their old perfume. You'd don't use it for scent, but it takes the grease odor away. And I put in glycerin. That helps to make it soft and nice.*

"*Now it's good for everything. The boys, they all went to the pond and used it to bathe. We put a tub of water out, take a bath in a big old tub. This is back there a lot of years.*

"*It's the size of Ivory. But, Honey, that soap don't compare to mine. That soap right there, in those packages, that's what my niece made. It's wrapped in freezer paper. Mine, I use aluminum foil. I couldn't afford to buy freezer paper.*

"*My mother, she learned from her mom; and her mother from her mother before her. I've always just used my own soap, never bought any at the store. Honey, it just makes your hair wonderful. Some people come and buy it and say that mine is the only soap they'll use. They'll never use that other stuff again.*

"*I've been all over Delaware and Maryland demonstrating. I started out at Old Dover Days, then I go to Trappe, then I go to Salisbury. I make one batch right in front of them, and they bought my soap. I'd take a couple of hundred cakes and sell it at 50 cents a cake. Well, Honey, the ingredients has gone up, so I had to put it up to 75 cents and now, this cake is a dollar.*

"*When I make my soap, the crowds come and stand around. They never saw nothing real like that. You pour it in the pan like you would fudge. It looks good enough to eat.*

"*I've been on television from Salisbury. They came up here to take movies of it. Once in a while, somebody will call me up and say, 'Miss Welch, you're on television!' I turn it on and watch. I never thought there would be this much fuss over cheap old soap. The lowest thing. But, Honey, my soap isn't cheap, and it is pretty.*

"I gave a demonstration to the Boy Scouts and Girl Scouts, over in Denton. I took a bucket for people to wash their hands. Later, a woman called me on the phone, and said she didn't know how she came to do it, but she only put her one hand in the bucket and not the other. On the way home she noticed how nice and smooth her skin felt on the one hand and the other one wasn't. She said she couldn't believe there was that much difference, just in washing your hands.

"Years ago, during the Bicentennial, I made little samples to give out to school children. That's when I decided to take my soap and put it out and see how it did. And it went overboard, went wild, and I put it on the market.

"Even today, they come up to me, and I don't even know their names. One young woman came up and said, 'Miss Welch, I still got my little cake of soap from 1976.' And I told her, 'I gave it to you to use.' But she said, 'We want to keep it for a sample. We're so proud of it.'

"I've made, I don't know how many, more than thousands and thousands. We have Heritage Day here and I sold 200 bars and had to go home and get 50 more. People came every year looking for me, and they say, 'I wouldn't a been here, but I'm out of soap.' Honey, I have people come to Salisbury every year, and they buy enough to run them a year. They buy four at a time. That's enough for a year. It lasts.

"I get letters from Texas, Alabama, all over. They write and buy 10, 20 cakes at a time. Pay me in the mail and I send it to them. I had a friend, used to be my neighbor, and she was married to an Air Force fella. I sent soap over to her and her friends over in Germany.

"Some of the bars float and some of them don't float. You don't know which ones, that's a mystery. But it's all a mystery, when you come to think that you can take six pounds of lard and some lye and it comes up with something so beautiful like this. I thank the Lord I don't have a burn on me from the lye. You've got to be careful.

"I give my recipe out to people, but people aren't going to make it too often. It's too much work. My daughter, Lillian, says she'll never do it. She knows how much work goes into it.

"I'm awful proud that I can produce something so valuable and usable, and they all come back for more. I love doing it. It's just a part of my make-up. It's just something I can do to help somebody else.

"Now, I can't do it anymore. My niece took it over now, since I've been in the hospital. Norma Jean Bradley, she's from Denton, a retired banker. So I'm the Soap Woman, and I've turned the Soap Woman over to Norma Jean."

Mildred Elizabeth Welch

Mildred Welch   July 12, 1996

Family Newsstand

Stanley's Newsstand opened during Woodrow Wilson's second term, just after the troops returned from World War I. For nearly 80 years, it delivered the news—through thousands upon thousands of copies of newspapers and magazines. While many of those publications have ceased operation, and many of their readers have passed on, Stanley's remained, serving the community for generations as an information outlet and informal meeting place.

Stanley's survived a building fire, the Roaring '20s, the Stock Market Crash, the Great Depression, World War II, the Cold War, Vietnam and periodic downtown Elkton flooding. It delivered the headlines when Lindbergh crossed the Atlantic, Pearl Harbor was attacked, Kennedy was killed, Armstrong walked on the moon, Richard Nixon resigned and a cowboy actor became President.

But competition from mega-chain corporate businesses, society's fast-paced, ever-changing lifestyles, increased government taxation and a decline in the number of loyal customers all combined to hit Stanley's Newsstand hard, forcing it to close on August 16, 1996.

The narrow, friendly storefront—opened in 1919 by A.F. Stanley—was operated by the family for 77 years. The back office contains mountains of records and the walls are covered with framed antique photographs of the store and downtown Elkton, the way it used to be, during better days.

In the end, the founder's two grandchildren—Philip J. Stanley and Debbie Storke—were forced to shut off the lights, lock the door, and walk away from Elkton's Main Street, for the very last time.

Silently and slowly, another Delmarva landmark—that affected the lives of so many in a very good way—followed the worn path taken by so many other small family businesses . . . and disappeared.

Philip J. 'Phil' Stanley, 44
Debbie Storke, 45

Owners and Operators
Stanley's Newsstand
From 1919 to 1996
Elkton, Maryland

"I've been here about 32 years, started when I was 11, doin' paper routes. We delivered the whole town of Elkton, I had one of 11 paper routes. It was all the area newspapers that were handled—the Wilmington papers, Philadelphia Inquirer and the Bulletin, the Ledger, the Baltimore Sun and the News-American. A lot of them are gone now. We're talking thousands of papers that were delivered. Sundays, I couldn't even tell you how many thousands of papers were delivered here.

"I started out at 4 in the morning. On Sundays I got done at 1 in the afternoon. I started out with bags, then I had a bike with a big basket. When I was able to drive, I was in the truck.

"Pop, that was John Stanley, and our Uncle Arthur, both had trucks, and they would drive on the Sunday routes. They worked out of the front of the truck and I jumped out the back door. I had a chair in the back. It was the old Ford Econoline van.

"Most people don't know, but our grandfather, A.F., was a real tobacconist. He made his own cigars. There was even a brand named 'Stanley's New Puff.' We still got one of the boxes. It's pretty fragile.

"Since we took over, I was the one who opened up here in the mornings, usually about five minutes late. But, 'cause I was the boss and the only one here, there was nobody who was gonna fire me.

"The enjoyable part of the business was the customers who came in and wanted to talk, even to me personally. Came from all over the county, really. They could have gone a few places other than here, but they didn't. We had that personal service, I guess. We didn't really go out of our way, it was just the way it was, the way we did things. I guess you can say we're losing a lot of good friends.

"We had a lot of regulars. If we didn't know them by name, we knew an awful lot by face and by what they bought. With about half of them, we'd share information. I sorta know my history about Elkton, of course my father was president of the historical society, plus he was mayor, so he knew the town well. With the paper routes, I knew every street and house. At one time, I had all the paper routes. People come in and ask me history, and where to find this and that all the time.

"I rarely get out of here, but I went to Florida a couple years ago, 'cause my cousin took me. I ran into not one, but a couple people that I knew. They said, 'Whatta you doin' down here?' I said, 'Same reason you're down here.' But it doesn't matter where you are, you run into somebody. I've even been down to Oriole games and people know me. Most of the time you don't even know their name, but you still speak. That's the way we were brought up.

"We've had a lot of wild things happen in here. Had a lady one time come in here and throw up all over my pens. I mean all over them, thousands of pens. Then, she just walked out the door, like nothing. I mean, it was a mess, and I had to clean it all up.

"Then, another time, on a winter Sunday morning, had a good many customers. And we hear this thump, bang at the front door. We looked out, and a man fell down, slipped on the ice, caught hisself against the front door. His toupee came off. He got up, grabbed his toupee, slapped it on. And when he slapped it on, he had the part goin' across his forehead instead of down the side. He came on in, and we're all under the counter laughin'. We couldn't wait on him. And the other customer says, 'OOPS! Man fell down. OOPS! Man lost his head. OOPS! Here he comes.' All those words. I didn't think I was gonna make it. I crawled under the counter. I think I busted both my sides laughing. Holy Mackerel! And he came in like nothing happened, grabbed his papers and walked right out. We must have a hundred stories about this place.

"But, you just can't compete anymore. Every 7-11, you name it, and all of them, WaWa—they're in my business. They sell my newspapers. And you can't compete any more with the stationery. You got Staples and Office Depot. They sell all of it cheaper than we can even buy it for wholesale.

"Everything we sell, the profit margin is small. But we could see it coming, with the malls and things. I don't think we saw the superstores coming, though. The only small businesses that will probably survive are the little Ma and Pa operations, where they live right in the back, or overhead. The old city style, where they're right there 24 hours a day.

"And the paperwork, it's just horrendous. It just goes up and up. There must be six times as much as there was 10 years ago. I tell you what I learned, we're paying taxes on tax, taxes on taxes. We thought of other things that we could do in here, to keep going, but it would still be havin' to be here nine days a week. We're just victims of a changing lifestyle.

"I'm going to miss the whole place, all of it. I been here 32 years doing this. I got to put it behind me. Of course, I was lucky I found this good job at Rodel. It's got the benefits.

"I know when we close, I won't see Main Street anymore. I'll have no reason to come down here. But, we can be proud. We built a name up, and we're going to close and take the name with us."

Phil Stanley   July 24, 1996

"Our grandfather, A.F. Stanley, had a brother who owned a newsstand over in New Jersey. He's the one who helped him get started in the business. You'll find that almost any Elktonian, I'm gonna say between 40 and 50, probably had their first job here as a paperboy. There were so many papers delivered, they couldn't bring them in the store. They had to assemble them out on the front sidewalk, in the late '50s and '60s.

"When they went to purchase a new vehicle, which wasn't very often, they had to make sure the windows were such that they could pitch the paper and it would go out the window. So it would go where they wanted it to go.

"The routes, they started to go out after our uncle died in around 1969. But I didn't have paper routes, I was just the emergency person, in case somebody didn't show up. I really came in here as a clerk, when I was about 14, I guess. We had a big soda fountain that went across the whole side of the store, with ice cream, milkshakes. I worked it more than Phil did.

"I would come in after school and went until about 9 or 10 at night. A lot of Elktonian teenagers did that, worked here at the counter. A lot of kids were employed here. We had a lot of employees really. Now, Phil and I are here, and Phyllis—she's been with us up front for about 10 years—and my son Michael is helping me out this summer. Our mother, Helen, does some of the bookwork.

"Phil and Pop took the soda fountain out in the '70s, when the health department came in and told Pop he had to wear a hair net, and he was bald. That's the truth. Then they said the bathroom door had to open a certain way. Little things that were too much bother. Pop worked in here until the end, when he was 68.

"We've met generations of people here. It was nice, working with the clientele, meeting with the people, personalities and working with the public.

"We had them come from Kennedyville, down in Maryland, and up in Oxford, Pennsylvania. We have a pretty large calling from both directions, Galena and down that way, Earleville. We have a fair amount of customers from that end of the country. They'd get oddball newspapers, like The New York Times, oddball magazines that you don't just pick up anywhere. We were a full line newsstand. We carried everything. They couldn't find the things they wanted between here and either one of those places.

"I'd have to say the business is in our blood. We were raised with Pop working seven days a week. I guess our whole family life was planned around this store. There's even a smell. We have it, especially at the front door, of the pipe tobacco and candy. We have people come in and just say, 'I love the way this smells.' When we open up in the morning, after it's closed up all night, is the only time we really notice it, 'cause we're here so much.

"I remember, Pop has always taught us that you never talk about anybody up front, because nine times out of 10 they'll be standing there. And that is 100 percent true. It's happened many a time, but you have to get caught doing it two or three times before you stop. We've had so many good memories and funny things that have happened. I'll always remember them.

"We had been talking about closing for a couple years. We never expected it to be easy, but we learned that the middle man's got a rough job. A lot of people have asked us what they could do to keep us here, but we didn't make a rash decision. There were a lot of things involved. The town has changed, but it's not just the town, it's all towns. Economic conditions have changed and retailing has changed greatly. Everything is sort of mall oriented. You go to the mall and everything is there.

"Benefits was the big thing. Phil didn't have insurance working here. I have coverage, 'cause my husband works at Acme. Phyllis' husband works for Chrysler. Phil had to pay for his own. It was impossible to find affordable health insurance. Whatever he made in here, he paid out of his pocket for his Blue Cross.

"After they heard we were closing, the nice people, they came in and said they're sorry we're leaving and they wish us the best. And they've been thanking us for being here. Then the other half say: 'What am I going to do without you?' And they haven't been here in five years.

"We had a lawyer from up the street come in and ask if there was anything he could do for us. Paul Schneider from the Swiss Inn came over and gave us free dinners. It was very nice, understanding. I was just totally surprised and touched. Some are genuinely going to miss us, I honestly feel that. "Well, I'll miss the routine of knowing what I'm doing every day, because I've done it for so long. Neither one of us know how to act with a day off. Usually, on a day off we're in here. Not having the responsibility or worrying about the place when we're not here, because it's always on your mind. And I'll miss seeing a lot of good friends that we've made, who I really don't think I'll see quite as frequently."

Debbie Stanley Storke   July 24, 1996

Bill Horleman, 65

Disc Jockey

WDEL-AM

From 1958 to 1996

Wilmington, Delaware

Disc Jockey

Bill Horleman was king of radio's airwaves during morning drive time in northern Delaware throughout the 1960s and '70s. His relaxed style and easy-listening music on WDEL-AM was a welcome wake-up call for thousands of faithful, daily listeners. Although he's been off the air since March of 1996 and officially retired, he's often stopped in stores and on sidewalks by lifelong fans, whose ears recognize the sound of their old friend's voice. When that happens, they often pause to tell him how much they enjoyed his show.

A Delaware native, Horleman entered radio in the late 1950s, long before FM stations became a major player in the entertainment medium. He worked, and thrived, during a time when station DJs were considered local personalities. They also stayed for many years at one station and established deep personal roots in their communities.

Today, radio, like everything else, has changed. Programs are more structured and formats are more rigid. Since most local stations are linked to national networks, they must adjust their schedules to coincide with the timing of news, stock reports and syndicated programming. In medium to larger-sized markets, the emphasis is on young, similar-sounding voices that have no trace of local color or distinguishable accent.

Hometown news, folksy conversation and spontaneous individuality are becoming rare. Ratings and advertising rule, and the personal relationship between a DJ and audience seems only to exist in smaller, out-of-the-way stations in special corners of the airwaves.

But, if you're lucky, you can still turn your dial and discover a reminder of radio's earlier days: when DJs were not ruled by the network clock, when voices didn't have that I-come-from-everywhere-but-nowhere tone, when they talked comfortably about their kids' birthdays, when they knew how to pronounce the names of the towns where their listeners live, when DJs had been on the air longer than you've been listening to the station.

"*I went to night school in Philadelphia for two years, after I got out of the Navy on the GI Bill, for radio and TV broadcasting. While I finished school, I worked for Atlas and had a part time job on weekends at WTUX. I played a little music and did the engineering for the Sunday church services and the ethnic broadcasting. I used my time off looking for a full-time radio job.*

"*After two years in Havre de Grace, Maryland, I got an offer to come to WAMS in Wilmington. I was there a month and they fired me. They said I just didn't have it, and suggested I get into another business. I was a little shocked at the time. I'd never been fired before. The same day, I went home and called Dick Aydelotte at WDEL. Luckily, he had heard me on the air, and said they were looking for someone to fill-in for a part-time fellow who did the weekends and the summertime schedule. He was going to Europe.*

"*They hired me, but they couldn't guarantee any work after the summer. I said, 'I'll take whatever work I can get now.' When the guy came back I was very lucky, because they decided to put in WDEL-FM. So they needed more staff and I was already there. I had been an on-air, fill-in, doing all the different schedules when people went on vacations. It was good experience. So I started working for WDEL-FM, six days a week from 6 at night to midnight, playing show tunes and operas. I was single and my night off was Tuesday night, so it wasn't very good for my social life. Tuesday night was a great night for girls washing their hair, or they'd have to bowl or something.*

"*After four or five years, I heard the morning guy on AM didn't want to do it anymore. At the time, in the early '60s, they were Number 1, everybody listened to WDEL in the morning back then. I kept bugging the boss, Harvey Smith, the station manager, to give me a shot at the morning. They finally gave me a chance and everything went great. So I had the spot from about the early '60s to the late '80s. I guess I did the morning show about 30 years, until FM really became popular. They figured they couldn't beat FM, because of its stronger power, and they decided music wasn't the answer. That's why they changed the format and went to talk shows. They figured that's how AM could compete. My type of broadcasting went by the boards.*

"*But I had been there so long, they didn't say, 'Thanks a lot. Good bye.' They were nice enough to let me do what I could do within their format. I knew it wasn't anything personal. It was just business. Our ratings were just not as good as they were in our heyday. They felt changes had to be made. I wasn't insulted.*

"*I always felt that my best kind of broadcasting was associating one-on-one with the listener, having them call me and talk to me. I'd always interject things about my family, and I'd hear about their families. The new style just wasn't my cup of tea. The fellow doing the show now does a very good job. He does news, weather, sports, interviews. It's much more restricted, the broadcasting you do now. You do this and this and this at a certain time. Much more structured. There's not really very much of a surprise in the programming, you know what's coming up all the time.*

"*I had music to draw from based on the type of easy listening music our station played. I would give a personal touch to things. I'd play a hymn in the morning, about 6:30. People would like a little touch of religion, then I invented a character called "Herkimer." I would get a tape and plug in his lines and we'd have a semi-spontaneous conversation on the air, with myself in the form of this elf, who was Herkimer. It became very popular, people enjoyed it. They would call up and ask 'Where's Herkimer today?' I even gave him a girlfriend. After a while, it got kind of old and I let him just fade away.*

132

"There was a tremendous amount of the individual DJ's personality reflected in radio programming before. Perhaps it was a little corny, and I tried to avoid being too corny, but every time my kids would have a birthday I would play some of their comments on the air. The night before, at home, I would ask them questions and kids would say funny things. Then I'd put them on a cassette and play them for the audience. People would associate me with my kids. They'd call and tell me how they felt. My audience liked that.

"We didn't do as many remotes back then. Now, it's every week today. Of course, you had bigger equipment to lug around back them. We did some remotes at Concord Mall and Wanamaker's. We'd have a whole setup of a studio right there in the mall—turntables, commercials, recordings. People would stand there and watch us.

"It's really a weird feeling to have people staring at you while you're broadcasting. You always have to look like you're busy doing something, even when you're playing a song and you have nothing to do at that particular time. We got to know a lot of our listeners that way.

"I'm a big Phillies fan. Every morning I'd announce the scores and moan about them or cheer them on. I had Phillies bus trips three or four times a season. We'd have a contest, or take the mothers one trip, and fathers or elderly on another trip. They'd meet at the station, we'd give them T-shirts and box lunches. We called ourselves Horleman's Hooligans. A lot of people still come up and say they went on those trips with me.

"We had an easy listening format, and would play the artists that our audience liked, Sinatra, Vic Damone, Peggy Lee. It was nice I happened to like that music, too. It was the music of my day. I don't understand the popular music of today.

"People wonder if I met any of the singers whose music I played. That didn't happen too often, but I did meet a lot of famous people. Along with the morning show, I did an interview show called 'Emphasis Delaware.' It used to be that every time a star would come into Valley Forge Music Fair, we'd give away free tickets. There would be a luncheon at Wanamaker's in Philadelphia, and they would invite all the press to promote the appearance, and the star would be there for an interview, and I'd use the excerpts for my show.

"I met John Wayne. He was plugging 'The Shootist,' his last movie. Four or five reporters would be at each table, and he would come around to each group and sit and talk for a few minutes.

"Joan Crawford was very interesting, she was plugging a book. It was around Christmas time. Two weeks later, I got a card from her at my home address, thanking me for the interview. I found out later that she was a fanatic about her fans. No matter how small the person was that she met—from an elevator operator to a person who interviewed her—she had someone find out who they were and get an address and she sent them a thank-you note.

"Well, her Christmas card had her address in New York City, so I sent her back a Christmas card, and she sent back a thank-you note for the Christmas card. She apparently always had to be one up on the fans. We kept a lot of those cards from her.

"I got Bob Hope's autograph. Barbara Eden from 'I Dream of Jeannie.' Soupy Sales in his heyday. I saw Tony Bennett at a luncheon and O.J. Simpson. A wide range. I enjoyed that a lot. I never got to meet Sinatra, though. I would have loved that.

"I started playing 45s, then went to LPs, then to cassettes. Now it's CDs. I resisted buying a CD player for many years. When I left WDEL, one of the gifts they gave me was a CD player with some CDs.

"I like this business. I think I liked being able to express myself on the air to people, and hearing from them. I've always said, when I talked to classes of kids on career day, that the most important thing in your life is doing what you like doing—even if perhaps you could make more money doing something else that you hate, because you spend three quarters of your life at your job. And if you're miserable in your job, you're going to be miserable in your life.

"Today, the radio work is technically much harder, and I think FM made a big difference in the programming. I never looked so far ahead that I saw the dramatic changes. I thought I would continue doing what I liked doing, in my style, until I retired.

"News people are the big guns now. Except for them, it's just having someone sit on the board and bring in the network programming. If you're going to have Gordon Liddy come in for two hours, push a button and he talks, play the commercials, push a button and you're back to Gordon Liddy again. It's still a bit more personal on FM, but even there they do a lot of commercials and a lot of long strings of five or six songs together. They say the station that plays the most music is the most popular, so they don't talk. I don't think the business is as personalized as it used to be.

"Making that one phone call, on the same day I was fired from WAMS, affected my whole life. What was rare is having worked for nearly 40 years in radio. But radio is such a vagabond life, so to work at the same radio station, and in your hometown, for 36 years, is almost unheard of. I don't think anybody will ever work at one radio station for as long as I did. And WDEL was a great place to work. I enjoyed the people.

"I really enjoyed getting up in the morning and going to work. To tell you the truth, I never really knew how popular I was, how many people listened to my show, until I quit. I knew we were Number 1, but I never thought of asking for more money or making any demands, because I was very happy doing what I was doing. I was very successful at WDEL, but I didn't bring them up from nothing. They were Number 1 when I came, and I was lucky to keep them Number 1.

"During the last few years, the type of broadcasting I used to do did not fit. I adapted myself to punching up the computers for commercials and talk shows. I'd run the board and bring the news in when it had to be done. Punch the right buttons, more of an engineering type role, as opposed to on-air work.

"In the end, the only time I was heard was doing station breaks and perhaps the weather, something like that. Perhaps if I'd been playing music, as I enjoyed doing, I don't even know if I would have retired, but it was a good time to go."

WM Horleman

Bill Horleman   July 27, 1996

Steam Show

During summer and into fall throughout much of Delmarva, farm folks, individual collectors, hobbyists and dealers show off their antique steam and gas machinery at organized, big-time exhibitions and at smaller area events.

From Easton and Federalsburg to Duck Creek in Smyrna, participants and visitors get a taste of what it was like when steam engines pumped water and wheat threshers did the work that sophisticated combines do today.

Since 1981, a more family-style gathering has taken place near Milford, at Horace and Norma Potter's place. On the fourth weekend in June, their Hickory Ridge Antique Farm show annually draws a growing crowd of family, friends and visitors to the Potters' five-acre spread.

As demonstrators make brooms, create baskets and cane chairs, passers-by—eating tasty homemade pies from Potters' country kitchen—get a concentrated glimpse of farm life as it was, not too long ago.

Displays of far away license plates and fancy, polished antique automobiles attract some, while others are amazed by the large collections of Indian arrowheads, old-fashioned penknives and miniature steam machinery.

Children enjoy the haywagon and stagecoach rides, and young men line up for a chance to toss bales of barley in the 1918 Red River Special thresher. After supper, live country music fills the air, and though most are happy to sit and talk, some are moved to kick up their heels.

Beside overnight campers and under outbuildings and temporary tents, participants spend the evenings renewing old friendships and relaxing in a world far removed from personal computers, fast food restaurants and anti-lock breaking systems.

Horace, 57, and
Norma Davis Potter, 51

Founders and Organizers
Hickory Ridge Antique Farm Show
From 1981 to Present
Milford, Delaware

"*I* grew up on my father's farm, near Felton. It was about 200 acres, back in the '50s, with dairy cows and corn and soybeans, so I got farmin' in my blood. We went over to Federalsburg, to that farm show, that's the Eastern Shore Threshermen's, about three or four years. I didn't have anything here then, only one tractor. That was the one my father had. We just had it for the garden.

"So my wife said, 'You oughta buy one of these old tractors.' So I went to the sale and bought one, an Allis-Chalmers W.C. 1934. And we fixed it up, redone it, painted it. Workin' on a farm, you kinda pick that up, too. We took it to Federalsburg in the '70s, and then went back every year. Display it over there, just like the people do over here.

"Then we started buyin' a little bit more, little bit more, and went to sales, and this is what we ended up with. Right now, I got 32 tractors and about 300 pieces of equipment. Everywhere. I had to build some new buildings to keep them in, and I have some in storage down the road here that I keep.

"We have gasoline engines, bunch of those. Lots of toys, farm toys, related farm items . . . corn shellers, feed grinders, corn meal grinders, a broom makin' machine, strawberry cup makin' machine, miniature sawmill, even some hog oilers. We have a lot of antique farm tools that are used on the farm. You pick up a lot over the years. You can always still learn somethin' along the way from all of them.

"I bought these over the last 20 or so years, at different places, farm sales mostly. Once in a while you run up on a collector that wants to sell somethin'. We go up to Pennsylvania, to that farm show every year, in Kinser, right on Route 30. In Amish country. Seems like every year we pick up something up there. I truck it back, and if it's a big piece, I get a bigger truck to haul it back.

"Once you start collectin', seems like you never stop. Keeps right on goin'. Got the bug right, I guess. It's sorta like a private museum.

"A few times, not too often, I'll just pull in a someone's yard. Don't even know the man, and say, 'I see you have an old piece of equipment down the yard,' and he'd say, 'Yeah!' Then I'll say, 'You gonna do anything with it?' and he'll say, 'No. Not likely.' I'll ask if he's interested in sellin' it, and a lot of times they are. Most of the time we get together, and I end up with it. Then once in a while, someone will donate something to us, for the farm show.

"The first Hickory Ridge Antique Farm Show was in 1981. I'm not really sure how it got started. I recall we were gettin' a few pieces of equipment together. We got a wheat thrasher, the big Nichols and Shepherd Red River Special. That's a top of the line. And when we got some more equipment, I told my wife, 'I'd like to have our own show,' and she said, 'You're crazy!' So the next year, we decided we were gonna have one.

"We had about 50 to 75 people here. Only about a half a dozen set ups. We did thrash wheat the first year, and a couple people brought tractors, but it wasn't many, 'cause it wasn't really advertised. Just word of mouth. The next year we made up posters and sent out invitations. People started comin'. And this year we had over 150 people that brought equipment here or had displays.

"That's a lot for a small place. We had 88 tractors, 32 of them are mine. That Huber is from around 1927, some older than that, all they way up to the 1960s. I try to redo one tractor every winter. I spend a lot of time with them, practically live with them. Get to know them pretty good, how each one starts different than the other.

"Most of all these companies are all gone. McCormick, Allis-Chalmers, Twin City, FarmAll, the Oliver, they're out of business. John Deere is the only one that's held her own name. All the others have merged. People come here and never heard of some of these names.

"We have a 102-year-old wheat thresher that was out here that day. That's a Champion, it's all wood. We use it every year since we had the show. The people, they bring their lawn chairs and sit and watch it operate.

"We don't charge anything. We're not into it to make any money. We enjoy meeting the people, and a lot of people like to come here, visit, and bring their campers and stay for the weekend. It don't cost them a thing, only if they buy somethin' to eat. They can come here, set up their table and have a good time. No charge, just like gatherings in the old days, the way they used to.

"A lot of the people who come know each other. They go from show to show and meet. And the one's that come here, they want the same spot they had last year. There's no problem, one will save it for the other one.

"When they come in we help them get set up, unload their equipment. We have the openin' ceremony at 10 o'clock, where we play the National Anthem and raise the flag, on Saturday and Sunday. On Sunday morning they play church music.

"We meet a lot of nice people. We never had any problem with anyone. People call up and ask to be in it. We have a lot of people that call and offer to help get it ready, mow grass, move equipment, put down fresh sawdust.

"People are always askin' what something does. We try to explain to them what it does and how it works. It's satisfyin'. I guess as long as the people like to come to it, and keep comin' like they did this year, and as long as our health stays good, we'll keep havin' it. Be lost now probably without it.

"When it's over, we help them load back up when they get ready to leave. Shake hands, say, 'See ya next time, or at the next show.' "

Horace Potter   July 25, 1996

Horace Potter beside his 1920s-era Huber tractor

"*This all grows on you after a while. Of course, I was raised on a farm, right over across that cornfield. This all started out as a hobby, now it's a bigger hobby. Horace grows more than two acres of barley before the show weekend, so they can toss it in the thresher. We also call the local dealers and let them bring their new equipment to display.*

"*On Saturday night we have live country music. We've had the Country Diamonds for the last few years, everybody seems to like them. People dance and listen and eat and talk. They'll stay up past midnight.*

"*This year, some of the people came with their campers on Thursday night and stayed until Sunday. A lot of them ask for the broom man and the basket man. It's for all ages. For children, we have a pedal tractor pull on Saturday morning.*

"*My family and his family all helps with servin' the food. My sister-in-law, Charlotte Davis, made 48 pies and 58 apple dumplin's. We serve breakfast in the mornin's. The people come up and eat and talk. We have four generations helpin' us in the kitchen the last couple years.*

"*We give plaques each year to the exhibitors in honor of someone. This year, it was in memory of my father, Jehu Davis Sr., who helped us so much. He passed away in February at 91.*

"*It takes us all summer to get ready, and then more time to get things cleaned up and put away. After it's over with, you don't want to get into it too soon. You're tired and seem to want to take your time.*

"*We get a lot of nice compliments. And people seem to enjoy sittin' out in the grove. There's always a nice breeze. This is a way of keepin' the old machinery and ways goin' so the younger generation can see how it was, because they don't know how it was done a hundred years ago.*

"*Every once in a while I say, 'I think we might not have it next year,' and people say, 'You can't give it up!' One time, I mentioned that I might want to get an organization to come in and do the food. My family said, 'What would we do, stand around and look at one another?' They enjoy it, and I don't have to call them and ask them. They just say when is it and they're here. It's almost like a family reunion.*

"*I never thought it would get this big. That first year, a fella from Harrington, Jack Short, said that this could really turn into something. I didn't believe him. Now I do.*"

Norma D. Potter

Norma Potter   July 25, 1996

Larry Compton, 78, and
F. Burgess Tucker, 71

Chairman and Co-chairman
Wesley Chapel Fish Fry
From 1961 to Present
Rock Hall, Maryland

Fish Fry

Go to Rock Hall, Maryland, on the last Friday in August and you'll witness an Eastern Shore institution: the Wesley Chapel Fish Fry. Ignore the modern automobiles parked around the church grounds and you are treated to a glimpse of the past: volunteers—from children who work as runners, to middle-aged fish fryers to senior citizen biscuit patters, cooks and crab cake makers—all working together.

Old-fashioned, Dutch-oven griddles rest atop blazing wood bonfires. As hot orange flames lick the sides of black iron pots and dented frying pans, fresh bread bakes and hot fish sizzles. Groups of church members, seated under tents, converse, gossip and laugh as they pat the dough to keep the biscuits coming.

Youngsters carry messages from the hall to the fields, ordering more fish, checking out the status of the bread and delivering cold drinks to hot workers. Other volunteers exit the church hall, ferrying empty trays toward the cooks, who pile them high with seafood.

All this activity serves the long line of visitors who arrive for a traditional, Eastern Shore meal.

Inside the coolness of the church hall, diners smile as they view the buffet table, featuring assorted pies, rolls, salads and, of course, seafood—all fresh and homemade.

When the event started in 1961 in a church member's yard, fish and crab meat were donated by area fishing crews.

For the last 35 years, the summer gathering and income for the church has grown, but the organizers stressed that increased "fellowship" is the most important product of the annual summer event.

"*I* guess I've been involved with it since it started. I remember helping park cars in the beginning, but I've been more active since 1970 on, but mainly as a volunteer. It started as a fundraiser at a church member's house, up at Miss Addie Jacquette, about a mile up the road from the church. I don't expect we had over two or three hundred people come to it. It was in the yard and parking was limited. It was there about 10 years, then they moved over to the shipyard, at Jim Buck's, who had a farm on the water—big yard, plenty of room. It kept growing, steady.

"I'd say our peak was three years ago, when we had about 1,500 people come to the fry. There's a good number of workers. Some of them just come up to help fry fish. They aren't even from our church.

"Our workers range anywhere from 6 to those in their 80s. But the majority are probably in their 50s and 60s. That means it's gonna peter out after a while. This is a community affair. We have help from the other two churches in Rock Hall. The Seventh Day Adventist people bake pies. This year, the banks and different stores in the area had people come up and help out, which is a big help to us.

"We have other people help us in different ways. Some watermen who have ice makers for their business will donate ice to us. One year, a local seafood retailer loaned us a refrigeration unit. Different organizations let us use things. Some families grow vegetables that they donate. We couldn't make it if we didn't have the help of the community. We couldn't do it with just the people from Wesley Chapel.

"A lot of the fellows who fry the fish are fishermen, and they've been doing this for years. Some have their own family fish frys. They're very common here during the summer. Now, when volunteers come in new, we have to help them get started.

"The fellowship we get out of this is wonderful. It's one of the highlights of everything that goes on in the church. People meet people here every year. They see their families and friends. The fellowship is worth more than the money that is raised from it.

"We see people we haven't seen since the last fish fry. We had one fellow from Baltimore, Mr. Spriggs, who would come every year and he'd buy 75 to 80 dinners. He paid for them, took them back home and gave them away. This is the first year he missed. He's in a nursing home now. He had a summer home over here. Lived here a month every summer. He came to church, got acquainted with everybody and would come over for the fish fry.

"I like the fellowship involved in getting it ready and working together, then seeing the people come. I guess I just like being a part of it. We have some guys who can't come out during the day to help, because of work or whatever. But they come out at night to help us with the clean up. And the majority of the guys who work here and are members of the church will stay here all night until the clean up is done.

"I consider it part of the church, but it's part of ourselves and something that's being taken away, because of less help, the passing of time, not enough people, or whatever. But if we ever think of stopping, the tradition kind of peps us up, I guess, to make an extra effort to keep it going. I'd like to think it will go on for a while."

F. Burgess Tucker

November 9, 1996

Past Chairman

"*In the beginning, the beauty about it was that the members of the church donated the fish and crabs. Mr. Hilton Crouch and his whole fishing crew, they were sand haulers, had nets out in the bay. When they caught the small fish that they couldn't sell, they would clean them on the way back in. Then they'd freeze them and give them to us for the church fish fry.*

"Years ago, watermen would donate bushels of crabs to us during the summer, and we'd get the women to come up here and pick them out and then freeze the meat for the crab cakes. Later, a man named Jessie Downey bought crabs and donated them to us. Now, we buy the crab meat already picked. We don't have the people to pick it any more. But we come here a few weeks before and will sit down for four hours a night and make crab cakes.

"We'll have probably 40 people here, working on crab cakes. We get 400 to 450 pounds of crab meat, and we made 3,200 crab cakes last year. We fried about 1,000 pounds of filets.

"To many, the fish fry was considered a homecoming for the church, but gradually it's gotten away from that. Now, it's seen as more of a fundraiser. That's what it started out to be, but it's more so now, since we don't have quite as many local people coming as we do people from away from here.

"We get people who come from Baltimore, Philadelphia. In 1995, we had eight buses from different areas. That's the most buses we ever had. Some people plan their vacation around this, so they can come back every year.

"We've been lucky, only got rained out one time. We rescheduled it that year, but that didn't work out too well. Now we do it rain or shine. Several times we've had to cook bread and fish in the rain. Outside. Put plywood over the coals of the fires. Put wood over the fish pans and bread pans. If rain hits the inside of one of those hot pans it will crack the metal.

Janet Lee Ashley and James W. Thompson make fresh bread while Gary E. Wilmer works over a hot outdoor oven fire.

"The fish pans were all locally made, and they used to get the bread pans from the prison foundry in Baltimore. More recently, Mr. Hilton Crouch made the bread pans we use now out of old tire rims.

"It's hard work frying the fish. It takes its toll. But we worry more about rain than the heat.

"I was chairman for a lot of years, from about 1980 to recently. Larry is in charge now, but we get together and work closely on it.

"Everybody complains a little about all the work that has to get done, but they're tickled to death, really. If we didn't have it, I bet we'd catch a lot of flack over it. It's something that not every church does. It's something you don't see every day. You're part of it and it makes you feel good.

"We're getting to the point right now where the older people are getting hard pressed to come out here and do it all day long. Fortunately, we still have enough young people coming out to help. But you worry about that day when you won't have enough young people to help and take over.

"As long as you can keep the young people coming out to help, and the community stays with us, we'll keep it going."

Bob Watson   November 9, 1996

Chairman

"Bob Watson had been chairman for 10 years and had a job change, so he couldn't spend the time it would take to keep running the fish fry. I was chairman of the board of the church, and he asked me to get someone to take his place. I went to six others and no one wanted to be chairman. But they said they'd all help. So, I was left holding the bag.

"I formed a committee of five, assigned jobs to them and split up the work. This made it easier for them and for me. As chairman, it's not that big of a job, just fill the slots as people die, disappear or move.

"It isn't that difficult, but I will tell you that I've found that a lot of our volunteers are getting older, and there aren't a lot of younger ones coming along. We can see the day when it will be difficult to continue the fish fry.

"Sometimes, when there are a hundred or so volunteers running around, I pause and try to take it all in. A lot of people would see the fish fryers and biscuit bakers and biscuit patters, and those people deep frying the crab cakes. But what I see is all these people having a fantastic time, laughing and joking. I don't see a dour expression on one of them. They're all just having the time of their life, and that's what it's all about—the fellowship—not only during the event, but over the four weeks before and as we prepare the food and collect the things we need.

"Working together and sharing in the fellowship, the way it's been done for all these years, is our true satisfaction."

Larry Compton   December 9, 1996

Clog Dancer

When Frankie Bartsch was very young, he used to accompany his grandparents to gas and steam engine shows throughout the peninsula. At the age of 8 years, he saw some Appalachian style cloggers dancing at the annual Tea Party Celebration in Chestertown, Maryland, and knew immediately it was what he wanted to do.

For the last 14 years, he's been entertaining audiences throughout the peninsula with his fancy footwork, featuring combinations of such steps as the bee, flea, frog, Alamo, big kick, Indian and North Carolina Triple. In the midst of a fast moving routine he'll toss in a chug (which imitates the sound of a chugging train) a few hand hits, several hitches (where he jumps to the side as heels hit together) and one or two Russians (both legs wide and up off the ground with both hands touching his toes).

According to the book *How To Do Appalachian Clogging*, it began when a mixture of Irish, Scotch, English and African styles were combined with American Indian dances a few hundred years ago.

The result was named buck dancing or flat-footing, because the performers kept their feet close to the floor. Later, as clogging developed, more involved and visual steps, jumps and turns were added.

Today, Frankie, who's won several awards for his skill, does most of his dancing solo. But, he said, it bothers him a bit that it doesn't look like there's anyone waiting in the wings to learn his traditional style of dance and carry it on after he's gone.

Frankie Bartsch Jr., 22

Clog Dancer

From 1982 to Present

Townsend, Delaware

"*Clogging is hard on your feet, because of the stomping. With tap dancing you hit it lighter. I use tap shoes, for the sound and because it's almost impossible to get clogging shoes made out of wood. They have to be especially fitted and made just for you.*

"*There's a few stories about how cloggin' got started. In Ireland, they say the church used to tell the people they couldn't dance. And the priest would look in the windows of people's homes. So they used to keep their upper bodies stiff and straight, so he wouldn't notice that they were moving their feet real fast.*

"*In England, they say the people who worked in the factories would be wearing wooden shoes and would be dancing while they worked, but they would imitate the sound of the machinery.*

"*Around here, some of the neighbors would get together and have a party, or a pig roast. Some of the fellows would start plucking a banjo or a fiddle and bass guitar. Then they would be up shuffling their feet. That's how it started out. I saw it done at the Chestertown Tea Party. I said to myself, 'Gee. I think I can do that.' We already had a lot of bluegrass music and I just got up and started shuffling my feet. Then I took some lessons in Queen Anne's County and some tap lessons down in Dover, then just started cloggin'.*

"*I mostly dance by myself and use a tape player, but a live band is a lot better. Most cloggers love to dance with a live band—with a banjo and fiddle and bass guitar.*

"*I never plan. I just go all out and do it. I throw the steps together. My dance is whatever I feel like at the time. With bluegrass, you sort of do as you feel. But the audiences seem to like it. And no dance is exactly the same. If the crowd gets into it, then I try to do the high stuff, like the Russian and hitch kicks.*

"*I usually start fast. I slow the middle down. And I speed it up at the end, 'cause that's what the crowd remembers. In the end of 'Orange Blossom Special' it really kicks. And I try to come back really fast with it and make it special.*

"*Sometimes the crowd gets to clapping. That's what keeps me going. That's why I love to do it, for the reaction from the crowd. Down at the Georgetown Hoedown, when I was 14, there must have been a thousand people in the audience. When I got done, I knew I gave it everything I got.*

"*I was dancing on a wooden deck at the Kitty Knight House, with a band, and the people loved it. They kept going, 'One more! Just do one more!' They were trying to kill me, but I kept going. It's like an emotional high, like you're addicted to the people clapping.*

"*I've danced at the Chestertown Tea Party since I was 8. The Pedantics, from Washington, they are there every year. There used to be 12 of them, but there are only four left now. They do something called the 'Hot Dog,' where they call everybody who clogs to come up with them. Then, we each go out and do the steps we do best. And they encourage young kids to get up and start clogging.*

"*That's how I got started. At the time I just had tennis shoes. But every year I got a little better. My grandparents were great. They'd encourage me to do it when I was little. My Pop Pop Bartsch made sure my cleats were tight and fixed up my board that I carried with me. He even came up with the idea of making it hollow inside, to get a better sound when I danced.*

"*I have certain fans at the Tea Party who know me. They'll come up and ask if I'm going to dance that year. One man told me I had the fastest feet he'd ever seen. It made me feel real good. I think people love to see action and movement. Deep inside, everybody wants to be up on the stage dancing.*

"I like clogging because I can do it well and it's easy for me. People tend to like what they can do well. At one time, I wanted to do it and go to Nashville or Dollywood and dance every day, but that would probably be bad on your feet and knees.

"So, I go around to nursing homes, events, parties when people call. It lights people up. But I don't see any other cloggers my age. There are a few older people who still do it, less every year though. No one young seems to be taking an interest in it. It's kinda like dying out. And it's not offered in dance studios. I'd like to teach it someday.

"I'm probably the youngest still carrying it on. I'll keep at it until I can't physically do it any more."

Frankie Bartsch Jr.   May 30, 1996

Country Musician

Harry "Lefty" McBride was born in Kent County, Delaware, near Blackston's Crossroads in 1924, one year before the beginning of Nashville's Grand Ole Opry. A lifelong, old-time country music fan, he worked on a farm, in a refrigeration plant, was a self-employed painter, a custodian and managed a pool room. "You can't get any rougher than workin' in a pool hall," he said, laughing.

In 1970, he started giving music lessons on his front porch, on Market Street in Smyrna. He outgrew the place, moved a few blocks, and opened his present, small town music store on North Main Street in 1984.

With racks of sheet music and rows of new and used guitars, Lefty's shop is a picture of the independent music studios that used to exist in nearly every town. Wooden and glass cabinets display Marine Band harmonicas, packs of guitar strings, stacks of drum sticks and even a bunch of old-fashioned Appalachian Jaw Harps, as they're called today.

Those expecting a modern electronic, high-tech sound studio, featuring fog machines, synthesizers and lighting displays, are in for a shock. Lefty's is a walk back to a simpler, more basic musical era, an operating museum complete with an owner who also serves as your real-life tour guide.

Prices are noted on handwritten signs, nothing fancy. It's a comfortable place, where quite a few regulars stop in from time to time, just to say hello, pull a guitar off the rack and try out a new rendition of an old song.

Sitting behind his counter, under an ornate metal ceiling and the slow-rotating blades of a ceiling fan, Lefty McBride is relaxed and content, doing what he likes best—talking country music, reminiscing about the old days, and, even sometimes, picking up his left-handed Martin and playing one of his favorite tunes.

Harry 'Lefty' McBride

Country Musician and Music Shop Owner

From 1949 to Present

Smyrna, Delaware

"*N*obody in my family played music, but they say every time I would get in the car in the 1930s, I would sing the whole time I was ridin'. Then, in 1948, I started to fool with the guitar. About a year later, I formed a band, called Lefty and the Hillbilly Pals. Back then, everybody was called 'hillbilly.'

"We played the honky-tonks all over, within 25 to 30 miles around—Marydel, Sudlersville, Dover, Middletown. Mostly on weekends in small taverns that would let, maybe, 40 to 50 people dance at a time. Remember, there was hardly any TV back then.

"It was five-piece group—lead guitar, background guitar, I played rhythm guitar, and there was a mandolin and fiddle. No drums or bass back then.

"In 1949, we had a radio program. It was on WDOV-AM. They had seven different bands come there and play all day on Saturdays. We was mostly on at 7:30 in the morning, and that's pretty early to try to get up and sing, you know it? That went on about a year, then Mr. Evans, he sold out and the new people, they sort of frowned on hillbilly music. So, that broke up the live shows.

"This happened in the greatest time of country legends, around 1950. We was singin' all Hank Williams Sr., Lefty Frizzell, Marty Robbins. That was a big time for us. We went for about two years and disbanded. There were problems. Some of the guys didn't want to practice. Some would show up late and with a broken string, and I got all the flack. So I just give it up. I didn't need that.

"I played with other bands. Some groups, I think, didn't have a name. They just got together and played. Anybody needed somebody I filled in. Freelancer. In 1970, I just quit playing publicly. I play for family barbecue picnics and jam sessions now.

"I didn't have lessons. I just learned with a book. I'd go over to a friend's house and watch him. Do what he did. Self taught. Determination's what done it, but it took me a year to learn. I guess I opened the shop because of my country roots. Music. If I'd been a mechanic, I guess I woulda opened a garage. But, country music, I just loved it all my life. There was two other music shops in town, but the owners passed away and they closed, so I started giving lessons in 1970.

"A lot of kids would take lessons then. I had around 10 students a week, anywhere from age 6 to teenagers. But it's just like the drive-in movie, how things have changed. Now, I might get one now and then, and just for five or six lessons, before they leave and go on their own. I just taught them to play by ear.

"There were more people interested in music lessons in the 1970s, and that was before VCRs came in. You see, with VCRs they could rent tapes that taught them how to play and learn themselves. Plus, they could rent movies and have something else to do besides music for entertainment.

"I actually started in the hallway of my other house. I had three or four guitars. Then I used my living room. Then I closed the porch in. It was a 7 foot porch by 22. It wasn't very big. When I came here in '84, I had plenty of room. It was like a castle. It seemed like it to me, alongside that 7-foot building.

"I actually done better since I retired, because when I was workin', I was just able to be open at nights, and this town kinda dies after 6 o'clock. Now, I'm open all day long, six days a week, from 10 until 6. I take Sundays for the Lord.

"There aren't many small town music stores around anymore. It's not personal now. You go to a shop, and they've also got computers and stuff like that. Here, I have people come in and just play and *just check 'em out. I talk. I guess you noticed I like to talk. I always been that way. I think the most friendly way you can show a person, when he walks into a place, is that you want to talk to him.*

"I have friends I've made through the years, some of 'em I work with and some of 'em I just know. You've heard of the old country store, well I'm the old country music store. That's about what it amounts to.

"They come in and pick one out and play a few songs and leave. But it's not a jam session. I still play jam sessions, couple times a week. On Sundays I go to Henry's place, out in Golts, Maryland.

"He's got a double car garage, and he takes everything out and has jam sessions. It's out by his house. He clears it out and puts chairs in there. Has music on Sunday afternoons for anybody who wants to come and play. I'd say I been doin' it for about 10 years. You meet old faces. You meet old people. It's 'Hi, Charlie. How you been?' The local music is what it's all about, with me.

"I would rather play to some of these places free, and have a little freedom to play a while, eat a while. I'd rather do that than play for somebody for money and they'd be your boss. Then you do what they tell you to do, how to do it, when to do it. I like the money, too, but it's not that important. I like to play the kind of music I want to play. If I play for nothin', I can do it.

"I don't really have a favorite song. I like all the traditional country songs. Old Hank Williams, George Jones, Merle Haggard. I like all those songs. I would say George Jones would be the favorite, and his song would be 'He Stopped Lovin' Her Today.'

"I got a guitar I bought in 1955. It's a small Martin, triple O-18. Not a great big body that you gotta go outta your way to hug.

"If I was to say there was anything I miss, I'd say I'd like to go back to the '50s. That was a wonderful time. I was in the band. I was 25 years old. Wasn't married. Oh, you know, it was more of a heyday for me. I wouldn't give up my family, or my grandchildren, you understand. But I would go back to the '50s. That would be my favorite time.

"Music was nicer. Mostly three chord songs, and maybe the song books was a little more complicated, but we heard 'em, and we could play 'em with three chord changes and make 'em sound all right.

"We could play some slow songs then, and, I'd say in the '70s, I played with another group at this place one night. We was playing a slow song, like 'Wedding Bells,' and the people, naturally, they was a little tipsy. They'd come up and say, 'Would you stop playin' that funeral

Lefty, in front of his Smyrna music store

music?' But that was the difference. Back in the '50s they'd eat it up. You could play a slow song and get away with it.

"I'm retired from the state, so I guess you'd say I'm semi-retired. I spend eight hours a day in here. If I didn't, I'd be travelin' or lookin' at the walls. You can get tired of that. This way, I can set in here and people come to see me.

"I love music. When I play, it's almost like going back to the good times, almost reliving it over again, except my age, as far as being entertained. It's the old days again. Back in the '40s, people would listen to hillbilly music real low, so their neighbors wouldn't hear. It was like it was from squatters or gypsies. Not accepted. Today, it's country and western and popular all over. Times change.

"I know quite a few people. When I see people from the old days, they'll ask, 'What happened to your black curly hair?' It makes you feel like you been remembered.

"I'll keep the shop as long as I can. I won't give it up as long as the Lord keeps me in good health. As long as I'm able and my health stays good. All I do is come down here, open up, run my mouth. Oh, and I dust once in a while.

"My outlook in life is, as long as you're satisfied with what you're doin', don't change it, because it could get worse.

"I've had fun reminiscing. The older you get, the more you depend on your memories. They can't take them away from you. And the older you get, the more years you have behind you than in front of you."

Harry "Lefty" McBride   July 18, 1996

Marlene with her assistant,
Sir Butler of Sanford

Marlene W. Marshall, 50

Postmaster

From 1978 to Present

Sanford, Virginia

One-Room Post Office

Try to find a real, old-time post office today you'd better be willing to do some searching. Years ago there were plenty of them. Many were small weathered buildings, often standing near the country store. Sometimes, they even shared the same building, and a number of these still exist.

According to Adolph Chiappa, manager of post office operations in Newport News, Virginia, who is responsible for Accomack and Northampton counties, "At one time the Post Offices served their people like grocery stores did. In the days when they were established—when there were no roads and no transportation, and before electrification reached some of the towns in the '30s—it was a necessity. There was a serious need for all these sites then.

"People would get there by horse and buggy, saddle horse or take "shank's mare," Chiappa said, "that means you'd walk."

Each site was an important area for meeting friends and catching up on the latest news. When the automobile and supermarkets came, things changed.

Even though the Eastern Shore doesn't move at as fast a pace as other areas, things aren't like they used to be.

Small country stores have closed, people are more mobile and, Chiappa said, "A lot of people don't have the time to socialize like they used to. Progress is catching up."

In some isolated locations, he said, the Postal Service authorized operations to take place inside private homes.

Today, on the Eastern Shore of Virginia—in an area about 12 miles across and 60 miles long, with a population of about 47,000—there are 51 U.S. Postal Service sites. Of those, only three are in private homes.

Chiappa described the Sanford Post Office, run by Postmaster Marlene Marshall for the last 17 years, as "real small." It measures about 56 square feet—including office and lobby—and was once her utility room. When L. T. Fisher's Grocery Store, which had housed the town's Post Office, closed in 1979, arrangements were made to move the service into the Marshall home.

When in-home offices were established, Chiappa explained, they served a definite need. Using homes saved the Postal Service the costs of constructing a separate building and insured that mail was accessible to small-town residents. But they won't continue to establish new in-house sites any longer. Today, when a postmaster from one of these smallest of sites retires, he said, they will not put the office in another home.

"The Eastern Shore is a unique area," Chiappa said. "During the last 10 years, I've seen an expansion of business up and down Route 13. When I started going over there 15 years ago, there were only two places to eat along the entire stretch in Virginia."

"*This used to be our utility room. My husband opened up the door to the outside and got it ready. The Post Office came in and put in the boxes and the window, and it's been here in the house ever since, and that was in 1979.*

"*I started out being open four hours a day. Then I built it up to six hours. Now, we're open 8 hours a day and half day on Saturdays. I have 124 boxes, and it's the box rent, stamps and money order fees that keep us going. That's what makes your Post Office.*

"*We service about 350 people, in the town and on the outskirts. I have a rural route also. Somebody else delivers, but I have to sort it and get it all ready for them.*

"*Daily, I would say on an average I'll have a hundred people in and out of here. I know them all by name, every one of them. All their family, all their children . . . grandchildren. If an older person doesn't come in for a couple days, I'll just give them a call or just check on them.*

"*We also have a campsite nearby, and a lot of people just have their mail forwarded here. Sometimes, they'll give me their itinerary for the whole summer, and on a certain day I'll forward their mail to Florida, North Carolina. Where I'm small I can do that for them, and they rent boxes here. I'm small, but I can handle any kind of mail you want to send, just as any large Post Office does.*

"*I love it. I just love the benefits. I love the people. I love it being here in my home. I wouldn't go to another Post Office if they paid me $20,000 more a year. We go to meetings with other postmasters, and they tell me they'd give anything to have it in their home. They tell me I have it made and I'm just so fortunate that I don't have to get up and drive somewhere to go to work.*

"*But there's a great amount of responsibility, and we do everything and follow all the regulations that the bigger Post Offices have to do. There have been a tremendous number of changes in the last 18 years, and the mail volume has increased. I'm in that Post Office eight hours a day.*

"*And, sometimes, after hours, people will come up and knock on the house door with a package to mail, or they'll ask me if I can get their package. I had one person call me, I know it was 2:30 in the morning. I was in bed asleep. Wanted to know how much it cost to send a package to so-and-so. Well, I wasn't too polite to them. They said they didn't realize what time it was.*

"*One time, my husband and I were out in the yard stacking wood on a Saturday afternoon, and people wanted their packages. That was my time off, and I just told them we're closed and they understood it. In the beginning, I had the lobby locked. But I told them I'd leave the lobby open if they wouldn't bother me after hours, and it's fine now.*

"*Everyone in town is so nice and they appreciate the one-on-one service. It's not so much a business, it's like I care and it's like they care.*

"*The best part of it all is the people, just getting to know them and their families. Sometimes, they just need someone to talk to, just to express their feelings. If they've had a bad day, they tell you all about it and I just try to listen.*

"*Let me show you my assistant. This is my dog, Sir Butler of Sanford. He keeps an eye out the window. Now, he can't get into the lobby, but when he sees you come in, he may go and stick his nose in your box. He can't get out, but he knows which box is yours. Seriously. And just say I'm in the kitchen, getting a glass of water, he'll come in and bark at me and turn toward the Post Office if someone's come in. Sometimes, he'll grab my arm gently and tell me to come.*

"This Post Office is very important for the town. There are no stores in town, the nearest one is about eight miles from here. People will come in here and ask for change. There's no fire department, no community center. This the focal point of the community. If anyone dies, or whatever, they always want me to know when the funeral's going to be, when the viewing's going to be. Whether they'll accept flowers. I pass it all by word of mouth.

"If there's some kind of function in the community or church, they'll usually ask me what time or about the details. We're like the information center. There are probably about 10 to 15 people out here who meet every morning at a specific time to chat. The lobby's crowded. Cars are lined up outside.

"There used to be a Post Office at Jenkins Bridge, a crossroads, there were hardly any houses. But they closed that maybe seven years ago, so I get some of that business now, too.

"When new people come into the area, they come here and ask where to get groceries, how do you get to Parksley, about the hospitals, doctors, how to get to find the different services.

"When I'm at the window and I see them come in for the first time, it's written all over their faces. They just can't believe that it's in my home and that it's so small. But when they see the service that I give them, they just love it.

"Some campers from Tall Pines Campground will hear about it and come here to see for themselves. They can't believe it's in someone's home. We've been written up once or twice in the papers.

"I'm always at work on time. I'm so thankful I don't have to get up in the snow or bad weather.

"But for the protection of the community, a year or two before I retire, I want to work to get it put in its own building. Because, before, when postmasters retired, they closed places like this. Everything is getting modernized, and I would hate for Sanford to lose its Post Office, because it means so much to the community and to the people.

"I've been in the other, new, big Post Offices. And sometimes I think I would love to have a bigger place with more room, on one hand. One-tenth, I'd love to have it. But the other nine-tenths, I love it just like it is.

"More space I'd like to have, but everything else I want to keep just the way it is. This place is very special."

Marlene W. Marshall

Marlene W. Marshall

December 16, 1996

*Josephine "Pina" Minuti, 80, and
Robin Mabrey, 44*

Mrs. Robino's Restaurant
From 1939 to Present
Little Italy
Wilmington, Delaware

Neighborhood Restaurant

Mrs. Robino's Restaurant is a friendly, family place. You can tell as soon as you walk through the front door of the converted city rowhouse. It seems like it's been there forever. The right side of the wall in the entrance waiting area is filled with framed, autographed photographs of Wilmington and Philly television and sports personalities offering satisfied testimonials about their visits.

Across the top of the opposite wall, near the long bar, are nearly two dozen certificates proclaiming the oldest of Wilmington's Little Italy restaurants as "the best" by readers of *Delaware Today* magazine and the *News Journal Papers*.

The business started in 1939, in a narrow rowhouse on Howland Street where Tersilla Robino began serving her pasta and sauce to Italian immigrants. Word spread about the fine quality of her cooking. Soon, customers were lined up outside, waiting to get in.

In 1940, the family opened the business at the present location, 520 North Union Street. Today, the single dwelling has grown to three times its original size, and the business continues to operate under the direct daily involvement of family members.

Most importantly, in the back corner of the entrance room—beside the swinging door where waiters and waitresses constantly pass with trays full of fresh pasta and salads—sits Mrs. Pina Robino Minuti, daughter of the original Mrs. Robino.

Described as the "true power" behind the restaurant, Pina offers a friendly smile while keeping a watchful eye on the employees and customers who visit her family business that has now entered its fourth generation.

"*I* was in the business from the time it started. I was 24 at the time, and I worked with my mother all the time, making spaghetti and ravioli. Now, I mainly supervise the operation, especially the kitchen.

"A lot of things were different then. We started in the living room with two tables. Every time my mother got a customer, she'd go in the back and roll out the dough, because she didn't know what they were going to order. She used to have people come from St. Anthony's Club and say, 'We're coming down,' and she would stay there and wait for them and make their orders.

"Next we got four tables. Then my father saw this place for sale and we moved here. When we began in here, we only had one rowhouse, not three like today. There were a few tables way down in front. We could fit about 16 people in here with four or five tables. Then my father extended it back further.

"I think it was 1965 when we added the second dining room. The third room, that came around 1980. The business started picking up and we added each room. Now, with the three dining rooms, we can get in around 150. Our kitchen is way bigger than it used to be.

"In the beginning, everything was made by hand. My father, Frank Robino, he put a motor with a belt on the hand crank machine for the pasta, so I wouldn't have to crank it. I did the pasta and my mother did the preparation in the kitchen.

"I used to work from 7 in the morning until about 2 in the afternoon, then come back around 7 at night and go until 2 in the morning. That's when I was young.

"My mother passed away in 1969. I ran the business for the family for a year, and I loved it. That's why I bought it in 1970. Now we're in our fourth generation. My mother, me, my son, Joseph, and his son, Joseph A. Then there's Robin, my niece. She came with the business. Then I have a sister, Mary, who worked in the business since she was 15. We have about a half dozen family members here.

"There were a number of Italian restaurants over the years. Some came and went, but we're the only one of the originals that's left.

"I guess we lasted on account of our prices, and our food was good. It's all homemade. Homemade pasta, ravioli. The same recipes as the original. I learned from my Mom, and the people working today are making it the same way.

"My grandson, Joseph A. Minuti, he started taking over the pasta. Now the new generation mixes the dough with a machine. But it's the same recipe. We couldn't keep up with it by hand today, not with the amount we have to do now. We even have a computer, that's something I would have never thought to have.

"We have a cook that's been here for many years, Yolanda. She's been here 40 years. My mother taught her how to cook.

"A lot of our other employees have been here a long time. Mary, my sister, on and off, had been here 55 years. Audrey's been here on and off about 20 years. Philomena, the girl who just left off her shift, about 20 years.

"People have been coming here for years—third and fourth generations. Their moms brought them here. They got married here. They say the food's still the same, and they keep coming back. Those who were kids are grown up and bring their kids.

"A lot of restaurants don't want to have the children, but we want to have the children come here, because it's a family restaurant. We'd rather have a family come once a week than come once a month.

"They come from all over—Rehoboth, Philadelphia, downstate, Florida. Some come down here for vacation, and their relatives bring them in.

"People come in and say to us, 'We've been away for such a long time,' or 'We were transferred, and we've just come back and you're still here. That's great!' Some of them tell us we're the first place they stop when they get back into town.

"One family was raised here and moved to Florida. They came back to visit and they were in five times in one week. I have a girl who moved to Spain, and when she came back home we were the first stop she made after getting off the plane. One girl joined the service. She was stationed in different places and she loved our raviolis. We packed them up in dry ice and shipped them to her.

"A woman came in and said her husband was in the hospital and he wouldn't eat anything but our raviolis, so we sent him up some. Then, I called him up and asked how he made out and he said, 'I made out fine. They were great. I ate every one of them.'

"The best thing I like is coming here and watching everything that's going on. I like to see the people come in. I like the kitchen. I like cooking. I enjoyed it. But I don't do it anymore. I never did like waitress work. Now my sister liked it, but not me.

"I'd miss it a lot if I couldn't come here. When I broke my hip, I was in here a week later. My doctor said I was a very strong woman. I sat in my chair, but I saw what was going on. People say, 'When you're here, Pina, things are different.' I guess they like me here.

"One of the most satisfying things to me is when I came in first in the *Delaware Today* magazine and in the *News Journal* surveys. We've always been first. That made me feel good.

"I'm proud of all this. I see it growing, and sometimes I can't believe it. I'm very happy. I wish my mother was here to see it. She would be so proud of this place, to see what she started."

Josephine "Pina" Minuti

July 23, 1996

Manager

"One of the reasons our business is still going strong is because a member of the family is always here, working. Because nobody watches your business like you're going to. You've got to be here. You can't own a business and be down to the beach. It works because you watch it.

"I think a lot of people who go into the restaurant business do not realize the amount of time you have to put into it. You can hire as many managers as you want, but nobody is going to watch your place like you are going to. We're lucky that our family has taken an interest in it.

"We've had so many funny things happen. We're open all the time, so, naturally, when it snows, everybody working in here is wondering when we are going to close. I remember one night, I was cooking in the kitchen, and we said: 'If we don't have a customer in an hour we're going to close.' It was a big snowstorm. Didn't two people ski down Union Street and come in to eat? We have the most loyal customers you ever would imagine.

"The last time it snowed, we were working with a skeleton crew. One waiter, one cook, a dishwasher and a bartender. I said: 'We'll stay open for a while.' We got so busy because we were the only place that was open. We had half the police force in here, I think. We were all waiting on tables.

"I try to take Pina out to lunch sometimes, because you can't sit in here without interruption, and we always meet someone. They come up and say to Pina, 'Don't I know you, from Mrs. Robino's? You're the lady that sits in the back all the time.' Then they say, real quick, like they're apologizing, 'I was just in there for lunch or dinner.' They feel they have to explain themselves to us why they're at another restaurant.

"We're proud that we're a family place with a relaxed atmosphere. It's not a chain. Our waiters and waitresses have come from the big chain restaurants, and they say it's different. We're like family. I guess we do get involved with our employees.

"Nobody is treated like a number. We all treat each other with respect. It's the same way with the customers. We're personal with them. You get to know a lot of them by name.

"Our biggest day is Mother's Day. We had them lined up outside and down around the corner. Saturday is your biggest night, it's date night. Sunday is your biggest to-go night. When you see these pots with the to-go orders. I mean, you just can't keep up with them. They bring in the pots and we fill them, depending on how many they need to feed.

"And the regulars, you know what they eat. The bartenders, they describe somebody by what they drink. They say, 'You know the two Smirnoff on the Rocks guy,' and the waitress will say, 'Oh yeah! The guy that gets the veal cutlet.'

"A lot of people say it's our sauce that brings them back. Some say it's the only sauce they can eat. The hotels send us a lot of business, especially on Sunday nights because a lot of places aren't open. We get referrals from the Hotel du Pont, Marriott and Radisson.

"I like it here because I like being with people, and I like the challenge. To make it go, to make it all work. I like getting to know the people and their families. It's all very satisfying. I really like the wedding rehearsal dinners. We're doing a lot of them. One guy got married here, and he had the reception here, 50 years ago. Then they had their 50th anniversary here. That really was a nice affair. We had a second marriage reception for one couple, in the third room. We decorated it really nice. They came in and they couldn't believe the place. They loved it and that made me feel great.

"There was a time when it was getting scary, with all these new Italian chain restaurants going up. I tried to get it across to our help that our customers have to drive into the city, first of all. They have to look for a parking spot, since we don't have our own lot. So I want to make their visit here the most pleasurable.

"But with all that, they still come back because the price is right, and they can't beat the food. They feel comfortable here. That's what we want. I think that says a lot for what Mrs. Robino's has been doing for more than 50 years."

Robin Mabrey   July 23, 1996

Joe Permar, 68

78 RPM Record Collector

From 1941 to Present

Wilmington, Delaware

Record Collector

Long before compact discs and cassettes, 8-track and reel-to-reel tapes, there were records. Colorful, artistic cardboard album covers protected the dark vinyl, long-playing 33-1/3rd, high fidelity recordings. And while teenagers liked the smaller and more portable 45 rpm, there was always a sense of nostalgia and even magic associated with the one-and-only original—the black, heavy, fragile 78 rpm record.

Today, few people under 40 have ever held a 78, but through the late 1940s these were the records that were the mainstay of the recording industry and entertainment business. The LP (long playing) 33-1/3rd disc wasn't invented until 1948. Unlike the 78, which only featured one song and had to be flipped over to play a different selection, the bigger "33s" were able to offer several songs on each side.

Up until a dozen years ago, 78s could still be found at garage sales and second-hand resale outlets. Today, however, they are as rare as the phonograph machines and thick, silver needles that are needed to create that distinctive, slightly scratchy sound.

In the early days of the century—when technology did not move at such a pace that the "latest" invention became obsolete before it was paid off—machines enclosed in ornately carved mahogany cabinets lasted for generations and provided musical entertainment for the entire family.

Joe Permar began collecting 78 rpm records when he was 13. At one time, he owned more than 20,000 of these sought after collectibles. While his assortment is still substantial, it now is slightly less than half that size. In the recreation room of his suburban split-level, an entire wall is filled with historic recordings performed by the greats of jazz, blues and swing from the 1920s through the 1950s. Each thick, black disk is individually surrounded by a thin, protective sleeve of light brown paper, a circular hole cut to display the record company label.

On the neatly stacked shelves are such recognizable names as RCA Victor, Columbia, Bluebird and Capitol, along with lesser known disks made by companies long gone, such as Black Patti, Herwin and Royal Blue Columbia, plus several of the unusually attractive picture records.

But to Joe Permar, each recording contains more than music. They hold memories, not only of the age when they were made, but also about the circumstances when they were discovered by the collector and saved from the trash heap.

"*I*
began collecting records in November of 1941. That's the day I received an old record player, an old RCA Victor wind-up machine, from one of my aunts. I was 13. I thought it was great. I had no player at the time. I had no records. I always loved music and I used to listen to the Big Bands, while I lived in the old neighborhood, in the 1200 block of Chestnut Street.

"My older brothers had the middle bedroom upstairs, so I had to sleep downstairs in the kitchen with the cats and the little radio. When I thought everyone upstairs was on their way to sleep, I'd turn on the radio and listen to the swing bands playing from Chicago, Philadelphia, wherever I could zip them in.

"I think it stayed with me, and when I received this player years later I was on my way. When I received records from the older '20s and very early '30s, I found that was my true love. Even today, music from that era is still my favorite.

"At one point, I just started collecting old records. I guess I went from outlet store to outlet store—the Salvation Army, different Goodwills, mission houses. What money I collected from my brothers and my Mom, from allowances, I used for records. There were so many artists, and so many I liked, that there was really no beginning and practically no end.

"During the very early '50s, I would jump in my car and ride through the old black neighborhoods on the East Side. I would take a square [block], and I would knock on doors and ask if there were any old records that they were discarding or no longer wished to have, and I would purchase them. Sometimes they just gave them to me.

"I'd mark off the square I covered and the next week I would be out there knocking on doors again. It extended from there into Chester, Philadelphia, I went to Baltimore, knocked on doors. Yes, indeed. A yield of records would be maybe a dozen to 75 or 80, maybe even a hundred. But I was being very selective if I was purchasing them.

"If no one was home, or if someone didn't have any, they often would tell me who owned a record player, and I would go back and try to see them at a future time. So I got leads as well.

"There were a number of funny things that occurred. I was carrying my valise on 7-1/2 Street, and I knocked on a door and this woman invited me in, a very chummy sort of a woman. She leads me to the back of the house and calls out, 'Company!' Then I noticed all these gentlemen and ladies sitting around. All of the sudden she turns and says, 'Can I help you?' and I said, 'I'd like to look at your records.'

"All of the sudden she got all upset and started shouting, 'Records! Records! I don't have no records! What are you a G-man? I don't keep records of what I do here!' Then I realized where I was. I was in a call house. The people started asking me what kind of records I was looking for. I was going through gestures of winding up a machine and going around with my finger like a record was going around. She eventually understood and told me to get out. They had a good laugh, but once she let me out the door, I couldn't stop laughing. I got hysterical and got the laughing jags. Even when I got in my car I was still laughing with tears in my eyes, so much that I couldn't drive.

"In Chester one day, a woman said I could get the records out the back. I went through the alley and she pointed to the ash pile and said if I wanted them I could rake them 'outta the pile.' Sure enough, I went out there with the rake and I would find one, blow the ashes off of it and put it aside. Then, I got the eeriest feeling that there were people looking at me, so I stopped and turned around and all her neighbors were in their windows looking at me as if to say, 'That guy's out of his gourd.' But I found some very good records that day. The black people collected a lot of the kind of music I *liked, the old blues, spirituals and the old jazz. I even went up to Harlem by myself and banged on doors and mission houses.*

"I'm still collecting, but 78s are much harder to find. The old records that I collected became more rare right after World War II. You see, there were always these scrap drives for metal, newspapers, tin cans, and there were also drives for old phonograph records. They were melted down and the shellac was used on the inner parts of shells for the big gunboats that fired on the islands.

"Movie houses would offer a free movie for five records. At that time, the kind of records you would take to get rid of were the records of the '20s and the very early '30s. Mainly because they were the five and dime record labels. You definitely would not take Vaughn Munroe's 'There I've Said It Again' or Tommy Dorsey's 'Boogie Woogie' or the current hits. You'd take grandpop's records. Who cared about his records?

"So you'd stand in line at the movie house with everyone else, give them your five records. They'd throw them in a pile and shove you in the door. After you saw the cartoons, news, serials, previews and movie, you'd come out and they were still shoveling record pieces into the dump truck. And this was carried on at every movie house about every second or third or fourth week.

"Years ago, when they were made, there were expensive records and there were very cheap records. The five and dime, the Montgomery Ward and the Silvertone, sold for about 25 to 35 cents. But the expensive ones, the elite, would you believe, sold for as much as $10. Those were the Red Seals, one-sided records and the Blue Columbia, too. After the War, the prices kept going up. They stopped making 78s about 1951 and '52, maybe some as late as '55. The majority, generally, were R & B, rhythm and blues. Elvis Presley and Fats Domino did some recordings on 78s.

"Today, the prices all depend on supply and demand, based on the artist and the label. I've sold them for as much as $300, $350 for one record. Those are generally at the record conventions. People still collect them, because of the rarity of them. But it all depends upon what an individual wants and is interested in. At one time, I had as much as 22,000. But I've got about 8,000 to 10,000 now. They're selected choices.

"Everyone asks me, 'Joe, do you play all those records?' I say, 'No! It's like anything else. You don't have time to look at your stamp collection, your coin collection.' In my case, there's something on each of those records that I like, that wants me to keep it. It has to be that melody, the love of that sound of that period. All of those artists were very talented.

"Every band had their top soloist and they had a following. Wherever Berrigan played, the Berrigan crowd would follow. Whether the dance hall was the Meadowood or the Sunnybrook, they followed Bunny in and out. But every band had its leader and its soloists. There was a time when I could name all the artists in the bands.

"There was a time when me and my peers would meet at a particular home, each would bring a record and play a number and try to spoof the rest of the crowd that was there. We'd try to figure out who was the sax man, who was the horn man, who's the vocalist? Or if it was a well-known title, who wrote that number?

"Each of these records brings back a memory. I can even remember the very first 78 rpm record I bought—'Someday,' by the Air-Lane Trio on the Deluxe label. I guess there are records I could play and I could tell you where I bought the damn thing—Philadelphia, Washington, D.C., Baltimore, South Jersey. It's amazing how a collector can build up a mental bank. Not all, but a good number.

"I've dealt in 78s and shipped them to all over the world. But, I've heard stories about this, and I think I may be one of the culprits. We're letting so much of our heritage slip out of our hands, and once they leave the States they may never come back. I've heard the Japanese are coming over to the big sales and buying up all the Morning Glory horns. Those are the record players that had a beautiful ornate horn, with the flower designs. They go to the auctions. And when they're there, there's nobody that can outbid them. They're here to get them, and they're not going to leave without them. And once they're gone, they're gone.

"You have to really seek out the old record players that will play 78s. A lot are in attics, and some people don't even know that they may still have them. Even the needles, the styluses, are hard to find. Few companies are making them. I've got three record players of my own that still play 78s.

"I'd say 95 percent of these records would be in the junk heap if I didn't get them, or they would have been sold or broken. In some cases I have nearly all of the things an artist recorded on 78. In the case of Cab Calloway, I've got everything but one. I think I'm only missing two of Gene Krupa's. Once I find those last keys, that's what I call them, then my collection is complete on what they've done on 78s. But it's like collecting anything, you get the later items first, and then go back to find the harder ones. But the joy of finding it is the thing. Sometimes I'll sit here, and I think it's an achievement. It was all seek and find, knocking on a lot of doors. I knew they were out there, you just had to use a little effort.

"You'd be amazed at how many of these have ended up in stoves. I found a family on the East Side, near Governor Printz, that had rare blues and rare jazz. They were exactly what I was looking for. At that time a quarter was a lot of money, and I got 18 of them. When I gave them the money, a quarter for each, they looked at each other and the man said, 'Ma, what did we do?' and the woman looked back and said, 'I don't know, but we burned up an awful lot of money this morning, didn't we?'

"They told me the fuel man who was to bring the wood for their stove was late coming and they took a lot of these records and threw them into the stove and burned them. When I heard that, I felt so bad, I didn't want to do anymore knocking. If I had just gotten out there a few hours earlier, who knows what I would have found and saved.

"There are a lot of people who don't know what the old records are. They'll ask about the 80 or 85 rpm,' and they speak in terms of 'the kind you can break.' The first thing they hit me with is, 'Where can I get the needles to play them with?' There's a reluctance to get rid of them, because their mothers and fathers have passed them onto them.

"When I play these records, I still have memories from those days, of being home and listening to the radio, to the serials and then the music would come on. I guess it just stuck in my mental bank.

"I guess it all started and grew from a fondness for that old music. I would have liked to have lived as an adult during the Depression years. The bands were always available. I think a lot about the past. There's a lot of nostalgia there and the music has a lot to do with it."

Joe Permar

September 16, 1996

Roadside Barbecue

You still see them, especially during the summer months, those extra large, dark metal barbecue grills that are set up off the side of the highways. Heavy iron monsters, black with age and coated with layers of baked grease from years of outdoor use.

Often they're perched beside gravel driveways, or in flat grassy medium strips. Straddling the fast moving lanes of passing traffic, they throw off clouds of gray smoke and waves of mouthwatering aroma.

The chicken has been cooking at the intersection of Delaware Route 16 and U.S. Route 13, in Greenwood, Delaware, since the late 1950s. About 1968, members of VFW Post 7478 got involved. Today, VFW volunteers split the barbecue with other organizations and work about half of the weekends during the roadside season that runs from mid-May through mid-September.

Tyson Cannon—a World War II vet, former post commander and VFW member since 1948—is one of the main cooks and has been working the grill since the beginning of the Greenwood VFW's participation. The menu has remained essentially the same, a half a grilled chicken, some pickles, a roll and a bag of potato chips.

Their sight and smell are signals to travelers, enticing drivers to interrupt their trips, take a short break and fuel up on a platter of barbecued chicken, coated with sauce that's made from a tasty secret country recipe.

As most major highway intersections take on an identical look, with competing chain restaurants anchoring every corner, independent eating sites are a welcome relief from cardboard burgers, thin pizza and Americanized tacos.

These side road barbecues may not be there much longer, and when they depart it will not be because of fast-food-store competition. The superior taste and reasonable prices of community highway barbecues beat the chain competition hands down. The problem has to do with a serious decline in manpower.

New club members are not willing to spend time at the grill and behind the counter. Without an infusion of new, younger blood, the current cadre of old timer volunteers may be the last to dish up that good-old, homemade, lip-smackin', finger-lickin' meal by the side of the road.

Tyson Cannon, 71

Chief Chicken BBQ Chef

Veterans of Foreign Wars Post #7478

From 1968 to Present

Greenwood, Delaware

"*I* remember when the Lions Club started doing it. They used to go out to people's cars when they were stopped at the lights and ask them if they wanted to buy the chicken. They'd hand it to them through the car windows in the late '50s. Today, we got a kitchen and covered grill, with tables out back, so people can stop, park and eat.

"This grill's about 28 feet long and can cook about 250 halves at a time. When we get it going, we have them coming off every hour and a half. We start about 6 in the morning when we light up the fire and charcoal, so we can get the chicken on about 6:45 and start cooking. By 8:30 the first batch is done, and then we keep them coming all day. A lot of people stop by early and pick it up to take to the beach.

"You've got to put the chicken on the grates and cook it to get the water out. Next, you start the basting and then take them off and put them in the cooler, to get the flavor in there. People don't realize it, but 15 minutes in the cooler is like 15 minutes on the cooker. We've got a special sauce. It's our own blend that we mix up. We go through 6 to 8 gallons twice a day. People like the taste. They're pleased with it.

"The cooking is the important thing. If you don't know what you're doing, you'll either burn it up or not get it cooked long enough. You have to know if you got enough coals to keep the fire going. Anybody can put a pickle on a platter, wrap it up and collect the money. The key is in the cooking. I like to cook. I'd rather do that then anything.

"On a regular weekend, we'll go through about 1,200 pounds of charcoal and sell about 1,500 to 1,800 halves. On a big holiday weekend, we'll go through 60 boxes, I'd say that's about 3,600 pieces. That's a lot of chicken. And it's fresh, not frozen. I can tell the difference. With frozen chicken, the bones are dark. We only sell fresh.

"It used to be a dollar. Last year, it was $4, and this year we had to raise it up to $4.25. But the customers still come. I got a man from Chestertown, he comes every day we're here . . . both Saturday and Sunday. I don't know his name. He's a farmer. He gets three platters and eats one here and takes the rest home. He said, 'If I had my say, you'd be open 12 months of the year.' He loves it. He can't wait until Saturday comes.

"A woman just came in and got six orders and said she's taking supper home. They come rain or shine, and we're here rain or shine. After all, you got to eat when it rains, too. They'll just sit in their cars and eat chicken, or they'll drive off eating chicken.

"I was down in Florida and struck up a conversation with a fella. When I said I was from Greenwood, he said, 'You're from up there with the barbecue!' I could have cooked his chicken. This is all volunteer work. We're doing pretty good, raising money for the programs we support in the community. I like to do it. I've been here and put in 12 hour days as a cooker, over the grill. It's rewarding, but I'm getting older now. It's starting to get to the point where it's getting to be a hassle.

"When I started, I was 44 years old. I'm 71 now. It makes a big difference. But we don't have the young people coming up. The younger generation isn't the same. The old ones die off, and the younger people aren't going to do it. The local fire company used to have a chicken and oyster dinner, but they couldn't get enough workers, so it's gone. Sometimes, we're going around asking people to help who aren't even members of the post. Wouldn't I just love it to see somebody young coming up and willing to take over."

Tyson Cannon   June 22, 1996

Joe Ragan, 50
The 'Accordion Man'
From 1961 to Present
Hedgeville
Wilmington, Delaware

Accordion Player

Quite a few people don't know what it is. Some think it's a portable organ. Others have never seen one up close. Tell them it's an accordion and a few nod, almost proud that what they thought was correct. Some even remember Myron Floren, smiling as he moved the gleaming black-and-white, box-like bellows across his chest on *The Lawrence Welk Show*.

Wilmington native Joe Ragan doesn't mind being called "The Accordion Man." He likes the nickname that he picked up sometime and someplace during the 35 years he's been playing the squeeze box.

He loves the instrument that for him is the source of hundreds of songs and thousands of fond memories. But he also realizes he's one of the few musicians left who can still play an instrument that has been deserted in favor of others considered more modern and stylish.

There's a low note of sadness in his voice when he recalls how respected and important the accordion used to be and how it's viewed today.

"**M**y father and mother, they bought me a starter accordion when I was 15. It was small, with only 12 buttons on the left hand. I took some lessons, stopped, then ended up teaching myself. I used to practice and play along with the records and I found I had a talent for it. Soon my parents, they were good to me, bought me a bigger accordion, one with 120 buttons. That was a really nice instrument.

"I played with a band called the Make Ups in high school—polkas, rock 'n' roll. Also did some weddings and other jobs. The accordion was a popular instrument in the 1950s. It sounded like two musicians, because it had a right hand and a left hand. It was very portable. You could take it anywhere. Remember, this was before advances in electronics made amplifiers and sound equipment smaller and smaller. Back then, the accordion was king. There were lots of kids playing it then. There must be hundreds of them today, just collecting dust in attics all over.

"Into the early '60s, people still followed the old Polish custom and hired musicians to go to a bride's house. Sometimes I went with a violin player, but most of the time I went myself. We played inside. Then when the bride left the house to go to the church to get married, we played the traditional Polish Wedding March. If it was a nice day, we'd follow her out to the car. It was nice. The mother would be crying and clapping along. I think I got $10. Once I remember I got a $5 tip.

"Then, the custom stopped. I don't know if there weren't enough accordion players or the brides didn't want it. Some thought it was too corny, old fashioned, not the new rock 'n' roll way. They didn't want to practice the old customs like they used to. For whatever reason, it's a tradition that's pretty much gone. And that's a shame, because it was really nice.

"Then I got drafted and went to basic training down South. We were having a talent show to boost morale. I was supposed to back up this black singing group. Somebody told them there was going to be an organ playing with them. I show up with this old, beat-up accordion and pulled it out of the box. They stood there looking. They didn't know what it was. This guy said, 'Where be the organ?' We all had a good laugh and it worked out. We did good enough to come in second place, playing 'Land of a Thousand Dances.'

"Later, when I was in Vietnam, I carried a harmonica with me. It was so hot, they wore out from the humidity. I think my mother sent me three of them. I was in an armored unit. One day our convoy was stopped in front of a service club near Saigon. I ran inside and saw a hillbilly pulling on an accordion. He didn't know what he was doing.

"I thought, I haven't played one of them in almost a year, since I got to Vietnam. A tear welled up in my eye, and I walked over and asked him if I could hold it. He said, 'Can you play it? You know how?' and I said, 'I think so.' I sat down in my dirty fatigues, laid my armored vest down, put my helmet on a chair and started playing 'Julida Polka.' I was so happy. It felt so good to be playing again. Those guys in there, they grabbed these Vietnamese girls and started dancing, trying to show them how to polka. One of them was a Polack from Chicago. He was stepping all over their feet.

"Then I heard a whistle blow outside. Somebody came in and yelled, 'Let's go! We're moving!' It hurt to take it off. They were kind enough to put it back into the case for me. I even turned and waved good-bye to it.

"In the early '70s, I got in with Joe Smolka and we started a band. All old neighborhood guys. It was fun, a lot of work, but fun, most of the time, anyway. There were always people you couldn't please. You found that out if you were in the music business.

"Over the years I've played some jobs myself, and a lot of people come up and don't know what it is. They say, 'I didn't know you played the organ.' When I tell them what it is, some say they couldn't think of the right name of it. That tells you one thing, that they aren't too many around anymore.

"I've got my fifth instrument now, a Sano Medi. It's got all these electronics connected to it, I could sound like a nine-piece band, all by myself. But it still looks and operates like your basic accordion. Today, though, there are too many whistles and bells.

"In order to keep up with trends and what people want in today's music, you have to carry all electronic equipment that's very expensive and also time consuming to set up. You used to pull it out of the box and play. No more. But, I know even if all the electric went off, I could still play a job and make some sound. I did it once, at an outdoor picnic at Our Lady of Grace Orphanage in Newark. I thought my arm was going to break off after four hours, but we got through it.

"But that's how they did it in the old days. They used to have weddings in homes. They would move all the furniture and roll up the rugs, and the musicians would come in the home and play all night. They earned their money, but it was a lot of fun. Every now and then you get to do a family party or picnic like that, and it gives you a sense of what it must have been like years ago, and how close people were to each other.

"I tell you, if I had a nickel for every time somebody asked me to play 'Lady of Spain,' I'd be rich. I got to the point where I just tell them I don't know it. When I need to get my accordion fixed, I have to send it to New York, North Jersey or Detroit. There's no place around anymore. Not even in Philly. If you went into a music store and asked to buy one, they'd laugh at you, if they knew what it was.

"Sometimes, when I open the box up and pull it out, I get, what I will describe as, unkind comments. Things like, 'Here comes the Polack Boy' or 'I bet he can't play Led Zeppelin.' I used to get a little insulted, but now I don't let it bother me anymore. These people have come and gone, and I'm still here playing today. We keep getting jobs, so some people still want us to come out and play for them.

"As long as my back and arms can hold out I'll keep it up. I used to stand when I play, but I had surgery, so I have to sit now. It's no big deal. I notice that Cajun and Mexican music are becoming popular. Look carefully, and you'll see some kinds of accordions in those bands. So its day is not completely gone.

"But good things come and good things go. I did a little more than I thought I would do with that instrument. Played a lot of good jobs, made some records and tapes and CDs. Actually, I'm sort of surprised I'm still playing today.

"I used to sit on the back porch, at 1414 Beech, and play for my Grandpop Frank Wierzbicki. He liked polkas and waltzes and obereks. That's a quick tempo Polish folk dance. I remember watching Dziadz, as my brother and I called him, and he would dance to an oberek so smoothly. It looked like he had air in his shoes. He'd mention a song, and I'd go listen to the record and then come back and play it for him the next day. He really liked that. He's gone now, but I can still remember those days, when I started. I guess I'm not ready to close the lid on the box just yet."

Joe Ragan

May 16, 1996

175

Capt. Otis Ray Tyler, 46

Mail Boat Captain
From 1983 to Present
Ewell, Smith Island, Maryland

Mail Boat Captain

Each day, at 12:30 p.m., throughout the four seasons of the entire year, the *Island Belle* leaves the Somers Cove Marina dock at the end of Main Street in Crisfield, Maryland, bound for Smith Island.

Located 12 miles west and surrounded by the waters of the Chesapeake Bay, Smith Island is known as Maryland's only inhabited island accessible only by boat. It was discovered by Capt. John Smith as he sailed up the Chesapeake in 1608, and its earliest inhabitants arrived from England in 1657.

Today, most of the several hundred residents are descendants of the original settlers and many still make their living from the water.

Supplying and feeding the residents is done entirely by boat, and, as has been the case for hundreds of years, the mail also must get through, and it does—over the water.

Capt. Otis Ray Tyler and his sons, Darrell, 26, and Dale, 25, pilot the family boats and make sure that U.S. Postal Service mail is delivered to post offices in Ewell and Tylerton, two of the three towns on the island. The post office in Rhodes Point closed a few years ago.

Members of the Tyler family have been responsible for getting the mail through for several generations extending back into the late 1800s, including John Whitelock, the present captain 's great-grandfather, and also his grandfather Ben Whitelock.

On a bright, sunny fall day, the *Island Princess,* one of the family's boats, carried a group of sightseers, regular commuters, supplies—including groceries, furniture, household goods, clothing and building materials—as well as packages and mail to the waiting residents who live out of sight of the mainland.

But even the isolation of Smith Island cannot halt the spread of the good and bad effects of progress. Standing beside satellite dishes and microwaves that add to the ease of living, there are an increasing number of "for sale" signs, plus old empty buildings, a closed school and, each year it seems, fewer and fewer residents.

Still the daily boat caravan of travelers and supplies continues, very much as it has for the last 340 years.

"*T*he mail work's been in the family just about a hundred years, except for just a few. My grandfather, he had three heart attacks and he retired from delivering the mail when he was in his early 60s. He would of liked that it would of stayed in the family then, but his son didn't have his Coast Guard captain's license, and I didn't have mine at the time. You need to have the captain's license to operate and carry passengers, freight and mail. You also have to have boats certified by the Coast Guard.

"As time went on—and the other captain, who had it for about eight years, wanted to get out of it—the chance came for me to take over. I had my license by then, and I was on the water at that time, crabbin' and oysterin'. I thought it was a good business to get into.

"We run 365 days a year. Well, we try to. Winds, heavy rains, freezin' rain, snows. It all depends on the combination. If it's out there blowin' and snowin', it's our decision. We need to go, but not if it's life threatening. We bring everything with us, food, merchandise, motorcycles, appliances. We even bring vaults when people pass away on the island. That's about 3,500 pounds. We have cranes to lift them.

"I like working with people. It's something different every day. You never know who you're going to meet. The island people are unique people. They're good to work with, and I love the water. This is not as much a water job as a waterman's. Even though we just cross it, you know, we have to be skilled and know what we're doing, because you've got passengers in your hands and you're carrying tourists. So, I guess you can call us watermen to a certain extent.

"I used to work with my grandfather when I was a little boy. It was him and his two brothers—the Whitelock Brothers. I used to work with them on the same docks, and my sons did the same thing working with me.

"The mail's been coming across for a long time, ever since there's been an island. When we get it here, we take some of it in the truck to the Post Office in Ewell, and the rest of it goes by boat to Tylerton. Running the mail goes every day—Monday through Saturday.

"I realize this is a bit unusual to people on the mainland, but not to us. I think there's only about three mail boats in the country. One goes to Tangier, Virginia. This one comes to Smith Island and, from what I understand, there's one up in Massachusetts. Now you might want to research that. My grandfather had the Island Belle. I have the Island Belle II and the one up in Massachusetts is called the Belle. I heard people talk about that.

"Some island people go with us. Some goes every day, some goes not every day. They've got doctor's appointments, shopping. We leave at 7:30 every morning, and they can come back with us at 5. I'd say the biggest majority of the island people have cars on the mainland, and some also have cars on the island. Some of them have new ones and keep them in the garages in Crisfield. They just get off the boat and get in their vehicle and go on.

"The worst thing we have to deal with is the weather. I got the judgment call. It all depends on the winds and the freezing rain and the snow. If the snow gets packed on your boat and the water is freezin', when that piles on your boat, that's more weight gettin' on board and you can lose the stability of the vessel. You also lose visibility a lot of time in the heavy snows.

"You have to watch what you're doin'. Even if you didn't have any passengers on, you've got you and your mate. We've got families and we want to get back home, too.

"Most of the time we may only miss one day at a time. Last winter, we hit some days when we would work a day and miss a day, because of the weather. We had so much bad snow and freezin' rain, a lot of ice in the water last year. See, when the water gets to the point that we have to have an ice cutter, that is provided by the state of Maryland, they escort the mail boat to get through. Of course, the other boats follow. When it gets to that point, we hit every other day. That happens just about every winter. That's not unusual.

"We'll get the ice and snow on the island, but we didn't get the brunt of the damage like they did on the mainland. Last year. we got a heck of a lotta snow. When we work with the state cutter, he gets here at sunrise. We have to follow him to Crisfield and he cuts us out and guides us back and forth, while we load and unload our merchandise. So it takes a bit of coordination, and that's why we will go every other day.

"There's times when I come across by myself. I sing to myself, whistle, pass time away. I sit there wonderin' about the island and the business. Different things.

"The biggest problem, the biggest thing I think about is the population of Smith Island. We're losing people. At one time we had between 800 and 900 population. We're down to 350. We have a lot of senior citizens on the island. We have a lot of young people leavin'. You only get one thing outta that. In time, your island's gonna be empty. . . . It's gonna be gone."

Capt. Otis Ray Tyler   September 19, 1996

"We go every day, seven days a week. The mail had to go through and the people depend on us. I guess the most embarrassing moment for me is when I've forgotten people and left without them, and they had to wait for the next day. That's an old hunting lodge over there. There used to be a lot more hunters come to the island. Today, you can't hunt geese and there are less duck. So, they figure it's not worth spending the money to hunt. Not like it used to be."

Dale Tyler   September 19, 1996

"Summertime is busiest, with all the tourists. Right now, in the fall, it's the most pleasant time. It's nice and cool and the weather's not too hot. A lot of people never heard of Smith Island, and a lot of people out of the city have never been near the water. We get some strange questions, like, 'Do people live on Smith Island? Do you have electric?'

"The worst part of the job is when it's raining, 'cause you have to protect the freight and keep everything dry. It takes a lot more work when that happens."

Darrell Tyler   September 19, 1996

Darrell Tyler, guiding the Island Princess across the Chesapeake Bay toward Ewell Island

Otis Huff, 72
'*Hardware Man*'
From 1957 to Present
Newark, Delaware

Hardware Man

Today, the national chain hardware superstores look like airplane hangers, that have been stocked to their 30-foot-tall ceilings with racks and shelves that workers need motorized extension ladders to reach.

Boxes and machinery line the walls, and endless aisles offer thousands of factory sealed packages containing bolts, screws, nails and widgets that confuse the human eye.

In aisle 76, rows of holiday decorations assault the shopper. In aisle 92, lamps and office furniture are for sale. Cassette tapes, CDs and snacks are available beside the computerized cash registers. Pet supplies are near the electronic doorway that leads to the outdoor yard, where decorative lawn sculptures and wicker furniture always seem to be on sale.

Young inexperienced clerks and shelf stockers roam the cavern, filling up the racks and avoiding eye contact with customers, who may ask a question about how to use the hardware or tools they just bought.

A key machine is nowhere is sight.

It wasn't always that way. There used to be real hardware stores, with open bins filled with nails and bolts and screws that you could scoop up and grab by the fistful.

The inventory was not computerized, but in the mind and soul of the husband and wife owners. They carried everything from bottle corks to roasting pans, from bicycles to auto parts and garden tools. In the back room and cellars were items that had not seen daylight for decades. In dampness and darkness they waited, patiently and silently, to be summoned by a frustrated homeowner who came desperately seeking help.

If you search, a few of these gems of the past can be located in one-horse towns and small strip shopping centers. They're not associated with any national chain, have been operated for decades by the same family and, at the front door, beside the key machine, you'll find a real, live, experienced hardware man.

Otis Huff arrived in Newark, Delaware, from North Carolina in 1970, and he never left. He never went to college. Didn't even graduate from high school. He doesn't have a wall full of framed diplomas or fancy advanced degrees with scrawled signatures.

Instead, his skills have come from the real world, a place where you learn through experience, careful listening and always trying to do the best for your customers . . . and many of them seek him out at Newark Lumber Company.

"*I* went to Newark Farm and Home and thought it was the most unique store I had ever been in. They had everything. It was just a one-stop store. You could almost get anything but breakfast and a tuxedo in there.

"They carried about 20,000 items on the shelves. I was manager of the fixtures department—which included nuts, bolts, locks and keys—and was responsible for about 4,000 items. I was surprised when the owner told me that one year I cut 12,000 keys for businesses and private customers.

"But times changed and the son started takin' it over, and he tried to convert it into a modern store. But people liked the old-fashioned store. As times change, things go different. It's gone now.

"I was in hardware and machinery work, together, for 15 years, down in North Carolina. Up here, I been in hardware for 25. So, all together, I been in the hardware business 40 years.

"They say more people know me than the mayor of Newark. If I don't know their names, I know their faces. You could talk to some of my customers, they could tell you stories. Frank, over here at Agway, he's a good fella. I help him out from time to time, with door locks and other things. He told me if I ever was without a job, I'd never be without work, just to come over with him.

"Instead of going to CardioKenetics, which I do now, I used to try to do my exercise walkin' through town, and every son-of-a-gun comin' down the street would stop me. For health, you got to keep movin', get your heartbeat right, ya know? Twenty people would stop and ask if I had somethin' in the store, how I was feelin' or whatever. I just couldn't' get my exercise done, and I had to go on the treadmill.

"Some people call me a hardware specialist, but I call myself just a hardware man. That's somebody who tries to help people when they come in the store. It's not somebody who just walks around and points that it's over there or somethin' like that. A hardware man is a salesman, he's not a clerk. It's somebody that if you buy lag bolts, he asks if you need the anchors and the masonry bit to go with it. If somebody comes in and buys an insert for a toilet tank and don't know how to install it, you explain to them how it goes—and that makes a customer come back to you.

"That's important today. Twenty-five years ago, you could pay somebody $10 to do most anything you needed. Now, a plumber won't come to your house for that. I take a lot of time explainin'. It's got as much to do with the business as the merchandise.

"It's different than a clerk. I don't even work the cash register. I let somebody else do that. I've had a lot of customers tell me they came to the store on account of me, and that makes you feel good, like you accomplished a little somethin' in life that way.

"I put up stock, I do the orderin'. I sweep the floor. I do anything. I don't care if you're the manager or the owner or the boss. If there's somethin' that needs to be done, you should do it.

"I been cuttin' about 14,000 keys a year. There's a way you cut 'em where they work and a way you cut 'em where they don't work. That's the reason I get as many as I do. There're a lot of people come in the store, and if I'm not there they won't let anybody else cut 'em. They'll come back the next day.

"I cut a lot of keys that locksmiths mess up. Customers bring them over to me. Lining it up is the main thing. I tell them to lay it in the track and put you finger over it and push it down. If you let it come up just one little bit, it won't work. If you're sloppy and don't care, it won't work. It causes the customer a lot of trouble, extra work, and it's bad for your reputation if they have to bring it back.

"I got the best key reputation of anybody in the country. I guarantee you that. You can hire a kid, and in three days he thinks he knows more than I do about it and I been at it 40 years. I still learn somethin' every day. Anytime you don't learn somethin' every day, you're outta the picture. I learn as much from my customers as they do from me.

"I kinda pride myself in what I do. I try to do it the best that can be done. Anybody that does anything should do the best they can. I don't see why you would just want to get by. There's too many things in the world that you can enjoy doin', and make a livin', instead of hatin' what you're doin'.

"I would hate to spend my life thinkin' that I had to make it to payday and quittin' time. You want to devote your life to something. I love my work. I love bein' able to help people. I like it now because I have no family up here. Through my work, I have all kinda friends. I call it my vacation, goin' in the store where I meet my friends, and talkin' with 'em and waitin' on 'em.

"Some people are surprised. They come in for somethin' they can't find anywhere in the country, and I can tell 'em where they can get it from or I can order it for 'em. They say, 'I been everywhere in the country and I can't get anybody to help me do this.' It makes you feel pretty good to be able to do something like that.

"The problem is, today, you come in and ask for somethin' and they tell you to go four aisles down on the left. You can go over there and look for 30 minutes and not find it. There's a lot on those shelves. We may be sold out of it, and the man can't find it 'cause he don't know what he's supposed to be lookin' for. I get up and go with the man to whatever he asks for. You don't find that happenin' in the stores any more.

"I've only taken five vacations in 15, 20 years. I may take off from Friday to Monday and go down home and back, but nothing long. I'd rather be here at work.

"I had my hip replaced. I was out about 15 days, and that was rough. It was good to back in the store. Fred came downstairs and saw me emptyin' boxes of bolts in the bin, and he liked to have had a heart attack. He said, 'What're you doin' back in here workin'?' That was in seven days after I came home. I said, 'I'm visitin' today, but these bins are empty and I'm gonna fill 'em back up before I go home.' I went home, but I went back next Monday and been there every day since then.

"But the business has changed and it's just sickenin' to me. Stores are doin' away with the things that they call dead weight. They want everything to move. If they don't think it turns over enough, they won't carry it. To me this was a part of my pride. It was what brought people back into the stores. In my opinion, they don't care about the walk-in customers, and they're caterin' to the contractors because it's less labor and bigger orders.

"The worst thing is tellin' a man we don't have somethin', that we stopped handlin' it, that we don't carry it anymore because it doesn't move enough. That's the worst. That hurts my feelings more than anything in the world.

"I always figured that if somethin' turned over three times a year, if it costs $10, it was worth carryin'. You got profit in it. If you got the one item people can't find, they'll tell somebody else and you'll have 10 more customers to come in to buy somethin', and they'll see somethin' else to buy. I think it's the best advertisement in the world. You keep the unusual and the hard-to-find items and it's a drawin' card. To have an item is better than an advertisement on the radio or in the newspaper, or television.

"There are very few of the old hardware stores, where the man had everything you needed and knew what was there and catered to the customers. Ogletown Hardware, over in People's Plaza, Tom and Paul, are still into it, and they got their family into it. That's one of the last ones you're gonna find in this part of the country now. They're the nicest fellas you ever seen in your life. It's old-fashioned hardware.

"Whoever goes into this work has got to have some training from someone else. But being willing is 50 percent of it. The future is going with the big companies. In 10 to 15 years, you won't see any independent local hardware stores. And I don't know where the people will go to find out how to use what's on the shelf.

"When I go in these big chain hardware stores, I think I wish I owned one of 'em and could hire 40 people, who had the interest in it that I did, to operate 'em. You go in them today and they don't help you with personal attention. You can pick up kids on the street, even college kids, anybody can work like that. They're just passin' through.

"If I didn't like it, I wouldn't still be doin' it. If you don't like people, you got no business working in a hardware store. You should have a job in an office, off somewhere by yourself.

"Nine out of 10 people are wonderful. That's what makes me want to stay in this job. We all have the customer who we would like to run from and hide, but you've got to deal with them. Sometimes, we say we should draw straws.

"If I was to hit the Powerball for $50 million, I'd be in the store first thing Monday morning. I've been working all my life. If I had my life to live over again, I'd do the same thing I've always done. I would get up tomorrow and go to work, just like today. I might live it up a little, give some money to the poor and get better clothes. But I would still want to go to work. Why should I change what I like doing? You've got to have something to do every morning.

"I'll keep doin' this until I'm unable to get out of bed and keep goin'. I'm not talkin' to you about this for the glory. I don't have a million dollars to leave anybody, but maybe I can leave what I know for somebody before I pass on."

Otis Huff   January 24, 1997

Butler

Travel the chateau country of northern Delaware, especially during winter months, and you can catch glimpses of famous estates that dot the countryside. Hidden most of the year behind tree-lined drives and landscaped acreage, their style and grandeur rival those erected by European royalty.

Their names--Granogue, Scarlet Oaks and Gibraltar, as well as Buena Vista south of Wilmington--possess a mystique associated with family fortunes and posh gatherings of society's upper crust.

A sample of how the well to do lived during the last century also can be seen along the main streets in the old-town sections of Easton, Dover, Snow Hill and Princess Anne. Stately homes, many now restored, reflect the character and pride of their first owners--mainly attorneys, businessmen and physicians, who came from Delmarva's old, monied families.

During the 19th century, and well into the mid part of the present, a large servant class worked in these estates--caring for children, chauffering, cooking, cleaning, gardening and serving guests at social events.

But times have changed. The number of butlers, chauffeurs, cleaning staff, cooks and live-in servants has declined dramatically. Catering, limousine and cleaning agencies now respond with temporary help to those who need such services. Today's rich want to avoid the tax and health insurance burdens associated with full-time, live-in employees.

But William "Marshall" Daniels, currently a resident of the Methodist Country House in Greenville, Delaware, can remember when serving the wealthy was an eagerly sought after profession. A native of Marydel, he is one of Delmarva's last remaining butlers. A remnant of another era, he began working in 1928, part-time after school at the side of his mother, Sarah Ethel Lee, who performed a wide range of tasks for the Mifflin family in Dover.

By the time he was 14, Marshall, as he is widely known, was invited by "Miss Edith" Richards Mifflin to work at the family's summer house as a "butler." The job involved assisting his mother, setting the table and performing other tasks. In black pants and shoes--topped with an eggshell coat to serve breakfast and lunch and a white coat to wear for dinner--he put out the fine silver and china and served dinner to the family and guests.

Even today, nearly 70 years later, Marshall still has fond memories. "To be among the wealthy, in that fine atmosphere, was wonderful," he said. "I always loved to see beautiful homes, and this job has taken me to some wonderful places. But all my skills and everything I know I learned from my mother. She taught me neatness, and she could organize and plan so she could get everything done."

An interesting character who willingly shared his experiences, Marshall spoke fondly of the wealthy he has served and the famous he has met. Casually, he recalled his daily personal encounters with members of the du Pont family, some with whom he still maintains contact.

Smiling, he remembered early morning conversations with Lena Horne and Bette Davis, while he worked at New York City's Copacabana nightclub, and, proudly, he talked of the thrill of shaking hands in Philadelphia, in 1944, with opera great Marian Anderson.

William 'Marshall' Daniels, 83

Butler

From 1928 to 1976

Greenville, Delaware

"*E*verything I learned was from being around cultured people and from my mother. In 1947, I came to work for the Dugdales in Wawaset Park. I'd have a white shirt on and tie on, and I'd arrive about 7:30. I could set the table in about 10 minutes. I'd serve breakfast. Immediately after, I'd clear off the table, shake the crumbs off the tablecloth, run the sweeper, then I'd come out and eat my breakfast. They let us work at our own pace. The parlor maid and I would go all through the downstairs, dusting and straightening up. That was a daily routine. After that, we'd take a little rest period, sit down for 15 minutes. Sometimes we'd laugh, talk with each other, take a peek at the paper.

"Then, it was almost time to set the table for lunch. Afterwards, we'd go ahead and clean the silver. Most places you did the downstairs silver on Mondays. Once a month we'd clean the chandelier. It was massive, beautiful and elaborate. We'd have to go up there and wash it, put a little bluing in the water, make it look crystal-like when it got dry.

"Now Buena Vista, I worked there for the Buck family about three years. That mansion is really something. It's so awesome, it's outstanding; 500 people could dance in the ballroom. We had to have a lot of help. Before my time, they entertained the late President Herbert Clark Hoover there. Mrs. Buck told me about that, every now and then she'd do a little talking with me, and that was the highlight of that place.

"The first du Pont I worked with was the late E. Paul du Pont Sr. He treated you wonderful. I would be out in the kitchen fixing cocktails, and he would come out in the pantry and talk and slice the oranges. The people I worked for were always smiling. They liked to see us happy. I never hated my job, I loved my work. I was just so glad to have employment and be able to make a living. I didn't have much education. I didn't have any trade. But I could fill in anyplace, do any job. My mother was my best teacher. And I'm not bragging now, but the late Mrs. E. Paul du Pont said I was the cleanest butler she ever had.

"Some of the mansions were so big that the guests could get lost in them. I'd see them looking around and I'd say, 'May I help you?' Then I'd escort them around the bend, and past the coat room and past the flower room. Some of the homes had two or three stairways. New help was hired by word of mouth, and we would be very careful who we recommended. I'd be so embarrassed if they messed up. If they did something very badly that would reflect on me.

"When I was in New York, at the Copacabana, about 1949, I was hired by the Moskowitz family to work at their house in Queens. They owned all of the Loew's theaters. They wanted another butler. They had their own private movies in the mansion. They had a big dinner every Friday night. They would have 20 to 25 relatives come in for three days. After they had dinner, they would go see the latest movies. They would allow all of the servants to come in on Friday nights, when the guests were there, and watch the movies. I'd go in there, since they ran a movie every night. I never had to pay to see a movie the whole time I was working there.

"Being a butler was a position of trust, something to be proud of. I never looked on it as being just a servant. I considered it an honor and a privilege to work for these people, to be in their homes and in their presence. I just can't understand this interest in me earning a living in an ordinary manner. I just wish my mother was living and able to enjoy the attention."

William M. Daniels

William Marshall Daniels

March 8, 1997

Bill Bartosh, 45
President, CEO and Founder
The Chesapeake Railroad Co., Inc.
From 1983 to Present
Greensboro, Maryland

Railroad Man

There was a time when shrill train whistles sounded throughout the peninsula, traveling across fields and forests even faster than the speed of the freight cars that raced across miles of matching strips of steel track. Engineers, brakemen and firemen kept the iron horses moving—delivering livestock, fertilizer, equipment and produce to small towns and larger cities along bustling rail lines.

Time conscious conductors consulted gold pocket watches, checked out their landmarks, then loudly called out the distinctive names of such stops as "Clayton!" "Hartly!" "Marydel!" "Goldsboro!" "Ridgely!" "Easton!"

From the 1830s to the middle of the 20th century, railroads were a vital transporation link throughout the peninsula . . . and then they died. Tractor trailers started to move produce and poultry along the highways, and private automobiles began carrying passengers. Once busy stations were boarded up, and these architectural treasures were lost to fire, became victims of vandals and were leveled by bulldozers.

In a few Delmarva communities, dedicated volunteers still work to preserve what's left of railroading's better day. They collect old equipment, renovate buildings and even restore cars and engines. In New Castle County, the Wilmington & Western Railroad offers weekend excursions and, in Parksley, Virginia, a small train station museum displays rail cars and artifacts that attracts visitors throughout the year.

In 1983, a unique preservation effort began. It was the resurrection of a real-life, operating freight line along 55 miles of trackbed from Clayton, Delaware, to Easton, Maryland, and a spur from Queen Anne to Denton. In 1995, after 12 years negotiating with government officials and private railroad representatives, the Chesapeake Railroad officially reopened the Clayton-Easton line.

Today, President Bill Bartosh—an experienced engineer and railroad man—continues to expand his private line's freight and excursion operations, returning much-needed railroad service to the center of the peninsula.

"*I grew up around the railroad, up in Marshalton, Delaware. When the B & O still had two main tracks running up to Philadelphia and New York, I was up there at the W. J. Tower, that's Wilsmere Junction, in Prices Corner, hanging around, throwing switches, doing whatever I could. I had a dream of being an engineer like a normal American boy back then.*

"*I was taking train orders by telegraph when I was 8 years old. I helped to start the Wilmington and Western Railroad. That's when I learned off the old mechanics how to rebuild, operate and maintain steam locomotives. I guess you could say I was one of the last steam locomotive engineers before diesel, because I learned on steam at the WWR. Later, when I hired on at the B & O, I went on to be a locomotive engineer from 1970 to 1990. I drove passenger and freight trains. My seniority district was Philadelphia to Baltimore, but I could work in other divisions as well.*

"*People ask me what it was like to run a 150-ton engine. It's a thrill to me. I love the business I'm in. It's exciting. There's a lot of technical skills to it. A lot of judgment is needed when you're running a train with cars that may weigh 20,000 tons, and you're projecting that train down the mainline track at 70 to 80 miles an hour. Of course, my shortline track speed is much slower.*

"*You have to use your judgment on braking, so you stop at a station or respond to a red signal. You have to know how to handle the speed and different conditions, be aware of the comfort for the passengers. There's a lot of pride in it. Some guys take it as a job, I took it as this is what I wanted to do with my life.*

"*The reopening of the Clayton-Easton line took me 12 years of negotiations with several parties to put into place. It's a privately owned railroad that moves over state-owned tracks. I have never received any operational subsidies, and CHRR provides much needed service to businesses and towns in the area.*

"*I've been asked why I got into the shortline business, and I'll admit I love railroads and I love a challenge. In 1982, some people wanted to run some excursions over the Clayton-Easton line, which was a Penn Central line for freight only at the time. I sent three passenger cars on this line, and it was only advertised by word of mouth and we were turning people away. So I started running some extra trips, but the line was slated to be closed and we had to stop. In February 1983, the last train was run, then the state of Maryland bought the line. Over a decade later, I reopened the line.*

"*Today, I run freight, predominately, but we have also run passenger excursions. Depending upon how much freight we have to move and what orders we have for that day, a run could be up to five hours round trip. Passenger excursions vary.*

"*Freight you take a little slower. You have different stops. The tonnage is different. Mainly, I haul agricultural products and ship some recycled lumber out. I believe we're providing a drawing card for economic development for the area. New and existing businesses seek freight service because of its reasonable cost, and as businesses grow, so will the towns along the line.*

"*Presently, CHRR has two passenger cars, 'The Defender,' a 1912 parlor/diner/lounge car, and 'The Catoctin,' a 1923 private business car. We also run dinner trains, and that has taken off very well. We prepare authentic recipes from the great railroads of the past on board as you ride. When my wife, Stacy, and I got married, we had our wedding and reception in 'The Defender.'*

"It's interesting when you meet people and they find out you're in the railroad business, they automatically assume that you're into model railroading. They ask me what scale I work with, and I just tell them '12-inches-to-the-foot scale' and they look at me like, 'What do you mean?' I explain that I mean the real thing.

"There are very few non-subsidized railroad operations like this. We also have a number of dedicated volunteers. Some are cabinet makers, others are electricians or mechanics. They may have a regular job during the week, but they come out to help us with projects or track work because they love trains. Volunteerism doesn't preclude professionalism. We follow all operating rules. We have to follow all the inspections and procedures that the Federal Railroad Administration and the state dictate. Everything we do out here is just like what Conrail or CSX has to do.

"There's a satisfaction in seeing something go that a lot of people said wouldn't. I don't know the words 'can't' and 'never.' If I feel there's a realistic chance to do something that I want to do, I'm not going to back down because of a bunch of negative attitudes. While I love railroading, I also look at this as a business venture that I believe can succeed.

"We've got these locomotives, the passenger cars, that we're making live again, and that's a good feeling. When they're sitting there, not running, they're sort of cold and dead. But when you put the lights on, they have a warm, soft glow. You hear the hum of the motors, the cry of the whistle. They're alive, and it's a whole different atmosphere. This is what we try to show our passengers and customers, the flavor of the railroad. It's part of our American heritage that should not die.

"Sometimes freight is run at night. When you're riding along, thinking about how far you've come, you look out. And when you get away from the lights of the towns, it's completely dark, and you see the stars and the moon. It's like you can reach out and grab them, they're that close. It's just a beautiful feeling out here. Even during the day, when you ride up the track, doing inspections and maintenance, you're often out in the middle of nowhere, no public around, no highways close to you. It's a whole different form of solitude.

"I guess I'm living proof that once railroading is in your blood it stays there forever."

Bill Bartosh   January 15, 1997

Jim Tartaglia, 45
Gravestone Cutter
From 1960 to Present
Wilmington, Delaware

Gravestone Cutter

For centuries it was the custom that a son would continue the work of his father. The innkeeper left his business to the oldest boy. The blacksmith, cooper, tailor, farmer and butcher passed on the secrets and tricks of their trade to members of the next generation, and those descendants were proud and honored to receive them.

Not too many years ago, signs above a majority of family businesses in both big cities and small towns ended with the bold proclamation: ". . . & Son." But in modern America, even this most honorable tradition is approaching its end.

Hard working parents want something better for their children—the good life with more money, a prominent position in the community and, above all, a profession. The unfortunate result of this form of progress is the end of the line of family occupations.

But in Wilmington, Delaware, Jim Tartaglia is an exception. In what some may consider an unusual work setting—at city cemeteries and in rural graveyards—he toils as a third generation stone cutter, working with marble and granite just as his father, Allen F., his uncle, Vincent F., and his grandfather, James Vincent, did before him.

The present day owner of Sand Piper Cemetery Lettering Company started working at the age of 9 in the family business—Wilmington Memorial Company—which was an independent monument manufacturing operation. Today, few of these small, family-owned operations are still in existence.

"*My father would go to the quarry in Barre, Vermont, and buy slabs of granite. They would ship them down and we would break them up into small pieces for monuments. We had full manufacturing capabilities. We could actually take a sawblock from the quarry and reduce it down to the size we needed to work with. We were able to pitch—or shape—the stone with a hammer and chisel, and polish it to give it the appropriate finish.*

"*We were one of the last of the fully capable manufacturing companies in Delaware. My grandfather passed away 15 days before I was born, so I worked with my father and my uncle Vincent. I helped around the shop, mixed concrete, set stones—took them out to the cemetery and placed them. We also did burial vaults.*

"*When I was 10 years old, I was running a 25-ton crane for my father, setting mausoleums in the cemetery. I've always been around equipment and handling things. I worked on weekends, after school, during summer vacations. In high school, I was one of the few kids who always had a few dollars in his pocket. It was my dad's and his brother's business, and I learned from them. I also had a lot of on-the-job training.*

"*Today, independent monument dealers have diminished because of several things—cemeteries themselves are now in the business of selling monuments, which they order direct from the quarry, plus the increased number of cremations and community mausoleums have reduced the demand for more traditional stone monuments.*

"*In Delaware, I'd say that in the 1950s, statewide, there were probably about 40 independent dealers. Now it's down to maybe 10. In this one-mile area from Elsmere to Cathedral Cemetery, there were five and now there's only one.*

"*There's still a big need and industry in flat stone memorials, and even in upright monuments, but these changes have reduced the ability for independent businesses to remain competitive. There even have been changes in mausoleums. At Wilmington Memorial, we used to build mausoleums on site. The industry had changed to where the prefabricated mausoleums are growing fast. You can order one from the factory. They ship it down on a flatbed trailer, deliver it in one piece and set it down on a foundation in the cemetery.*

"*The reason why I chose cemetery lettering is because—even if they were to stop making any more monuments today—there would be a backlog of work. Typically, it's the situation where the husband passes away first. The wife buys the stone for both her and her husband. When she dies, instead of having to pick the stone up out of the cemetery and ship it back to the quarry to get her name added, I just go out on site and do it.*

"*That also pertains to large family plots. It's not uncommon for some family plots to have as many as 20 names. And every one has to be lettered as each one in the family passes away. I work with a range that goes from 2-foot by 1-foot flat markers to mausoleums. I also do work on large buildings and signs, plus cleaning and restoration work.*

"*In cleaning, it's chemical cleaning, sand blast dusting or high pressure wash. In restoration, a stone may fall over,*

or they may break in half—whether they be tabloid-type or flat ledgers—I work on them all. They're affected by the weather, lawnmowers run over and into them. If you get several inches of snow, the crew will go out to open a nearby grave and drive equipment over a nearby stone without knowing it.

"I'm the only full-time cemetery letterer in Delaware. There are still a number in Philadelphia. I've done work from New York to Baltimore and down as far as Rehoboth, Berlin and on the Eastern Shore. I've been in large city cosmopolitan operations and to small private, family cemeteries.

"I like my work. I like the idea that I'm doing something that my father did, that I'm carrying on a skill that's been handed down from generation after generation. It's also not something that too many people do. Every once in a while I'll do a job and I'll meet someone in the family who appreciates very much what I've done for them. That gives me a real sense of satisfaction, because it's a very personal business. Whenever you deal with death in any capacity it's very emotional. The rewards for the times that I've made some people happy and touched them mean a lot to me. There are some families that will come back to me to work for them every time they experience a tragedy.

"I also do whole layouts, depending on what special needs there are requests for. Sometimes, I'll work for dealers who have stones that need to be cut or need special designs. They'll get me to do it rather than going to the factory or the quarry.

"At one time it was an old tradition for the family to go to a monument yard or a monument dealer and select the very stone they wanted to be placed at the gravesite. Emotion and tradition played an important role in the past. They would put their hands on a stone and say, 'I want this stone.' Years ago, prior to 1900, your undertakers were also stonecutters.

"In the early days of this century, the family would go to the funeral parlor together and after the service they would go to the stone cutter. He would have his wares in the yard and they would make a selection. Then he'd letter it and put it out in the cemetery. Today, as so many things have changed, people have gotten away from that to a degree. They just place an order and don't really care where it comes from. Most people do 90 percent of their monument buying from a catalog or pictures.

"Individualization has diminished, and the cookie cutter mentality in monuments has gotten stronger because of economics and convenience. But if someone goes to a monument dealer and sees the stone that they want, the monument dealer will have me cut the lettering on it.

"When I'm out there working, one of the things I think about is not making a mistake. I like the fact that whatever I do will, literally, last for hundreds of years. Even though people in today's Dixie Cup society are used to things being used and then discarded or thrown away, everything I do stays forever, and that is a nice feeling.

"The one thing I put off thinking about is: Who is going to letter my name on a piece of stone when I'm gone? The way things are going, there might not be anyone around. But if there is, I hope they do as good a job for me as I would do."

Jim Tartaglia   January 13, 1997

195

Piper, Dick's Guiding Eyes for the Blind dog, stands at attention during the playing of "Taps."

Dick Hires, 72, and John Murphy, 66

Bugler and Honor Guard Captain
VFW Mason Dixon Post #7234
Ocean View, Delaware

Bugler and Honor Guard

Since it was first played beside a Civil War battlefield in 1862, "Taps" has been associated with peace and quiet. Originally, the military lullaby alerted Union soldiers that time for sleep had arrived.

Eventually, the solemn bugle call became a grateful nation's "Thank you" to its war dead, a call to eternal rest for those in the military who had served their country.

As the veterans of World War II, the last generation of true American heroes, pass on, they take with them secrets and a precious legacy . . . the experiences of common men and heroes, of professional soldiers and volunteers who answered freedom's call.

But today, at a time when these old soldiers are dying by the hundreds each day, the 24-note bugle call is sounded less frequently. Few Veterans of Foreign Wars posts still maintain honor guards, and there are a limited number of military musicians available to perform the ceremonial salute to the dead.

Local graveyards and funeral homes do not have the resources of Arlington National Cemetery. While active duty personnel, retired general officers and Medal of Honor recipients are guaranteed full military honors, the families of the average veteran must depend upon the goodwill of aging comrades—and a few younger vets from more recent conflicts—to fire the volleys and sound the bugler's call at the gravesite.

In Downstate Delaware, members of Ocean View VFW Post #7234 still pay final tribute to their fellow veterans' deeds of valor. In every season of the year, the echoes of three rifle volleys still race between the tombstones. And as Honor Guard Captain John Murphy salutes, and the firing squad members shift their weapons to Present Arms, post bugler Dick Hires, accompanied by his guide dog, Piper, sounds the solemn notes of "Taps," over the flag-draped coffin . . . offering a last farewell and proper thank you to an American veteran.

"In the 1930s, I started playing the bugle for a drum and bugle corps in Salem, New Jersey. When I went in the Navy I didn't play in the band. I was in the Navy Air Force. I was an aerial gunner and aviation machinist mate in a combat aircraft service unit. I joined up the day after Pearl Harbor and served in the Southwest Pacific.

"I actually joined the VFW from overseas in 1943. It was a post in Sacramento, California, but I never got to see it. When I got home I transferred my membership to a post in Salem, New Jersey. When I moved to the Bethany Beach area, I joined the Ocean View VFW.

"I got started playing the bugle after I attended a funeral in 1982 for a veteran who had passed away. There was a high school girl who played 'Taps.' Bless her soul, she did a good job, but it just didn't seem quite right. I guess I sort of felt guilty. I knew I could do it. I was a fellow veteran. I wanted to do it, and I just knew I would feel better doing it myself. So, I've been doing it ever since. Every patriotic holiday, Memorial Day, Veteran's Day that used to be Armistice Day, Pearl Harbor Day and every funeral, which seem to be increasing. I've played at hundreds of funerals.

"I feel I am paying respect to a departed comrade who has fought for his country. It gives me a satisfied inner feeling. It's my way of saying, 'Thank you' with my heart. I play it from the heart instead of from the lips.

"When I get ready to play, I think of my father a lot. I think of the family of the deceased. I think of all the veterans that fought and died for this country and have served this country. That's where I think playing it from the heart comes in. I have a lot of emotional feeling about it.

"I've been asked to play for different veterans organizations when our firing squad is involved. Our honor guard will help out during ceremonial activities and on patriotic holidays for American Legion Post #17 in Lewes. They adjust their time so we can complete our responsibilities and get over here for their events.

"We're out in all kinds of weather. I participated in a funeral in Wilmington two years ago for a former state commander from Delaware. They had a dual firing squad, from the Rehoboth VFW and Ocean View VFW. I played 'Taps.' It had to be zero to 10 degrees above zero, and the wind was blowing 25 to 30 knots.

"I had the mouthpiece in my one hand and the trumpet close to my body, around the valves, 'cause I knew what was going to happen. Well, I got through the 'Taps.' I had had my hand frostbitten many years ago while fighting a fire in New Jersey and it was in pain. I thought I was going to pass out. It was a bitter, bitter day. And they had another bugler that played the 'Echo.' He got the first note out and that's all, because the moisture inside of the horn froze. It was a very unfortunate thing, but, thankfully, I got through my phase of it.

"I started losing my sight in the mid-1970s. I didn't realize I had glaucoma. Since I don't drive, Mr. Murphy, who's captain of the honor guard, or Mr. John Somerville, who's a member of the honor guard, they come and get me.

"On December 4, 1993, Piper, a yellow Lab, and I graduated from the Guiding Eyes for the Blind School in Yorktown Heights, New York. Everybody thought that Piper wouldn't be able to handle the noise from the firing squad, but it hasn't been a problem. I gradually broke him in. Now, he stands right along side of me. He doesn't jump. He almost stays at attention, and it doesn't bother him a bit.

"I'll do this as long as I can. But we're getting up there in years. I'd like to get a young boy from the area and teach him how to play. That thought's been running through my mind for the last year or so. That way, there'll be someone to continue it on."

Dick Hires   December 16, 1996

Honor Guard Captain

"*I'm a Korean War veteran. I'm retired Army with 22 years. I was in the infantry and combat engineers most of the time. I went to Korea in September 1950, and I was in Vietnam in 1968-69. After I retired in July 1970, I went into the U.S. Capitol Police and stayed there until '92.*

"*Being retired military, I've done drills and ceremonies. I watched the honor guard when I came up here and I got interested in it. So, I told one of the fellows that I'd like to be involved and that was it. I knew drill and I can give commands. I knew I could help out instead of just sitting there. They're always short of people. I've been doing it since 1994.*

"*This is my way of showing respect for the people who have served. We have 11 members in the honor guard right now. They're from World War II, Korea and Vietnam. I'd say about half are from World War II. Down the road, we have to get some people. I'm a Korean vet and I'm 66. The World War II guys are in their 70s. We have a hard job ahead.*

"*Most of my calls are from the funeral home, and often they'll say the family has requested that the honor guard be there. Sometimes we'll attend and stand beside the casket at the funeral home providing the full military service, and other times it's the basic military service at the cemetery.*

"*I'm not the kind of person who likes to go to any kind of funeral, but it's important that someone be there. You use the word respect, and that's what it is, showing respect to the person, the veteran and to the family. I feel very good about what we do. Inside, I can say when I leave there, 'If somebody's going to be there, why shouldn't I be there?'*

"*The district also has an honor guard, but there's not one at every post. We've responded to requests from other posts.*

"*I went to a state meeting last month and they said they had 17 funerals in a month. There's going to be a new veterans cemetery opening up near Georgetown for Southern Delaware. But, if the funeral's scheduled, we'll be there. That's it. I'll be there as long as I can, and we'll keep trying to recruit. Our Ocean View Post is the largest in the state, and it's a retirement area, and many residents and members are at that age.*

"*But whenever anybody calls up for us to participate in a ceremony, it doesn't have to be a funeral, the first thing they ask me is: 'Is Dick Hires going to be there?' He doesn't realize he's the highlight. We can fire the volley, but they all want Dick to play. Dick is concerned that we have to come up and get him. But, in truth, if we didn't want him, we wouldn't come up and get him. He's an important part of this and we enjoy having him with us.*"

John Murphy   December 16, 1996

Afterword

All is not lost. Dedicated individuals and active organizations throughout the peninsula have been making a serious effort to preserve the distinctive culture of Delmarva. In private shops, some still make products by hand. Small businesses serve regular customers despite competition from nearby chain stores. Family restaurants continue to offer breakfast specials, and regulars drive past fast-food outlets to meet at the "good old place" to talk about the "better days" over morning coffee.

Local and state arts councils and historical societies sponsor talks, promote research and publish books about the past. They also organize programs and invite speakers to discuss regional customs, area culture and local lore.

To experience the essence of the Delmarva Peninsula—its people at work and at play—turn off the wide highways and travel the narrow back roads. Ignore your clock and map, and let instinct and luck be your guides.

Buy gas at a single-pump country store, eat a platter of pancakes and scrapple at a firehall breakfast, buy a handmade creation from a side road vendor, pick up some vegetables at a roadside stand, ride the carousel at a small town summer carnival—take time to talk with the person behind the counter.

Space and time limited the number of people who were able to be included in this book. I had hoped to spotlight a crabber, fisherman, migrant worker, midwife, goose caller, crabpot maker, gravedigger, cook, orchard owner, chicken plucker, blacksmith, country doctor, potato sorter, biscuit maker, crabmeat picker, undertaker, circuit preacher, clock maker, bookstore owner, racetrack groom, horse trainer . . . .

The list is a lot longer.

These people, and others who I was unable to locate—or who declined to be interviewed—could certainly fill another volume or two.

But they are there for you, and me, to find, to meet and to enjoy.

Make a point to take the time to do so.

You'll find the effort and experience worthwhile.

Author's note: *Disappearing Delmarva* is a beginning rather than an ending. We have plans for other books about the unique culture and colorful characters of our peninsula. We're open to suggestions for more people to meet and other places to visit. Drop us a note in the mail and we'll get back to you. We appreciate your interest, help and suggestions.